W9-AOZ-560

LEGEND

LEGEND:
THE STORY OF POCO

AMERICA'S PREMIERE COUNTRY-ROCK BAND

By Jerry Fuentes

Groundhog Press

Copyright © 2008 by Jerry Fuentes

All Rights Reserved.
No part of this book may be reproduced in any form or by any elec-
tronic or mechanical means, including information and retrieval systems, without written permission from the publisher, except by a
reviewer who may quote passages in a review.

Published by Groundhog Press
619 Fordham Drive
Stockton, CA 95210
Email: booksatgroundhog@sbcglobal.net
Website: www.booksatgroundhog.com

ISBN: 978-0-9817592-0-3

For Kim

My Love and My Life

TABLE OF CONTENTS

Introduction

They say you could sense that something special was about to happen. The air was filled with anticipation. It was a Monday night at the popular watering hole known as the Troubadour in October 1968. Mondays were hoot-nights, where performers looking for their big break would get up and do a couple tunes in front of a mostly disinterested crowd. But that night was different. The crowd was eagerly expecting something more, something special. What most in the crowd didn't expect was the debut of an innovative rock group that would still be performing 40 years later. To think that among those five nervous young musicians that took the stage were two future Rock and Roll Hall of Famers, a *Guitar Player* Hall of Famer, a founder of the Eagles, and a founder of Loggins and Messina is almost too much to believe. But it's true.

This book traces the history of that band, Poco, from that relatively obscure beginning in 1968 to the present day, a span of 40 years. Two decades in the making, *LEGEND: The Story of Poco* uses a variety of sources to chronicle the group's musical career. I've interviewed nearly all the former members of Poco, as well as three members of the current band, to tell their story. Only Rusty Young was reluctant to let anyone else tell his story. I've also spent years diligently perusing stacks and stacks of magazines, newspapers, microfiche, and microfilm, and spent hours and hours surfing the internet (at first just a novelty!) to document their thousands of concert appearances and dozens of album and single releases.

   I discovered Poco shortly after the release of their second album, POCO while on a family vacation to Los Angeles. Living in the
small Gold Rush town of Sonora, California it was not easy to stay up
with current music trends. I had lost track of Richie Furay after the
Buffalo Springfield's breakup and was delighted to find that he was
still making music. It took over two years for DELIVERIN' to appear
in our local department store and its one bin record section. Seeing
some Buffalo Springfield tunes on the back cover, I immediately
plunked down my $3.99, took it home and I was hooked for life.
   Over the years it has been frustrating to hear them constantly
being referred to as a country-rock band. While Poco was originally
credited with developing an accessible form of country-rock, I feel
they have displayed the talent and versatility beyond the confines
of the genre. You could put together a pretty good sampler CD including the bluesy *Nobody's Fool* from their debut album, the disco-
esque *Never Gonna Stop* from 1977's trilogy *The Dance*, the Caribbean flavor of *Barbados* on 1979's LEGEND, the slick production of
Save a Corner of Your Heart in 1984, and the rhythmic styling of
Shake It in 2003 and hear elements that extend far beyond rudimen-
tary country stylings. Sure there are plenty of country influences
throughout Poco's recorded legacy, but listen carefully and you'll
also find blues, jazz, bossa nova, folk, rock, and classical. Anyone
who claims that Poco is simply a country-rock band couldn't have
been listening. Toward that end, I've tried to include an appreciation of Poco's recorded work as documented in contemporary reviews, as well as more modern interpretations through the eyes of
the band.
   As a fan of Poco, I used to rail against the gods when yet another album failed to hit the top of the charts or still another single
didn't even appear on the *Billboard* Top 100. I couldn't understand
why no one seemed to "get" them the way I did. What I didn't realize was that anyone could be a Peter Frampton or Elton John fan,
but it took something special to be a Poco fan. I remained a solitary
Poco fan for years until the mid-1980s when I discovered other fans
through corresponding in record collecting magazines. We were few
but mighty, and with the emergence of the internet, the ability for
Poco fans to discover each other and stay in contact grew by leaps
and bounds. The term "Poconut" popped up as the age of the
internet grew and those who were fans sought a unique identity,
and I consider myself to be a charter member. I mean, who else
would spend 20 years of their life on this stuff except a nut! I assure
you that this book has plenty of new information for even the most
die-hard Poconut.

Hopefully, this book will prove to be an eye-opener for any fan of rock music. Poco's struggles with the uncertainty of the world of rock and roll are an amazing example of what not to do and still manage to triumph. I'm convinced that a lesser band could not have weathered the challenges. The members of Poco were so clearly devoted to their passion for making music that no obstacle seemed too great. Yet despite their ability to persevere, Poco is often referred to as an under-rated band. It's true that their influence extends more to fellow musicians than to music fans in general. However, commercial success is never guaranteed in the music business, and musical ability isn't always the yardstick used to measure it. If it were, there would be no way that a bunch of dogs barking *Jingle Bells* would outsell or outperform Poco on the charts. But it happens, and I've tried to unravel some of those mysteries. Not all the answers are contained here, but within these pages is a story of triumph and perseverance in the face of a rock and roll world that didn't seem to understand their greatness. Oh yeah, and sometimes it was just bad luck.

Jerry Fuentes
October 2008

1
Early Times

Although typically categorized as a California or West Coast band, Poco's roots were firmly planted in America's heartland. Richie Furay, founder of Poco, was born and raised in Ohio. He entered Otterbein College after high school and formed a local folk trio called the Monks. After some regional success, the trio began setting their sights for greater success. With great anticipation, Furay and the Monks traveled to Greenwich Village in New York City and secured a two-week stay at the Four Winds Club. "It was the summer of '64," recalls Furay. "Two Otterbein classmates and I deced to take on New York City to start our folk careers. We managed to create some interest in several folk clubs. Steve [Stills] was playing in one of the basket houses, and we became friends." Although folk music had been the rage, the Monks found the Village had changed in the span of a few months. "By the time we got to Greenwich Village to do our folk music the folk scene was already over," Furay asserts. The impact of the Beatles and other British Invasion bands had clearly made its mark. The Monks found themselves playing to scattered crowds and barely made a living as the tourist trade declined and the novelty of folk clubs wore off.

As Furay and the Monks toiled, another folkie drew Furay's attention. Stephen Stills recalled his introduction to Greenwich Village. "I hit New York right after my 18th birthday and stayed there a couple of years," Stills recalls. "The only real ambition I had there was, for a brief time, a fantasy of playing bass for John Sebastian's band, the Spoonful, because I thought I could play, but I didn't really get on so well with Eric Jacobsen, who was in control of the situation at the time." Stills jumped right into the folk scene, forming a duo with John Hopkins. This folk trio fell apart in August 1964 and Stills was looking for work.

The result was the formation of the Au Go Go Singers. Composed of the Monks, Stills, and the Bay Singers, this grouping played an off-Broadway review, recorded an album, made a national TV appearance, and broke up all the space of six months. With the collapse of the Au Go Go Singers, Furay found work at a factory and Stephen Stills moved to California. A year later, Richie Furay and fellow musician Gram Parsons began hanging out in Greenwich Village and marveled over the first album by a California group, the Byrds, that melded folk music with Beatle-esque rock. Furay recalls, "It was so different from what I was writing. I figured I had the talent and ability, but I didn't have a clue about how to go about it, so I immediately thought of Steve." Hearing this new blend of musical styles, Furay wrote a letter to Stills in hopes of putting a group together. By the time the letter found Stills, the year 1966 had dawned. Stills eagerly invited Furay to join him in Los Angeles and they formed Buffalo Springfield, along with Canadian guitarist Neil Young (who Stills had met in Canada on a short tour after the breakup of the Au Go Go Singers), bassist Bruce Palmer, and drummer Dewey Martin.

The band's career began as the house band at the legendary Whisky a Go Go. By the end of their stay at the Whisky, the Buffalo Springfield was a live act with a hot reputation around Los Angeles. When their managers booked them to open at the Hollywood Bowl for the Rolling Stones, it seemed that superstardom was just around the corner. Unfortunately, that was not to be case. Their first two singles failed to chart and then bassist Bruce Palmer was busted in New York and deported. As the Springfield contemplated their future, a tune the group had recorded and added to the album after its initial release began climbing the charts. Stephen Stills' reaction to the riots on Sunset Boulevard in November 1996, *For What It's Worth*, proved to be a hit. It eventually settled at #7 on the national charts and provided the foot in the door that the band had been seeking.

At the same time, as California nurtured the new music exemplified by the Byrds and Buffalo Springfield, other areas around the country began to feel the pull of a new sound. The music scene around Denver, Colorado, was originally heavily influenced by the British Invasion. Everyone wanted to be British, and bands that wanted to be successful were quick to copy the latest releases from British rock bands.

It was in this environment that Böenzee Cryque was formed. The band fit in with most other groups in the area, playing the Top 40 hits of the day. The band took its name from the Benzi-Kricke Sporting Goods store on South Colorado Boulevard in Denver. Massaging the spelling, Bush and company came up with Böenzee Cryque. "We did it grammatically incorrect," points out keyboardist Bill Delugt, "Everyone mispronounced it - it's Ben-zee Crick." They quickly became very popular and played gigs throughout the state. As with most Denver bands, they were enchanted with the music of the British Invasion and began working up letter-perfect renditions of songs by the Beatles, Stones, Hollies, and the Animals. They also worked up a couple of tunes by a San Francisco group who sounded very British, the Beau Brummels.

By 1967, both steel-guitarist Rusty Young and drummer George Grantham had replaced original members in Böenzee Cryque. By the time Young and Grantham joined, the band had become influenced by the Buffalo Springfield and began to explore a more country-oriented sound. "Böenzee Cryque was the only rock n' roll band I was ever in," Young asserts. "I was in that band a brief period of time. That was my first rock n' roll experience." Grantham recalled Rusty's arrival in the band. "Rusty brought the country influence in. We were a rock and roll band. We were in the group together for about two or three years. It's funny, but he didn't play steel guitar with us because people weren't ready for it. He stood up and played regular electric six-string. But he did play the steel towards the end of the group, and I'm sure we had to be the first rock n roll group with a steel guitar."

Meanwhile, another Denver band challenged Böenzee Cryque for local supremacy. The Soul Survivors were an R 'n' B oriented band who had released a couple of local singles. They had the support of local radio DJ Hal "Baby" Moore, who played their releases religiously. Still, the Soul Survivors success remained regional, and they began yearning for greener pastures. In February 1966, the Soul Survivors entered a "Battle of the Bands" competition in Denver, Colorado. They easily won the competition, but one of the participants caught their ear. A young band out of Nebraska, the Drivin' Dynamics, boasted a bass player with a stratospheric voice. Randy Meisner had joined the Drivin' Dynamics at 14 and had quickly taken over as lead singer. "One night in 1964," Meisner recalls, "we played a talent contest up in Denver, at the Cow Palace. A group called the Soul Survivors had just lost their bass player to the service. He sang high and played bass. So did I. I sat in with them, and about two weeks later a guy from the band drove over to Nebraska and asked me if I wanted to go out on the road with them to open for an L.A.-based group called the Back Porch Majority. They convinced the other members of the Soul Survivors and me to come out and try our luck in L.A." Having heard the California sounds of the Buffalo Springfield and the Byrds, the Soul Survivors had a destination in mind. The Soul Survivors headed for California to seek their fame and fortune.

They originally called themselves the North Serrano Blues Band, but quickly assessed their true station in life and christened themselves the Poor. "When we first got out there, one of the [Back Porch Majority] had an apartment in Encino, off Ventura Boulevard, behind a Ralph Williams Ford dealership." Meisner recalls. "So we all took apartments there, or rather one apartment, unfurnished, for all of us. We used mats they left outside the dealership as beds. And it went downhill from there." Once in Los Angeles, the Poor hooked up with Charlie Greene and Brian Stone, who were managing the Buffalo Springfield, among others. Meisner explains, "But we were like the ones at the bottom of the totem pole. We never really got anywhere." The Poor's recording career consisted of four singles over a two-year span. Why? Guitarist Randy Naylor recalls, "Greene and Stone kept moving us from one label to another so that they could collect all of the advances! We would be left with some paltry little hand out."

Greene and Stones prime clients, the Buffalo Springfield were struggling as well. Despite having a Top Ten hit, Buffalo Springfield was never able to fully take advantage of their break. A steady stream of replacement Buffaloes began passing through the band in the wake of Bruce Palmer's deportation. Love's bassist Ken Forrsi sat in for one date at the opening night at Gazzarri's. Ex-Squire Kenny Koblun was called in from Canada to replace Palmer temporarily, but after a brief 10-day stay, he was let go. Jim Fielder was next in line (although Young considered Guess Who bassist Jim Kale) to play the bass. Fielder lasted until May when Palmer managed to get back into the country. Unfortunately, that was the exact moment that Neil Young chose to opt out of the band and a new guitar player had to be found. Buffalo Springfield's managers brought Doug Hastings of the Daily Flash into the band but the fit was not a comfortable one.

Without Neil Young, the Buffalo Springfield began to splinter. After a shaky couple of dates in Colorado, Stills brought in Byrd David Crosby to sit in for the important set at the Monterey Pop Festival. Unfortunately, Crosby didn't help, and the band's set was ignored by most of the media and left out of the theatrical film of the festival. Almost right after the festival, Furay suffered an attack of tonsillitis and the band canceled several engagements, including the

Newport Folk Festival. In Furay's absence, the band did a couple of local dates at the Hullabaloo with Crosby taking his place.

Although the summer was filled with concert dates and a few recording dates, it was clear that Doug Hastings was not the answer. Young had tried to launch a solo career, but Atlantic would not let him out of his contract, and they were not interested in him as a solo artist. Financially down to almost nothing, Young returned to the group in August, and the band completed their second album with him a month later.

However, the year 1968 would not treat the Buffalo Springfield well. In late January, tensions between Stills and Young increased. After a gig at UC Irvine on January 26, the pair began fighting backstage after a spirited guitar duel onstage. Dewey Martin leapt into the fray and lectured the pair about acting like "a couple of old ladies." Bemused, Bruce Palmer hopped in his car with a young girl and sped away. On the freeway back to LA, the police stopped him and arrested him for having an open container. The band's lawyers secured his release, and Palmer headed for home at the Tropicana Hotel. Within hours, police arrived there and arrested him for possession of marijuana. While in jail, representatives for the group arrived and insisted that Palmer sign away his rights and royalties to the group. He was too much of liability to keep in the group. He reluctantly did so and Palmer was subsequently sent to a detention center in San Diego to await deportation.

The band was back to square one again. With shows booked in the Los Angeles area, the group needed a bass player quickly. They held auditions immediately, and midway through the parade of applicants, a familiar face appeared.

2
Last Time Around

Hopping up on the stage, surprisingly, was their engineer-producer Jim Messina. The 19 year old had been a crucial part of the band's support team in completing their long-awaited second album. But his musical talents were never called upon during the sessions. Bemused, Furay and the rest of the band called out a tune from the second album and began to play. Already familiar with the material, Messina jumped right in. A few bars into the song, Stephen Stills began to smile and Messina knew he was in. Messina recalls, "The moment the music started up, I just knew this was great! I was having a great time. And they all knew it was the right feel too." Stills gave his approval after the audition and the others agreed and shook hands all around.

After working on the BUFFALO SPRINGFIELD AGAIN album, Messina was in a perfect position to help the band out in the wake of Palmer's departure. Aside from filling in on the odd live date, Messina helped the band put together a number of tracks that he had helped produce in December and January, along with some left over from the spring sessions in 1967, and submitted it to Atlantic Records as their third album in mid-February. Disappointed with the effort, Atlantic rejected it and told the band to do some more work on it. Label president Ahmet Ertegun also asked that the group, obviously demoralized, to consider booking a tour to support the album. They did, signing on to another Beach Boys tour, this time of the Southeast. It was a grueling tour, 33 shows in 17 days. The tour got off to an inauspicious start when the first four dates were canceled after Martin Luther King was assassinated and tensions in the South rose. The band eventually completed the tour, although the Springfield had to pay back money advanced to them for the shows that were canceled.

During one of the canceled dates, Richie Furay and new bassist Jimmy Messina found themselves in the back of a taxi in Nashville. "Richie and I were driving along one day in the back seat of a taxicab," Messina explains. "I asked him if he was interested in purising music, and he said he was. So I said, 'Well, whey don't we get a band togteher, a small band, part country and part rock and roll?' He said, 'I'm willing to give it a try.' So I said, 'Why don't we start thinking about it now before this band busts up?'" It was no secret to both of them that the group was undeniably on its last legs. Although Messina got along with everyone in the group, he naturally gravitated towards Furay. Their personalities seemed to mesh, and Messina felt that both Furay and his wife were exceptional people. As the cab carried the pair through Nashville, Furay agreed that Messina's idea appealed to him, but both were content to wait for the right time to put this plan into action.

They didn't have to wait long. During the tour, Neil Young let it leak that after the tour he was through with the Buffalo Springfield. Dewey Martin went through the roof upon hearing the news. He sought out Young's room and pounded on the door, screaming that he was going to kill him. After returning to California, the Springfield collapsed due mostly to apathy of its remaining members. By the time the band returned to LA, it was broke. The cancellations had forced the group to return money to the Beach Boys, who had promoted the tour themselves. The members of the Springfield were unable to get airline credit or rent cars upon their return.

Following through on his plan, Young announced again that he was leaving once they were back in Los Angeles. This time there would be no attempt to keep the band going. Stills was spending nearly all of his time with David Crosby and Jimi Hendrix. And unknown to his band mates, after doing some session work for Judy Collins after the Beach Boys tour, Stills had laid down a number of acoustic demos in anticipation of a solo project. Clearly Stills was looking beyond his group. When approached about replacing Young yet again, he told Furay, "I don't want to break in another guitar player." Since he was no longer interested, the Buffalo Springfield ceased to exist.

Unfortunately, the album was not completed so recording sessions continued after the band was back in Los Angeles. Neil Young was finished with the group, and Stills had also abandoned the effort. Messina and Furay gravitated even more towards each other while continuing to work on the album.   Although Messina had some preliminary discussions with Stephen Stills about working together after the Springfield broke up, Stills chose to work by himself on his material. After recording material together at Atlantic's New York studio, Furay and Messina brought the tracks back to Los Angeles. Messina explains, "With Ahmet's cooperation, we got most of the last part of the material, like *Kind Woman*, recorded in New York but it still wasn't complete. So when we came back to California, I still had some work to do. Richie had a roadie at one time who knew Rusty and George, and I was looking for a steel player to play on *Kind Woman*."

Now working for the Turtles, roadie Miles Thomas offered his help. Still sure that Furay's talent was worth backing, Thomas continued to maintain an interest in his career. Thomas had told Furay that he played steel guitar when they were first introduced. When Furay approached him about playing on *Kind Woman*, Thomas begged off, claiming he hadn't played in years. Furay tried to cajole him into playing something on the track. Rather than offer up a less than acceptable performance, Thomas presented Furay with an alternative. He told Furay and Messina that he had gone to school with one of the best steel players back in Colorado. With Furay and Messina's approval, Thomas contacted Rusty Young.

Meanwhile, Rusty Young held down a day job at Music City, a Denver music store, to make ends meet. Böenzee Cryque was slowly winding down. In fact, by the time Young was contacted about the Buffalo Springfield session, he was actively seeking a new gig. "Miles called me up and said, 'I got this thing set up for you,'" Young relates. "'The Springfield need a steel player on a song they're recording, and I've got an audition for you with this guy named Gram Parsons who's putting together a new band, and they're looking for a steel player too. So come on out.'" Young knew that his answer to Thomas was a lifetime decision and it wasn't a tough one. He considered the Springfield to be his favorite band, and the opportunity to play on one of their records was too much to pass up. Young arranged to come out to California immediately.

Furay picked Young up at the airport in his little red Volkswagen, shattering any rock star myth that Young had envisioned. Furay took him to Sunset Sound and introduced him to Jimmy Messina. Young recalls, "Jimmy was pretty much running the session, but it was always a partnership between Richie and Jimmy, right from before Poco." Rusty Young had some apprehension when he found that the airline had broken his steel guitar in transit.

When informed of the damaged instrument, Messina found a steel guitar belonging to Stephen Stills packed away in a closet at Sunset Sound. Upon inspection, Young agreed that it would work, although the pedals were installed backwards. After briefly explaining what they had in mind, the pair ushered Young into the recording studio and let him play. Messina smiles, "We flew Rusty out. I set the mikes up and recorded his performance for that song. And it was during that session, on the other side of the glass, that Richie and I had a conversation which followed up on a heart-to-heart talk we'd had during the Springfield's final tour. I said, 'Richie, here's our opportunity. He's got enough country and enough rock 'n' roll in him to where we should consider talking to him about working with us.'" Furay agreed. After Young laid a sparkling steel line on the track, Furay and Messina asked him to hang around for awhile. Young chuckled, "We went to breakfast together, the three of us, and talked about playing together. So they asked me to stay and get a new band going. There was even talk of keeping the Buffalo Springfield name. I didn't do the Gram Parsons audition because when I went into the studio with Richie and Jimmy, we really hit it off."

The Buffalo Springfield played several final shows, including concerts in San Diego and Sacramento, and played their final concert on May 5, 1968, at the Long Beach Arena. Backstage, Rusty Young hung out with Furay and Messina, anxious to get started with a new band. After the breakup, both Stephen Stills and Neil Young left to pursue solo careers, leaving Furay and Messina to assemble the group's final album from previously recorded songs. The pair took the material from Stills and Young and added some of their own songs.

With Furay and Messina still busy putting the final touches on LAST TIME AROUND, Young returned to Denver to prepare for his move to Los Angeles. He quit his job at the music store, got married, and then headed back for California. After returning to southern California, Young found Furay and Messina struggling to put together the remainder of their new band. Messina recalls, "Richie and I wanted every player we got to have the potential for being a star in their own right. We didn't want any weak links."

After the Springfield's breakup, Furay's house became the focal point for auditions for a new band. The end of the Buffalo Springfield did not leave the Furay's in a strong financial position, but with some royalties coming in, they were able to make ends meet. Furay was still signed to Atlantic, and he made a request to have the label front his proto-group some studio time to demo some material. Although Ahmet Ertegun loved the Springfield, after their breakup he knew Atlantic would not be able to retain the services of everyone. So, he chose to hang onto Stephen Stills. Already wary of Neil Young's stability, Ertegun allowed him to move to Reprise Records. He also wanted to make sure that anyone interested in Furay's services would offer Atlantic terms that were advantageous to the label. When Furay's request came through, Ertegun approved it, knowing the demos would be used to interest record companies in signing Furay's new group. Furay, Messina, and Young cut some material in June 1968 at TTG Studios in Hollywood. They used session drummer "Fast" Eddie Hoh and keyboardist Lee Michaels. Among the songs the proto-group recorded were *What a Day*, *Do You Feel It Too*, and *I Guess You Made It*, all holdovers from the Buffalo Springfield, as well as *Tomorrow*, a tune recently written by Furay and Skip Goodwin.

Documentation on these sessions indicates were booked as Buffalo Springfield sessions likely for billing purposes. Messina recalls that although booked as Springfield recording sessions, they were really for Poco. "Those were demo sessions to try to get the band together for Poco because *Tomorrow* I don't recall ever being considered for Buffalo Springfield. *I Guess You Made It* had been around for awhile, but I don't know how long. I don't know if that was the beginning of it or whether that song had been recorded as a demo for Buffalo Springfield." Rusty Young maintains that the proto-group flirted with the idea of continuing as Buffalo Springfield, and in fact it was reported in the press as such. Thankfully, Furay decided that a break from the past was necessary.

Back in Los Angeles, Gram Parsons returned from London after quitting the Byrds. Word got around that Parsons was putting together a group aimed at blending country and rock more effectively than the Byrds had accomplished on their album SWEETHEARTS OF THE RODEO. Furay decided to see what was happening with his friend from the Village. Furay recalled, "Gram and I had conversations about picking and choosing players and making one band. But that never worked because I wasn't gonna give up Rusty for Sneaky [Pete Kleinlow], and he wasn't going to give up this guy for that guy, so two bands evolved."

Furay decided that his vision was the one he wanted to follow. Rather than form a band together, Furay and Parsons each decided to continue putting together their own bands. Parsons went off to form the Flying Burrito Brothers. Rusty Young has long felt that Parson's later work with the Burritos was heavily influenced by what he heard at Poco's rehearsals. Parsons strongly disagreed. "The difference is that [the Burritos] started out playing country music and Poco started out playing Buffalo Springfield music."

The Flying Burrito Brothers and Poco would often be mentioned together in critical discussions of the emerging genre of country-rock. However, members of Poco never felt there was a comparison between the two groups. George Grantham maintains, "The Burritos play what I'd call barroom country music; they sound like all those bands that play country standards in honky-tonk bars." Furay agrees, "Yeah, they're always doing that ol' shuffle beat. We don't play that kind of country music. We play progressive country music."

One of Furay's goals for his new group was to find a drummer who could sing. He and Messina had tried several drummers without success. Jon Corneal and Jimmy Ibbotsen also auditioned. According to Corneal, he was actually hired, but soon left when the band continued to take its time getting together. Finally, Young helped by bringing in Böenzee Cryque drummer George Grantham. Young assured Furay that his friend from Böenzee Cryque would be perfect. Messina was quick to listen. "I know for myself that when I find a musician that I really like and I like their style, I like them, and if they make a suggestion, I say, take it!" Rusty Young made the call and his friend was quick to answer. "George had been out looking for a straight job," Young recalls. "So when he showed up in penny loafers and short hair, Richie and Jim thought I'd lost my mind. But he played just the kind of drums we needed and he could sing. He was perfect."

Since Young had split for California, the Böenzee Cryque had collapsed. Joe Neddo's erratic behavior had led to him leaving before Young. Sam Bush's recent marriage spelled a winding down in the interest of keeping the band together. They had been unable to break beyond Colorado, and now it seemed the band was marking time. Grantham remembers, "When Rusty decided to go out and do [the Buffalo Springfield session], the band pretty much kind of crumbled around that. People pretty much decided to go on home. After Rusty left, I got into another playing situation. Malcolm Mitchell had a friend named Huey. They'd put a band together and I was playing with them. It was more of a Paul Butterfield kind of thing." Grantham joined the group, and they recorded one single for Dot Records with producer Frank Slay. The single *Sightseer/Feather* was released in early 1968 and did not chart nationally. *Sightseer* was a rocking blues-oriented tune with some atmospheric slide guitar work. *Feather* was a mellower psychedelic ballad arranged with strings and organs by Frank Slay. Both songs were originals written by Mitchell. Grantham confirms that Mitchell also wrote a song called *Candy Coated Lady* that was never released. A demo of the tune performed by Böenzee Cryque has recently surfaced.

A few months after the release of the Malcolm Mitchell single, Young contacted Grantham. "Rusty got in touch with me," Grantham enthused, "and said they needed a singing country-rock drummer. That was pretty much right up my alley. They had tried a couple of guys and for some reason it didn't click, and I think Rusty wanted to get me out there. I was kind of excited, scared, and yet I had my doubts about myself, 'Oh my god, L.A., Buffalo Springfield!' I was scared to death about going out there. But at least I knew Rusty and I felt good about that." Grantham's enthusiasm was tempered by his nervousness. He arrived in Los Angeles, and Young took him to Furay's house in Laurel Canyon.

Furay and Messina didn't exactly fall all over themselves over Grantham, as they had with Young. Grantham recalls that it was a nerve-racking wait. "We got together, ran through some tunes that Richie, Jimmy, and Rusty had been working on with the band. I remember going into a studio and playing along with some drum tracks that Dewey had recorded on some songs that Richie wanted to use in Poco and stuff like that." It wasn't just his drumming that Furay and Messina were evaluating. The new group was to have a strong vocal component. "Yeah, singing was a big part of it," Grantham recalled, "When I was in Denver, I was the high harmony guy. I was Graham Nash, you know? I got to L.A. and what they needed was low harmony parts. I had to go from one extreme to the other, which really didn't suit me. But I did know parts and that helped a bit." It took several weeks before Furay and Messina committed themselves and asked Grantham to stay. Relieved, Grantham moved out to L.A. and set up at Miles Thomas's place, along with Young and his wife.

The quartet began rehearsals at Furay's house in Laurel Canyon in mid to late summer. Furay and Messina started seriously looking for a bass player after sending off the tapes of the final Buffalo Springfield album to Atco Records. Although Messina had been the Springfield's final bass player, he made the decision to return to the guitar with the new group. Messina had played guitar in a couple of surf groups in the mid-60's. Messina started off by trying to emulate Stephen Stills' guitar style. He picked up some fingerpicks and tried to work out picking patterns in a country style. It was different from the surf riffs that he'd come up with as a teenager. Messina ran into trouble immediately when the metal fingerpicks began cutting into his fingers. "Eventually I just threw them away," Messina told Steve Caraway. It was clear that Messina's struggles on guitar were going to keep the group close to home for a while.

By contrast, Rusty Young's abilities made them realize that he would be the lead player. During their jam sessions, he showed them the versatility of the steel guitar by imitating the piano, organ, and banjo on it. Young also played the banjo, dobro, and mandolin. Furay's guitar skills were modest in comparison, so he chose to stick to basic rhythm guitar. Grantham's skills were certainly acceptable. The questions were limited to how well Messina would jump back into guitar and what other instruments would be needed.

Initially, the group was open to other instruments and auditioned several musicians. "You have to remember," explains Young. "In those days there also weren't synthesizers. So if you wanted an original sound, you had to play real instruments that weren't rock instruments to get different sounds." Furay's fledgling band also auditioned Gregg Allman of the Hour Glass. The jams added some textures to the group that were enticing. Rusty Young told Kurt Loder, "It was amazing. Gregg and Richie really did sing well together, it was a style that sounded real unique." Furay recalls, "We started Poco and rehearsed for what seemed like forever. We even tried Greg Allman when we were trying to put the band together. That lasted maybe a couple of days." But the group wasn't comfortable with Allman and his personality. During the short time they played together, Allman often would jam for hours, suddenly leave, hop on his motorcycle and scream back and forth down the street outside Furay's house, and then return to play. This unpredictability, plus the biker image, didn't fit with what the group wanted to project. After a few days, Allman was told that there wasn't a spot for him in the group.

Young noted that many of the people that the band auditioned and didn't offer a spot went on to form groups of their own using variations of what Young and company were doing. The struggle was somewhat puzzling for Rusty Young. "I thought that Jimmy and Richie would know some big time stars to bring into the group, but it took a long time to get Poco together." It's doubtful that Furay's approach was to bring in known names. He was openly critical of his former partner Stephen Stills' approach of snagging ex-Byrd David Crosby and ex-Hollie Graham Nash to partner with.

As Furay continued to hunt for members, his former partner Neil Young appeared on the scene. He was about to put his first solo album together and wanted some assistance from Jimmy Messina. Young's relationship with the Rockets had yet to blossom into the formation of Crazy Horse, so Young needed additional musicians to help him record his first album. Messina was a sympathetic companion during the final months of the Springfield, and

Young gave him credit for the successful sound of *Expecting to Fly* on BUFFALO SPRINGFIELD AGAIN. Rusty Young recalled, "I remember Neil coming over to Richie's house in Laurel Canyon a couple of times when we were rehearsing Poco. He sat down and played us songs he was going to do on his first solo record and hung out with us. That's where he picked up on Jimmy and George for his solo album." Since his new band wasn't ready, Messina happily obliged. When Messina found that Young needed a drummer, he brought along George Grantham to the sessions.

Young began his solo album at Sunset Sound in August 1968, and Messina proved to be a willing partner. When Young heard the rough mix of *If I Could Have Her Tonight*, he wanted to re-cut the track. Messina recorded an entirely new bass line while Young re-cut the various guitar lines. Grantham recalled this diversion did not cost Poco any time. "I think it took only two or three days. It was real quick. Neil liked to work quickly in the studio." Despite Messina's efforts to aid his friend, when NEIL YOUNG was issued six months later, both Messina's and Grantham's names were omitted from the liner notes. It took nearly 15 years before Young acknowledged Messina and Grantham's contributions to his first album.

Messina has some vague memories of the rather brief experience. "I recall one session in particular where I came in – it may have been after we'd already recorded or they'd recorded something else and asked me to play bass on it, overdub some bass. I'm the kind of person that has to write a chart on something because, not that I can't remember, but it's too taxing to sit there and try to remember and also focus on creating parts. They played the song and I wrote out the chart very quickly, double-checking it, went out and sat down, and I said, 'Let's do one run-through and let me make sure I have the right chords.' I played and then I said, 'OK, you can roll it now.' And they said, 'We already did.' I said, 'Well, I...uh, I can play better than that.' 'Nope, nope. It's fine – we love it!' And they took it."

During the sessions, Messina also made a swap of guitars with Young that benefited both musicians. "The first set-up I used in Poco was a Gretsch that Neil gave to me," recalls Messina. "I had a Les Paul, but I didn't like it, and he had an extra 'Horseshoe' Gretsch. So I traded him and started out on that guitar." The Les Paul Messina surrendered was to become Neil Young's signature electric guitar "Old Black" after Young modified the pickups. The Gretsch lasted for only the first couple months of live performances with Poco before Messina switched to a custom made Fender Telecaster that produced his distinctive guitar sound.

Messina and Grantham's extra-curricular activity did not stop the efforts to find the missing pieces of the new group. Grantham revealed, "We had a couple of people in mind for the bass. Chris Ethridge was one player we looked at." Despite a solid audition, Furay and Messina determined that vocal skills were a key ingredient in their band and Ethridge didn't measure up. Ethridge went on to become a charter member of the Flying Burrito Brothers, Gram Parsons' band. The group's search for a bass player came down to two musicians, both recommended highly to the fledgling band. One was Randy Meisner, bassist for the Poor. Miles Thomas had suggested him to Furay, who told Thomas to bring him by the house.

Meisner told rock historian John Einarson of this audition, "I went up to Richie's house where they were having tryouts for the group. I had come out to California with the Soul Survivors who became the Poor. Miles Thomas was the guy that pretty much got me into the tryout with Jimmy and Richie. Rusty was already in the group. I don't know what it was, but I played about three songs with them, and probably it was my voice which was real high and strong and with Richie's which was strong so that kind of worked. We didn't use any falsetto in those days, just full out blasting. And with my little bit of R 'n' B bass playing, it worked." However, Meisner did not seem anxious to jump into another situation. Messina recalls that once they had decided on Meisner for bass, it took some persuasion to convince him to join. "I think there was a little bit of courting and seduction used in getting Randy. Courting meaning spending time with him and seduction meaning giving him the music and hoping that it had its addicting effect." Indeed it did and Meisner soon agreed to join the fledgling band.

The group eventually realized that full out blasting on vocals would do irreparable damage to their vocal cords once they started touring. So they made the decision to tune their instruments down a half-step so the Furay and Meisner didn't have to strain to hit the high notes night after night. Poco maintained that practice as part of their musical arrangements until the 1980s. .

The other major candidate for the bass playing position was Timothy B. Schmit, bassist for the Sacramento-based group called the New Breed. The band had released several local singles and made a couple of TV appearances during their career. By 1968, the band was calling themselves Glad and recording an album in Los Angeles. During the sessions, several girls who were fans of the New Breed followed them down from Sacramento. When these girls relocated to Los Angeles, they made friends with the Buffalo Springfield. They played their New Breed records for the Springfield, and Furay took an instant liking to Schmit's voice. The girls kept telling

Glad that Richie wanted to jam with them, but the group stead-fastly refused. "It was too intimidating," guitarist Tom Phillips explains. Finally, just before Glad left for Sacramento, Schmit decided to accept the invitation. He and Phillips drove to Furay's house. Phillips picks up the story:

> So the two of us drove over to Richie's house not knowing at all what was going on. And when we got there it was Poco. It was Messina, Rusty and George and Richie. And they handed Tim a bass and said, 'You wanna play some songs?' And Tim said, 'OK' and they started playing and then they took him into the bedroom. I remember that's when I re-member seeing Rusty play steel guitar 'cuz Richie and George and Jim went into the back bedroom and I could hear them harmonizing. I can't remem-ber what they were singing but they were teaching Tim the harmony part or something. And Rusty and I were in the front room and I just watched him play steel just completely enthralled. I bought a steel when I came back. So I remember driving back to Hollywood and Tim was going, 'Wow, they're start-ing a new band. What if they want me to play bass? What am I going to do?' And I said...I remember plain as day, I said, 'You'd be crazy not to go..'cuz what are we doing? We can't even get a job!'

Furay did invite him to audition for his group. Coincidentally, Meisner auditioned the same day, immediately after Schmit. Schmit's audition was encouraging. It was a tough call, and it ap-pears that Furay and Messina were leaning toward Schmit. But after some investigation it became clear that Schmit couldn't join be-cause of his draft status. He was classified 1-A and would surely be drafted if he didn't remain in school. That situation worked for Glad, but not for Furay's new band. Instead, the pair offered the position to Meisner after his audition.

Schmit, although he had some reservations about leaving his friends in Glad, was crushed when Furay and Messina failed to select him. "I felt like I was a failure." Schmit remembers. "I was only (about) 20 years old, but I felt old in the rock 'n' roll world. I felt like this was my one big chance and I blew it. It wasn't a great time." Disheartened, Schmit returned to Sacramento at the end of the summer with his band mates in Glad only to find that the time they had spent away from the local scene had cost them the loyalty of their local fan base.   They also discovered that their manager was having trouble booking even local dates for them. Before long, Schmit's apathy was brutally apparent to his band mates. Phillips explains, "We used to ask him, 'What do you want to play next?' and he'd say, 'Who cares.'" Schmit agrees. "I felt really low and I was really getting depressed because it would have been just what I wanted to do, and in fact I never stopped thinking about it."

In Los Angeles, Furay and his new band began assessing their pool of talent. Aside from his solid bass playing, Meisner's vocal talents were his strong suit. Grantham says, "Randy wound up taking the high harmony parts I was used to singing. But Randy could do it better. He sang higher than anyone I'd ever heard in my life. So that was ok with me."   Additionally, Meisner's punchy R 'n' B-influenced bass playing gave the band a solid bottom. George Grantham's drumming was solid and his versatile vocals were a true asset. Rusty Young's fluid and innovative pedal steel guitar work was clearly going to be the band's signature sound. Messina's Bakersfield-style guitar work and production skills were an obvious strength for the band.

Furay was satisfied with the band and rehearsals began in earnest. At first, they played in Furay's living room. However, as the volume increased and the visitors such as Glenn Frey and Gram Parsons continued to crowd the place, it was clear the band was going to need more room. It was time for the band to take a step into the world outside Furay's door.

3
When It All Began

By the fall of 1968, rehearsals had quickly outgrown Furay's house, and Dickie Davis arranged for the band to use the Troubadour during the day to rehearse and learn tunes. Davis, the former road manager for the Buffalo Springfield, had previously worked at the Troubadour, and was friends with the owner, Doug Weston. As a result of the agreement, the band had the run of the Troubadour during the afternoon for several months. Doug Weston had the band promise to play his club for free as part of the deal. It was a typical Weston deal that obligated the band to a number of live appearances at the Troubadour for no fee until the "rent" was earned back. Still, the band couldn't afford commercial rehearsal space, and the deal did guarantee them a venue to showcase their band when they were ready. "Before our first showcase gig," Grantham sighed. "We rehearsed a lot. We rehearsed a lot at the Troubadour long before we ever played live there. That was the way they wanted to do it - to get the songs down, try a lot of different things, really polish it and make it shine." Richard Perry, Troubadour bouncer and bartender, recalls, "They played the Troubadour every afternoon for the entire summer. They didn't even have a name for themselves yet."

They continued with rehearsals and the level of frustration proved to be a challenge. They were all fairly young and inexperienced. Although Furay and Messina had more professional experience, Messina was struggling with regaining his skills on guitar. It

19

seems clear from subsequent comments that Messina's inability to jump right back into lead guitar playing was one source of the frustration. Messina confirms, "During that year of transition - from being a bass player to playing guitar in Poco - I had a lot to learn and a lot to create. Fortunately, the beginning of something is always the best place [to learn] because you all learn together. The country-rock style was the new thing so I had to learn how to play and fit into that. It took me a year to get that particular thing together as a player."

Grantham agreed. "I think it took him awhile. Of course, he had played guitar before. Jimmy, I would say, wasn't an improviser, an Eric Clapton-type, a soloist who improvises licks. Jimmy was one to work up parts, kinda like writing a song. He and Rusty would work up twin lines and stuff. It was a different kind of approach. So things were much more worked out instead of playing off each other. That was the way Jimmy was." Despite Messina's optimistic evaluation of his guitar playing, it bothered Rusty Young. "Part of the hassles throughout was the fact that Jimmy just couldn't pick very good guitar. He got a bit better, but in the beginning he was just terrible. But he's a brilliant bass player, so good that I hate to see him play guitar - though his playing has really improved."

Another difficulty was that Young and Grantham's experience, for the most part, had been to work out arrangements to cover British rock songs. They were much less prepared to offer creative arrangements to original compositions. The band spent months working out arrangements to a handful of Furay compositions. Furay had nearly a dozen songs left over from his days as a member of Buffalo Springfield. In fact, several tunes eventually used the arrangements that the Springfield had worked up for them. Furay encouraged Messina to write songs as well, but there were few to work with in the beginning. The band continued to struggle as 1968 waned. Of these early days, Furay recalls how hard and long it took for the group to get tight. Young agrees, characterizing themselves as kids who weren't very professional.

Despite the difficulties, it was clear that the band was forging some exciting new musical forms. Musicians from around the L.A. area began dropping by rehearsals and paying close attention. The longer Furay delayed the public debut of his group, the more anticipation seemed to build among the musicians and others who frequented the L.A. club scene. The time spent rehearsing allowed the band to forge an exciting and dynamic new sound with a consistant performance. The vibrant energy of the five young musicians translated directly into their arrangements and live performances.

As the band grew tighter and more proficient in their execution, the more solid a unit the band became. Unique to their situation was that all five of them contributed to their sound and to their approach.

As the musical side of things began to come together, the business side needed attention. The group needed management and they immediately made an unfortunate mistake. The fledgling group saw themselves as anti-establishment and therefore ignored going with a professional management company or manager. As Furay was to recall in a 1973 interview, "I used to think, I'll just play my music and leave the business to other people, I'm not gonna worry about that stuff at all." Instead, Furay wanted someone who would be more sympathetic to the band. He also wanted someone that he could talk with and influence. His experiences with Greene and Stone during his time with Buffalo Springfield had soured him on Hollywood managers. Furay chose to offer management of his group to former Springfield road manager Dickie Davis. Davis had served the band in several capacities over their brief career before being fired shortly before the band's breakup. Davis was certainly not professional management by Hollywood standards. However, he had some experience with the Springfield, and that was enough for the new group. He fit in well, and they were left to put together material and tighten up their chops for live performances.

One person frustrated by the choice of Davis was Miles Thomas, who was relegated to the role of road manager. Although he felt strongly that his efforts were largely responsible for getting the Colorado contingent together with Furay and Messina, he had been unable to get the group to accept him as their manager. Rusty Young also expressed his doubts about using Dickie Davis but conceded, "We didn't want to be part of the establishment. We wanted a band that didn't have to play by the rules. We chose the route of going with a friend managing the band who had basically never done it before. That really hurt the band in the beginning."

After Messina and Grantham finished up the last of their sessions with Neil Young in October, Furay agreed that the band was ready to make their debut. They auditioned for a spot on the Monday hoot-night lineup at the Troubadour and got a spot early in October. They were set to make a name for themselves.

In order to do that, the group needed a name, of course. "Our first name was R. F. D.," Grantham was to recall wistfully in *Crawdaddy*. "It stood for Richie Furay's Dream or something like that." Rusty Young recalls that they seemed to have a new name every week. Among the names reported in the underground press that the band considered were Fool's Gold, Popcorn, Red Wing,

White Lightening, Douglas Leader, and Flintlock Pepperbox. Troubadour employee Richard Perry witnessed the band's early rehearsals and says, "They were first called Buttermilk and R.F.D. Then
one day they showed up and were calling themselves Pogo" Young
said it was their manager, Dickie Davis, who offered Pogo. According to Young, Davis identified with the comic strip character so it
seemed perfectly natural to him for the group to use the name.

Early one Monday evening in October, Furay and company
packed their gear and headed down to the Troubadour on Sunset
Strip, a popular music industry hangout, to play their hoot-night.
Session bassist Arnie Moore was there that night and recalls, "I
walked into the Troubadour in LA one night and saw all these record
company people standing about - so I knew something was going to
happen. It was a Monday night, which is 'hoot night' - anyone can
get up and play. Anyway, this group came on...and it was Poco,
who had never been seen before; they'd been rehearsing in Topanga
Canyon, but no one had heard them yet...Well, they did five songs
and just blew the place apart! Nobody could believe it." Pogo's
five-song, 20-minute set created such a sensation that owner Doug
Weston immediately booked them for another engagement. Richie
Furay would later call Pogo's debut one of the most memorable
moments of his musical career. The crowd's reaction nearly reduced him to tears. After all, Pogo was his baby and his responsibility, and he rightly felt the pressure.

Each of the members has special memories of that first live
performance. "That was our coming out party there," beamed
Grantham. "Everyone in town knew about it because they knew the
talk was on the street - Richie and Jimmy from the Springfield - it
was an incredible night. So exciting! The place was packed with all
these record company people. Man, I think we played about 20
minutes. We were all scared to death. It wasn't too hard to get up
for that." Rusty Young boasted, "People loved the band!"

Jimmy Messina also has vivid memories of that night. "Well,
it was an incredibly exciting evening. Record executives were all
over the place. The place was buzzing. It felt like the Beatles
could be in the room. And just seconds before they said 'Ladies and
Gentlemen,' there was this big "BONG!" and my fingerpick had shot
off because I was holding it too tensely on a string, and it shot off
into the audience. Suddenly, I'm missing one finger to play. So I
remember stumbling through the first song. It was such a drag,
such an embarrassment. That was my own narcissism, my own self-
consciousness coming through, but the rest of the evening all I recall was I was scared out of my wits, nervous, but it was exciting

and everyone loved the music. There was a wonderful vibe in the room. They loved us. It doesn't get much better than that."

Furay felt that he and the band had done their best to prepare. "We had put a lot of hard work into making our debut be a memorable moment, both for us and those who would be there when we took the stage," he recalls. "There would be nothing short of the highest professionalism we were capable of. There had been a lot of talk about our debut, and the last thing I or any in the band wanted to do was 'wish we had been ready' – we were and it was exciting. We were stepping onto the stage with a new kind of music. We knew we had something special but only time would tell."

One member of the audience was guitarist Paul Cotton. His band, the Illinois Speed Press, had recently moved from Chicago to Los Angeles. Hearing through the grapevine about the first spin-off from the Buffalo Springfield, Cotton made sure he was there. "It was quite an up evening," Cotton recalled. "The audience was blown away. I know I was. They were really well rehearsed. Most of the songs that night ended up on that first album. You could just feel the excitement. George was amazing, a singing drummer. I was really intrigued by George's and Randy's voices. It was the freshest music I'd heard since the Byrds' debut album – impeccable harmonies, Richie's voice, and Rusty's steel. Nobody plays like Rusty, then or now. The marriage of country and rock was there."

A few weeks later on October 24, the band appeared again at the Troubadour, this time billed as R.F.D. Playing a full set, the band thrilled the crowd again with an energetic set of country-rock music. Reviewer Michael Etcheson of the *Los Angeles Herald-Examiner* noted, "They do something between country and rock, authentically both, with leanings one way or another. They are the Richie Furay group. Furay, who also brought Jim Messina from the Buffalo Springfield with him, took the trouble to rehearse them well before the public saw them, a gesture that the packed house appreciated." R.F.D.'s set included *What a Day, Just In Case It Happens, Yes Indeed* and *Short Changed*, all of which would subsequently wind up on their first album. R.F.D. went over so well that Troubadour owner Doug Weston promised to have the band back for a longer stay.

Fresh from two acclaimed shows, R.F.D made another surprise appearance at Bovard Auditorium at USC on November 2 to play a benefit for the LA Free Clinic with Hoyt Axton, Bobby Lind, and Three Dog Night. It was another dynamic performance that gave the band even more confidence.

True to his word, Weston brought the band back to the Troubadour about a month later. The band officially debuted at the Troubadour on November 19, 1968, with Biff Rose as the headliner. By then, they had retreated to using Pogo as their name. Dickie Davis had come up with R.F.D. When someone in the band decided that the initials really stood for Richard F. Davis, they demanded the name be changed. Their two-week stay proved that their initial gig had been no fluke. Reviewer Pete Johnson in the *Los Angeles Times* gave them glowing marks, especially praising the singing of Furay and Meisner saying, "Both have high, flexible voices which melt together in delightful harmonies and separate for strong solos." The Troubadour gigs quickly got their name around L.A. Michael Eitchison was back and observed, "Pogo has broadened their material since their one night stand a few weeks back. They are still a seamless combination of rock and country but there is a bit more variety now." Included in Pogo's set were Furay's ballads *First Love* and *Crazy Eyes*.

In December, Pogo continued to play the local club scene. They returned to the Troubadour for a couple of shows on December 6 and 7. Just before Christmas, Pogo appeared at the Anaheim Convention Center as part of a Sam Riddle *Boss City* show. The concert was filmed for later broadcast on local LA television. A few days later, Pogo made their first out of town appearance at San Francisco's Fillmore West, third billed behind Steve Miller and Sly and the Family Stone. The trip to the Bay Area was somewhat of a surprise to most of Pogo.

They ran into the provincial audiences during their stay at the Fillmore. Grantham was shocked. "I didn't know it, but they didn't like L.A. bands much. There was this conflict between L.A. bands and San Francisco bands. I don't know if we knew that or not. I know I didn't know that. There was a little bit of friction there with Bill Graham too." Furay, of course, had dealt with the situation as a member of the Buffalo Springfield. "I don't have a lot of fond memories of San Francisco," recalls Furay. "I didn't like the music or the town, even though the Fillmore was the happening place on the West Coast."

Pogo would actually have a short life – at least as a band name. Walt Kelly, creator of the comic strip Pogo, objected to the group's use the name of his iconic cartoon strip and threatened to sue. Upon their return to Los Angeles, Pogo was booked to open a show for Canned Heat at the Shrine Auditorium. The group found itself served with papers to cease and desist using the Pogo name. This was a bit of a shock to Furay, who recalled the owner of the Buffalo-Springfield Roller Company's approval to use its name for his previous group. "Walt Kelly took immediate offense even though the name had nothing to do with the comic strip," Furay told Pete Fornatale in *Jazz & Pop*. "So we just dropped the line from the 'g' rather than hassle and try to find another name." With such a successful debut and good publicity, changing the group's name was not advantageous to their career. Still, being forced to change their name wasn't the worst thing that could have happened to them. The change was made to Poco. It was close enough to their former name that the recognition they'd gained wouldn't totally be lost. They spent a considerable amount of time in the press downplaying the change and insisted that Poco had no special meaning whatsoever to them. Although the group began referring to themselves as Poco, the change in the public eye took awhile to take hold. Shows were advertised up to four months later still using the name Pogo. But no one in the band really missed the name. Furay today says, "Thank you Walt where ever you are – Poco is such a much better name."

Despite the shock of the cease and desist order, the New Year's Eve show garnered Pogo some additional positive reviews. Michael Ross of the *Herald-Examiner* noted, "Pogo - the musical heirs of the lamented Buffalo Springfield - entered and introduced itself as the sound of 1969. That's very true. The group, led by Springfield alumni Richie Furay and Jim Messina, certainly combined the tight, intricately-woven harmonies of the Springfield with the brittle, metal ensemble playing currently popular, to a completely contemporary (if eclectic) effect."

In the beginning, Pogo's set consisted almost exclusively of Furay material. Furay also did most of the lead vocals. Meisner got to solo on *Anyway Bye Bye* and *Calico Lady*, although Furay wrote both songs. "*Anyway Bye Bye* was a killer song for us at the Troubadour," contends Meisner. "It was one of those really high songs that Richie and I did. I was just grateful somebody was writing good songs." George Grantham recalled Pogo playing a song of Furay's called *Crazy Eyes* during one of their initial concerts. But the song didn't fit well into their set. This song, written about Gram Parsons, was quickly removed from the set and resurfaced years later with a radically different arrangement. Furay also did his best-known Springfield tunes *A Child's Claim to Fame* and *Kind Woman*.

Rusty Young's steel guitar was instrumentally the focal point of the early Pogo live set. Young explains that the novelty was just one aspect of it. "When we talked about a new band, taking it more towards experimenting with country instruments was a natural. Remember, there were no synthesizers at the time so if you wanted new sounds, you had to go to real instruments that hadn't been widely exposed." Meisner offers, "Rusty didn't play it a lot like a steel. He made a whole different instrument out of it playing it through a Leslie speaker. That was really unique. He could get a B-3 organ sound so we could get that R 'n' B feel, and when we did strictly country stuff, he could go back to that."

The return to Los Angeles also precipitated the search for a record contract. Pogo considered the Beatles new label, but overtures to Apple Records went unrewarded. Young recalls auditioning for George Harrison, but he wasn't interested. This brief encounter with the Beatles led to a spurious story circulating that John Lennon had been responsible for the group taking the name of Poco. Not so, says Rusty Young. "I have no idea where they came up with

that. Lennon was around, but I don't think he was around until after we started playing as Poco. Harrison was there. In the beginning, we even auditioned for him, but at any rate it didn't happen like that at all."

The group also considered the Buffalo Springfield's label as a natural home. Messina recalls, "Richie and I had met with Atlantic Records. At the time Irwin Spiegel, who was the group's attorney, or at least he was Neil's attorney, Neil had suggested we meet with him to see about getting a deal for us. So Irwin Spiegel had talked to Atlantic Records about signing Poco. At the time, as I recall, the numbers that came back were not enough for us to be able to record and survive." Sure that the Atlantic connection was not going to provide for the group, they began looking elsewhere.

Dickie Davis suggested that the group consider both Columbia and A&M as possible homes for the band since they had indicated interest. *Rolling Stone* and the underground paper *Open City* reported that A&M Records was on the verge of signing Pogo, but Atlantic had blocked the move by refusing to let Furay out of his Buffalo Springfield contract without adequate compensation. A&M certainly appealed to at least one member of Poco. Prior to being tapped as Buffalo Springfield's final bass player, Messina had been prepared to join A&M as a staff producer.

"It was touch-and-go," recalls Messina. "It was like an airplane being in the air and trying to land, went to touch down and had to go back up again. And we were running on empty as far as the deal." Davis invited representatives from A&M, Columbia, and Atlantic Records to the band's Troubadour showcase. Pogo's performance was top-notch, but the field of interested labels dwindled. Atlantic Records still wouldn't come up with enough money. Messina recalled, "There was some things that were said to A&M Records by our manager at the time that was insulting so that lost the deal. Atlantic was too low, but Epic Records, which was sort of the step-child of Columbia, came to bat and said, 'We'd like to have a shot.' Quite honestly, I kind of liked the idea of Columbia Records. It was CBS-oriented, established. I'd never heard bad things about their accounting or anything. I felt it was a reputable company and felt we were lucky to get it."

Ahmet Ertegun wanted some compensation for the loss of Furay, and Epic had someone he wanted. Former Springfield guitarist Stephen Stills was putting together a new band with former Byrd David Crosby and Hollie Graham Nash. Nash abandoned the Hollies in December 1968, and the trio was rehearsing in New York. The Hollies' American label was Epic, and Nash's Hollies contract was in the way of Atlantic's signing the trio. After some quick negotiations, both labels came to an agreement that would give both of them what they wanted. Atlantic agreed to swap Furay's contract to Epic Records for the contract of Graham Nash. Epic agreed and Pogo signed their contract on December 5, 1968. The baseball trade, of sorts, allowed Nash to join forces with Stephen Stills and David Crosby on Atlantic and for Pogo to enter the studio. The trade agreement for Furay's services was signed on January 15, 1969. Another critical part of the deal was that Ertegun insisted that Pogo record several songs that Furay had written for Buffalo Springfield since Atlantic held publishing rights to them.

Pogo was initially very happy to have signed with Epic. Everyone seemed to agree that Epic offered them the most money and the best opportunity for success. Epic Records, a sister label to Columbia Records, had an excellent reputation in the country field. Unfortunately, in the excitement of getting a contract, Pogo allowed Dickie Davis to enter them into a difficult situation. The Epic contract called for Pogo to deliver 12 albums in four years! The group eventually had to call in a lawyer to get the number reduced to nine, which wasn't much better. Pogo were also told they had to repay Atlantic for the studio time it fronted them to produce their demos. The band found itself in a big hole financially before they had barely begun. Furay felt that the lack of good communication between Epic and Dickie Davis was never rectified and caused Pogo many problems in the future.

As news of Poco's recording contract circulated In February, Poco returned to the Troubadour. The LA *Free Press* wrote, "We heard them a few months ago, and in the interval they seemed, to me at least, to have really gotten up and away. The voices are marvelous, alone or together, the whine of Rusty Young's steel guitar astonishing, the songs enjoyable, except for the tendency to overloudness." Michael Etchison of the *Herald-Examiner* said, "Pogo

is not quite the house band of the Troubadour: it only seems that
way. Most clubs should have a house band that good. The high
point of the set I saw was bassist Randy Meisner's singing of *Anyway
Bye Bye*, in which he started out sounding something like Rusty
Draper in *Night Life* and rising to a falsetto climax that sparked
cheers from a partisan audience." Pete Senoff of *Open City* noted,
"Pogo, led by Richie Furay and Randy Meisner, ran up to the stage,
yipping and yelling their Minnie Pearl-like "howdies" and proceeded
to do a set of material that perhaps could best be labeled 'uptempo
Buffalo Springfield'."

Randy Meisner's memories of those early shows still bring back
a smile. "Every time we played the Troubadour it was just packed.
People hanging out of the rafters. We'd go up to Doug Weston's office and maybe have a shot of tequila and some beer, then we'd
start yelling, hooting and hollering, which is really great for a group
to get together just before you go on, like a football team psyching
up. We'd come out the door hooting and hollering and down the
stairs to the stage. By the time we'd hit the stage, the whole audience would be yelling by then. We'd have 'em cranked before we
even started playing, so when you know the audience is with you it
gives you that extra boost of natural energy. It was just so much
fun!" Rusty Young agrees. "I loved going on stage and couldn't wait
for people to hear us. When we played the Troubadour, we could
see in the audience all these people who we'd idolized or recognized as big stars – Ricky Nelson, the Smothers Brothers, Waylon
Jennings, various Byrds, on and on.", many of the group's fans were
anxious to hear the results. Their live shows had attracted excited
crowds and the energy was incredible. John McEuen of the Nitty
Gritty Dirt Band contends, "Poco was one of the most underrated
groups. What they did for country rock was to take it to the max.
There was one night Poco opened for the Dirt Band, and boy did we
feel tiny going on after them." Fans were sure that the group would
top the charts as soon as their record was released. As the band entered Columbia Studio in Hollywood, supporters expected Poco's
exciting brand of country rock to yield results that could be nothing
short of revolutionary. There were high expectations and plenty of
anticipation on the street.

But even before they got into the studio, the band began to
experience problems. Jimmy Messina was taken aback during the
signing of the contracts with Epic. "This was something that affected me personally. When we went in to sign our deal – I felt I
was the producer. I had not been paid in Buffalo Springfield for the
efforts I had put out, in my opinion. What I was given to produce
the group was very, very little. We're talking about one-half of one

percent. And as I said, it wasn't about the money for me. I had accepted that and realized this was a great experience. But when I went to produce Poco, Dickie Davis and Richie had decided that the production royalties should be rolled into the artist royalties so everybody gets more. And I said, 'Well, that's all fine and dandy, but I'm the one doing the work. I don't think it's fair.' They said, 'Well, if you don't think it's fair, then you're gonna have to leave.'"

Messina was astounded by the reaction. "By this time I had already put all the time and energy into Poco, and I remember feeling really betrayed. And at the same time, I'd committed to this; I'd signed my name to this contract. I believe that kind of knocked the wind out of me. I just felt betrayed by people who I had given my time and energy. Those were demos that I was putting my effort, energy, and talent together to get this group a deal. And all the rehearsal time and effort. I really saw it from my point of view, right or wrong, I really saw this group having gotten together because of myself and because of Richie. And I felt deep down inside, again rightly or wrongly, if I hadn't really pushed Richie to do things, get songs written, and let's get into the studio, I don't know that Poco would have happened. So part of me was upset about that, internally I expressed it. I didn't feel it was fair, as I told you, and the ultimatum was – leave. So that left a nasty bite on my spirit. But with that in mind, I'd made a commitment, so I kept going."

Another decision by Furay was to share the publishing on all songwriting. "It was my way of saying 'thanks' to the rest of the band for contributing their part to the music," he explains. "Yes, in the beginning I was writing most of the music, but I believed the rest of the group was entitled to and should have a portion for their contribution. When you're a group, you're a group. My only regret is that I wish some of those songs could have made us all a little more money." Little Dickens Music was formed and split the publishing income five ways.

Anxious to record its first album Furay shepherded his group into Columbia Studio on January 15, the day the agreement between Atlantic and Epic for Furay's services was finalized. As with the final Springfield album, Messina served as producer. Furay had a large volume of songs he wanted to record. Since no other member of the group was as prolific a writer, it was easy for Furay to dominate this area. In fact, the group felt Furay's songs were a major strength. Rusty Young says, "I think a great part of our originality was Richie's amazing songs. They weren't like anything else I'd heard before and I loved them." Meisner concurs. "Richie's songs were a lot different and a lot better than what I'd heard."

During their first session, Poco cut two songs destined to grace the A- and B-sides of their first single. There was some difficulty as the group's rookies were a bit intimidated by the recording studio, but nothing that some experience wouldn't cure. Some frustration was evident as Grantham recalled, "The first album took a long time. It was all new to me. I mean, I was a Denver drummer from a local band, so I was just blown away all the time. The sessions were all unionized. You had three-hour recording times that you could play. You'd just get going, getting your sound down, and the engineers would take a break!" Young concurs, "I'd never been in a professional studio before except for the Buffalo Springfield session for *Kind Woman*. We recorded at CBS Studios. It was interesting, we would be in one studio and in another room we would see Dean Martin, Johnny Mathis, or Dan Hicks and his Hot Licks recording. I was just awestruck."

Grantham also says that there were other adjustments to make. "Of course, Jimmy was producing the record, so he was wearing two hats. That was a little different, producing and being in the band. I think that because of all the stopping and starting, and it was the first time we were all working in the studio together, getting the sound that we wanted took a long time. And Jimmy had this way of doing the record, building it layer by layer, so it seemed to take a very long time." The way Messina had of doing the record was to record individual instruments and layer them into master tracks. Very little of the sessions were done live. Basic backing tracks were recorded using the bass and drums, and then individual instruments were overdubbed one at a time. It was a lengthy process. Still, within the first six days, Poco had cut six songs. They returned to Columbia Studios on January 27 and worked for another week. They conducted a number of overdub sessions with Messina and Young adding on their guitar solos and finished the album on February 25.

The recording of the first album was not an enjoyable experience for Jim Messina for a variety of reasons. "Now we get into the studio and suddenly one of my talents, which was engineering, I was told I can't touch the board. I said, 'What are you talking about?' They said, 'You have to be a union person to touch this board.' So I said, 'OK.' I went out and signed up for the IBEW. Come back and said, 'Here's my IBEW card, now let me touch the board so we can get to work here.' 'No, you have to be an employee. You have to be part of the union, and if you are a royalty-bearing artist, you have to give those royalties over to the union.' Part of me thought, 'I just gave 4/5 of my royalties to the band, and now they want to take what's left and give it to the union.' I said, 'Dammit!' You know? So all of a sudden I'm stuck with an engineer, who's not a bad person. Terry Dunovan was a good person, but he did not have any experience cutting rock and roll music. He had been involved with Andy Williams. He did a lot of string dates, things that were the generation before us. The sounds were flat; there was no dimension to them. I can only recommend. I'd have to say, 'Right there - equalize that! Please, a little high-end. We need some bottom.' And not being familiar with the studio and what it could do or what it couldn't do or knowing the circuitry and where they were. They wouldn't give me schematics. I didn't have any idea how the system flowed or whether I could patch around an amplifier to get into a different pre-amp. It was a nightmare. So when the record finally got done, I was disappointed in the sound quality of it. It just didn't meet up to what I felt it could have. And not being able to touch the board was such a disappointment. I think that combined with feeling a little bit of betrayal there at the beginning left me with an experience at the end of it that I was kind of glad it was done."

An astounding turn of events took place during the mixing of the album. After the recording was complete, Furay and Messina began mixing down the tracks as they had done on Buffalo Springfield's LAST TIME AROUND. But at least one member of Poco was concerned. Listening to playbacks during the recording sessions, Randy Meisner wasn't pleased with what he was hearing. "I really didn't like the sound we were getting on tape. It just didn't sound like us. I didn't hear the bass and drums." One day, Meisner called down to the studio and asked to be included during the mix. He explains, "I called in and said, 'I want to come down and listen to the mixes.' Richie for some reason thought he and Jimmy Messina should just do it alone. I said, 'If that is the way it is going to be then I don't feel like a member of the band,' and Richie said, 'Okay, and you quit kind of thing.' So then I left. [Laughs.] It was just as simple as that."

That was the end of Meisner's Poco career. No effort was made to bring him back and smooth over the differences. Furay told the others only that Meisner had quit but not why. As the years have past, all involved claim it was a terrible misunderstanding and some real management could have preserved the group. Indeed, some calm and rational thinking on both Meisner's and Furay's parts could have prevented the split. Messina offers some interesting insights after decades of reflection. "Randy is a very sensitive person. Extremely sensitive. So I don't know what happened. I think sometimes in my opinion, Randy would get under pressure, and the pressure gets to be too much and his tendency is to back off. It

could very well be something as simple as that. I don't know."
Rusty Young's reaction was fueled by a different perspective.
"They fired Randy without even talking to me," insists Young.
"Randy was my friend. I just didn't think the whole thing was right.
Jimmy and Richie were asserting their authority. They'd do that
every once in a while."

But with the album essentially in the can, Furay didn't seem
worried about the loss of Meisner. What was of concern was that
the group decided to eliminate as many of Meisner's contributions
as time and budget would allow. Grantham recalls, "We might have
left one or two [bass tracks] but we redid most of it, and a lot of
the background singing Randy did we redid too. He's on a few cuts.
I can tell where his voice is, but we redid as much as we could, time
allowing." Young recalled, "All his leads - he sang lead on a couple
of songs - we went in and replaced them." Furay and Grantham re-
cut some of Meisner's harmony vocals while Messina recut many of
the bass tracks before delivering the album to Epic. According to
Grantham, Meisner sang lead on *First Love, Calico Lady*, and *Short
Changed*, as well as the second lead vocal in *Pickin' Up the Pieces*.

The album was already behind schedule because the band was
pretty slow in recording the songs due to their inexperience. Besides delaying the completion of the tracks, Meisner's departure
caused a delay in the delivery of the album, because the cover art
and interior artwork had to be altered. The cost of the redesign ultimately was charged back to the group. The label also was not
pleased that the perception would be that the group had broken up
as its first album was released. When Epic balked at all the changes
being proposed, Dickie Davis stormed into Columbia Records and
demanded the cover be retouched to remove Meisner's likeness. It
was just another in a series of disputes the combative manager had
with the label. Clive Davis eventually approved the change, but
remained angry about Davis' attitude.

When the album eventually appeared, the liner notes credit
Meisner's contribution, but no photo of him was included. They did
something even worse than removing him. "They put a dog on the
cover," Meisner told KTTV's Richard Randall, "but that's ok, 'cuz I
like dogs." Grantham explains, "That's Jimmy's dog, named Jasper. I don't know who decided to use that, but originally that's
where Randy's face was. Maybe Jimmy said, 'Just put my dog on.'
I don't know." Messina disputes that saying, "My dog was black.
That wasn't Jasper. I don't know what that was." Jasper was a
familiar face to fans that regularly attended club dates where Poco
allowed him to roam free on the stage during their sets. Most now

credit Dickie Davis with the decision to put a dog on the cover in Meisner's place.

Meisner had his supporters among fans and the media. After the release of the first album and news of Meisner's departure hit the streets, *Teen Screen* wrote, "Rumor has it that Richie Furay and Jim Messina are nearly impossible to work with...Richie's ego gets pretty high sometimes. Randy Meisner split from Poco to play back-up behind Ricky Nelson and the group lost an important addition to their sound. Too bad." Meisner quickly hooked up with Rick Nelson, as *Teen Screen* noted. Having seen Poco at the Troubadour and wanting to explore country-rock for himself, Nelson asked Meisner to put together a band. Meisner explains, "Rick was looking to form a country-rock band and wanted to know if I was interested and I thought it was an opportunity to the guys who got me out here." Meisner called up ex-Poor band mates Alan Kemp and Pat Shanahan, and they picked up former Buckaroo Tom Brumley on steel guitar a few months later. Nelson dubbed them the Stone Canyon Band. They debuted at the Troubadour on April 1, 1969, to solid, positive reviews. Meisner never regretted his decision to leave Poco. "There wasn't really much money at the time so it wasn't like I was throwing anything big away."

Although Meisner's departure was quickly covered as far as the album was concerned, Poco still had to play live to pay the bills. That meant that some changes had to be made and quickly. Messina immediately returned to the bass, and Poco continued on the road as a quartet. For all intents and purposes, the band wasn't hurt by Meisner's absence in the short term. To test the waters as a quartet, Poco played several local shows. On April 10, Poco opened for Canned Heat at UC Santa Barbara. They also played a pair of dates at the White Room club in Buena Park. Opening for them was a band out of Chicago called Illinois Speed Press. Their lead guitar player Paul Cotton caught their eye, and when he came back stage to introduce himself, they became casual friends.

After the local shows, Poco headed east for their first show-case gigs in Boston and New York. Poco played a three-night stand at the legendary Boston Tea Party in May. From there the band traveled to New York City. A review of Poco's first East Coast show at New York's Bitter End club on May 12 indicated their act was still tight and together. *Billboard's* Fred Kirby wrote, "Poco's solid vocals and instrumentals could carry the unit far, especially with country music becoming increasingly in." It is interesting to note that while most of the songs in their set would appear on the first album, they also played *Hurry Up*, which appeared on their second album, and

Do You Feel It Too, which didn't appear until their fourth album. Obviously, Furay was in the midst of a songwriting frenzy.

Later that night, Poco did a guest set at Steve Paul's The Scene. *Variety* reviewed that set under their New Acts section. "Fronting a wholesome and study image, the combo will be quick to catch with middle-of-the-roaders as well as the hip set. Furay's vocals stand out on the slower, bluesy ballads while the uptempo bids are via excellent three-part harmonies. A plus to the group's sound is Young's rock 'n' roll steel playing. Young does not have purist reservations about 'selling out.' He will readily employ any sound effect that fits the material, including wah-wah and fuzz, to make his instrument mimic anything from Indians on the warpath to a dive-bombing plane. His upfront antics add a distinctive drive to the group and his background playing gives a unique fullness. Messina, who formerly picked lead guitar for the group, now adds bass lines that show overall understanding of the total sound and serve as a firm anchor. Grantham produces an exceptionally bouncy beat with nicely syncopated foot patterns and sizzling cymbalism. At present, the unit's tour de force lies in their closer, *Short Change*, which builds to breathtaking climax. Judging from where they have come within a half a year, they are sure to carry their music into many more interesting areas while further fusing as a team." Poco finished a weeklong engagement at the Bitter End and returned to Los Angeles.

The summer concert season proved to be a good one for Poco. They secured the prestigious opening spot for the Who at the Hollywood Palladium on June 13. Pete Johnson of the L.A. *Times* noted, "Poco [is] smaller by one number since I last reviewed them. Good material, good harmony singing and an exciting live act." Michael Etcheson of the *Herald-Examiner* was less charitable. "The use of falsetto in rock began with the Everly Brothers, to all practical purposes, spread to the Beach Boys, the Beatles and the Byrds. In Poco it reaches its conclusion: At times they sounded like a bluegrass band record played too fast. This has always been a little annoying, and the absence of original member Randy Meisner shows that he contributed much in giving body to their stratospheric excursions. Other than that, Poco has two virtues: Richie Furay's buoyant songs and Rusty Young's marvelous steel guitar. Their arrangements are simple, allowing ample opportunity for both virtues to be exercised." Pete Senoff of the *Los Angeles Image* noted, "Poco emerges as just four guys having a hell of a good time singing. The audience couldn't get enough. They performed most of their new Epic album material, dropping Richie's Buffalo songs that they were performing a couple of months back

After short stints at the Golden Bear in Huntington Beach and the Troubadour, Poco appeared at the Newport Pop Festival in Costa Mesa on June 22 and the Denver Pop Festival on June 27-29. Barry Fey, the promoter for the Denver Pop Festival, wanted Poco so bad that he arranged to have a Lear jet fly the band into Denver for their appearance, then fly them back to Los Angeles to make their Troubadour show. "We had to fly in a Lear jet, play that show, and fly back to the Troubadour that night," Grantham recalls with a smile. "Steve Martin was opening for us. We were late. I remember getting off the plane, getting on a bus. We walked in and there he was playing banjo. He was playing one of our songs. I think it was *Short Changed*. But he was singing - you know how Steve Martin is - he was singing it off-key and everything. It was a long day and night." The critical reaction to their Denver performance was lukewarm. The *Minneapolis Flag* observed, "Poco did a set of their country-rock. Interesting, but the group needs more than Furay. Every song sounded like a derivation of *A Child's Claim to Fame*."

Poco completed their weeklong stay at the Troubadour and made an appearance on the ABC-TV late-night *Joey Bishop Show*. They performed *Pickin' Up the Pieces* and *Just in Case It Happens, Yes Indeed*. They spent a few minutes chatting with the host, who commented on Richie's fringed jacket and asked the obligatory questions about the Buffalo Springfield.

Poco next traveled to the Northwest for their first appearance in that part of the country. They opened at Eagles Auditorium in Seattle in July. Their set exists on a collector's tape taken from a radio broadcast. The material from the Seattle show drew almost exclusively from their first album. Poco performed a full version of *A Child's Claim To Fame*, the Buffalo Springfield outtake *My Kind of Love*, and several unreleased tunes, *Nothin's Still The Same* and *Hurry Up*. Poco did an extended jam in the middle of *Nobody's Fool* that they eventually recorded. The most striking aspect of this live tape is the energetic, almost frantic style of drumming by George Grantham. It provides an interesting look at what Poco was playing live, especially with only one album recorded and in its first few weeks of release. This version of Poco was as exciting as any lineup in concert. However, the four-piece arrangement put tremendous pressure on Young as the only lead instrumentalist. He recalled when Messina moved over to bass and he played "every guitar I could get my hands on." This is never more apparent than the version of *Grand Junction* that this lineup played, since Young had to play all the lead lines that he and Messina had traded off on the recorded version. Janine Gressel of the Seattle *Times* wrote, "The most striking musician in the group is Rusty Young, who played pedal steel guitar. After hearing Young, one can only wonder why pedal steel guitar hasn't been an integral part of hard rock all along. [Poco] songs had soul, but it was a simple, uncomplicated feeling that was enormously refreshing after being bombarded and blasted by the violent psychedelic sounds that were upon us so recently." Patrick MacDonald of the Seattle *Post-Intelligencer* said, "There's no redneck, hoedown elements to their music, only the goodtime 'pickin' and a'singin' variety. Hopefully, their Western tinge won't hold them up from pursuing other elements of pop music. They have the talent to go beyond the narrow definition of country music."

During June, Epic finally released Poco's first album. PICKIN' UP THE PIECES marked another watershed in the relatively new area of county-rock. Both the Byrds (SWEETHEARTS OF THE RODEO) and the Flying Burrito Brothers (GILDED PALACE OF SIN) preceded Poco into the market. But for the Byrds, country-rock was but a passing phase, and the Burritos leaned towards a more traditional country sound. Poco actually fused the two styles in an exciting and lively new way.

The album established what was to become the Poco "sound". The opening track was a poem by Kathy Johnson set to music by Furay and aptly entitled *Forward*. It segued into Furay's up-tempo *What a Day* and established a lyric mood with the opening line "It's a good morning and I'm feeling fine!" The song also showed off the considerable talents of Rusty Young on pedal steel, who used the instrument to imitate the sounds of a banjo and piano. Furay wrote the song while still a member of Buffalo Springfield. Although most of Meisner's contributions were removed prior to release, his vocals remain on this track. "*What a Day* was saved from the Springfield because we never really worked on an arrangement," Furay explains. "It was a beginning, a new day, a happy time for us and it fit Poco more than the Springfield." The next song, *Nobody's Fool*, is another tune performed live by the Springfield. Poco's arrangement of this song turns it into a slow blues with horns arranged by Nick DeCaro and Ken Easton. Young plays his steel through a Leslie speaker, affecting an organ-like sound. Drummer George Grantham took the lead vocals for *Calico Lady*. Skip Goodwin wrote the lyrics while Messina and Furay wrote the music. A nice bass line and sharp acoustic guitar work by Messina are featured. It is an excellent vocal showcase, and it is a shame that Grantham was never again allowed a solo lead vocal for an entire song. Furay's pretty *First Love* followed. It is a ballad along the lines of his *Sad Memory* from BUFFALO SPRINGFIELD AGAIN. However, Furay later revealed that the song was about the Springfield's breakup.

Side one was rounded out by a two-song medley. *Make Me a Smile* opened with a hot acoustic guitar lick by Messina, who co-wrote the tune with Furay. Again it sounds as if Meisner's harmonies remain on this track as well. *Make Me a Smile* segues into the most rocking track on the album, *Short Changed*. Both Young and Messina showed off their instrumental talents as Young plays "fuzz" riffs on his steel and Messina tosses out a very weak guitar solo. A tempo and key change after the instrumental break slows things down. Anyone who listened to *Nobody's Fool* and *Short Changed* and still called Poco a "country-rock" band just wasn't listening.

Side two opened with the title track. Undoubtedly *Pickin' Up The Pieces* summed up Furay's hopes for Poco. It signaled his anxiousness to carry on after the frustrating demise of Buffalo Springfield. Poco even had the lyrics printed on the inside cover to emphasize the song's message. Grantham alternated with Furay on the vocals. It was followed on the album by the high energy instrumental *Grand Junction*, written by Rusty Young. It featured trade-off solos by Young and Messina. *Oh Yeah* marked the vocal debut of Jimmy Messina with Poco. Written by Messina and Furay, *Oh Yeah* is close in tone to *Carefree Country Day* on LAST TIME AROUND. Young plays some fine dobro on the cut, with some soft electric rhythm and heavy bass low in the mix. High harmonies by Furay and Grantham on the choruses contrast with Messina's sleepy delivery. *Just In Case It Happens, Yes Indeed*, another Furay song, was an upbeat country tune with Messina on electric guitar and Young on dobro. The tempo betrays the country blues lyrics. This became a Poco trademark in the early days, singing the blues to an upbeat and energetic pace. The team of Furay and lyricist Skip Goodwin were responsible for the final two songs on the album. *Tomorrow* was a more classic county-style song except for some interesting string and horn arpeggios in the bridge arranged by Nick DeCaro. The album ended with another of those upbeat country tearjerkers, *Consequently, So Long*, with some sharp solos on steel by Young.

Skip Goodwin, co-writer of a couple of the albums songs, was an acquaintance from Furay's brief time in Connecticut after the Au Go Go Singers broke up. Furay explains, "I met Skip when I was living in Wilbraham, Massachusetts when I was working at Pratt and Whitney in late 1965. I lived with a family and Skip was a neighbor. We just kind of became friends. Then Skip started writing some poems and I tried to put them to music. Around the time near the end of the Springfield, Skip came out to visit us. He ended up staying several months with Nancy and I not long after we were married.

That's when he presented these songs." The pair's collaboration consisted solely of Furay putting music to Goodwin's lyrics.

PICKIN' UP THE PIECES was covering relatively new territory and as a result didn't sell exceptionally well. It did get as high as #69 on *Billboard's* charts. *Guitar Player* gave the album a glowing review calling the music "very tight and definitely funky." The review also highlighted Rusty Young's prowess on steel guitar. But the influential *Rolling Stone* chose not to review the album in spite of their earlier enthusiasm for Poco's music. Even worse, the fan magazine *Teen Screen* wrote a scathing review for their Put Down section echoing Meisner's objections to the mix of the album. "The LP was over-produced and consequently, dead sounding. To get to the nitty gritty, Rusty's steel guitar was buried to accommodate Richie and Jim's little music things. What's so disappointing is that Poco are much better live. They stomp a little life into their songs when they get on stage."

PICKIN' UP THE PIECES was certainly a groundbreaker. Furay recalled, "Certainly it was an innovative album. I think the most dominating thing was the fact that we had this country sound. We were pioneering the country-rock sound at the time with the introduction of the steel guitar, the high contrast harmonies and all. It wasn't that we were really country folk, but we did enjoy that style of music. It had a lot of energy, and I think that's what Poco was well known for over the years, just the high-energy music that we put out."

A month after the album's release, Epic tested the singles market by releasing *Pickin' Up The Pieces/First Love*. It was an obvious choice but failed to make the charts. The singles charts especially were largely reflective of radio airplay along with sales figures. Poco ran headlong into a dilemma. Rock Top 40 stations considered Poco too country, for airplay and the country stations were still very provincial when it came to rock acts and so ignored their work. It was a situation that Poco would never fully resolve. Young recalls that Epic initially remixed the single to eliminate the steel guitar at Clive Davis's direction, but Furay insisted that the album's mix be used.

One aspect of PICKIN' UP THE PIECES' less than spectacular chart performance was Poco's inability to tour nationally to promote it. Late in the summer, Poco returned to the clubs around Los Angeles, playing Thee Experience and the Golden Bear. They also headlined at Cal State Fullerton before heading east for a big show at the Flushing Meadows Pavilion in New York. The bill, featuring the Chambers Brothers and Albert King, drew a record crowd of 14,700 fans. Poco's set was a good one and was reviewed kindly in the New York *Times*.   Mike Jahn wrote, "What Poco has done, really, is to take light country singing, pepper it with Rusty Young's good steel guitar work, and pour it over a firm and polished rock background. The result combines country charm and happiness with a rock beat, with none of the notorious country and western lyrical corn." Despite the regular good notices in the press, Dickie Davis couldn't land them a spot on a national tour, and the group was forced back into the local clubs just to pay the bills. Young bitterly recalls, "In the early days we had very little money. Epic weren't too eager to give us any, and even when we needed to buy equipment, we had to fight for them to lend us the money...we just about made enough to survive." Grantham concurs, "We had a lot of problems getting off the ground our first year...getting together with our management, our booking agency, record company, our tour schedule. It just wasn't as together that first year, year and a half, as it was thereafter. And those things made it go slow."

Decades later, Furay looked back on those early struggling days for Poco and noted, "We got little tastes of the touring scene, and it would help to offset any disappointments or discouragements of 'things not happening fast enough.' I believe the excitement of making the music on a national level helped ease the reality of not very large paydays in the very beginning. We knew it was gonna take a little time, but truthfully we also believed any financial difficulties we were faced with would go away as soon as the first record was released. With the 'buzz' going around town – we were sure it was just a matter of time before we took to the big stage and the national scene and that would take care of any of the struggles a lot of bands just getting started were dealing with. Things don't always work out the way you think they will."

Poco played many rock festivals in the summer of 1969, but they were absent from the most prestigious – Woodstock. Rusty Young explains, "I was at our manager's apartment one day when the phone rang. They called to ask us to play the Woodstock Festival. I was jumping up and down. I *knew* everyone who was anyone was going to be there. The manager, Dickie, said 'no thanks' and hung up the phone. I couldn't believe it. What was he thinking? He told me Poco had a 'better offer.' We then played a high school gymnasium instead of Woodstock for $500 more than the money Woodstock had offered us." It's interesting to speculate on what appearing at Woodstock might have meant to Poco. Not all bands that played the festival emerged as major stars. Certainly, bands like Crosby, Stills, Nash, and Young, Santana, and Ten Years After garnered considerable praise for their sets. But groups like Sweetwater passed across the stage virtually unnoticed. Whatever exposure Woodstock might have generated for Poco, the point was moot. Their manager went for a sure paycheck.

Unable to sustain any sort of national tour, Davis booked the band back into the clubs around Los Angeles. After New York, Poco played another round of shows at Thee Experience and the Golden Bear. They also did a number of college shows including MiraCosta College in Oceanside. Unfortunately, their set was cut to only four songs when a downpour sent electric shocks through the stage. On November 13, they opened a new club on Sunset Strip called Thelma's. The lack of publicity resulted in a less than packed house, and the poor sound system reduced their performance to mud. However, the reviewer in the Los Angeles *Free Press* still had good things to say about the band. "They really fit the description of 'good time music,'" the *Free Press* said. "Their set includes several new tunes from their forthcoming album. They have abandoned most of the heavy country licks in favor of a subtler influence underlined by the fine steel playing of Rusty Young."

Poco continued to struggle to make ends meet. With a sizeable bill to Epic Records, Poco made the decision to take only $125 a week each and use the remainder of their income to pay down their debt. It was enough to live on, but just barely. Grantham recalls, "I don't know how we made it. Probably did some mooching from family. Times were really tough."

The inability to crack the AM radio market caused the band to have second thoughts about the direction they chose for themselves. Although Messina was sure that Poco would find a way to interest their audience, Furay began having doubts. He decided that Poco needed to tone down the country aspects of their sound and head for a more recognizable commercial rock sound. That summer, Furay took Poco back into Columbia Studios to record a song that would allow Poco to display some of the more subtle touches on their next single.

4
Picking Up the Pieces

The first month of concerts after Meisner's departure showed that Poco needed to be more than a four-piece band. Although no one outside the band seemed to notice much difference, the group was not clicking like it had during Meisner's tenure. Rusty Young in particular was not happy with the situation. "I thought we were crazy for leaning so hard instrumentally on the steel," contends Young. "At one point after Randy left, we were a four-piece band with the steel as the only lead instrument." Furay admits he wasn't happy with the band's sound at that point either, but Furay wanted Tim Schmit to replace Meisner and was willing to wait for him to become available. Grantham explains, "We couldn't think of anybody else we wanted so we waited until Tim's status changed. His band would always come and see us when we played Sacramento, where they were based. Tim really wanted to be in the band."

After missing an opportunity to join Poco in the summer of 1968, Schmit remained a fan of the band. "I saw Poco perform in San Francisco," Schmit revealed. "When they were still called Pogo – this was after I knew them and was up for the job with them but they had to tell me 'no.' But I saw Pogo that night and thought, 'My god, I could' a been part of that. I gotta go back.' But I wrote *Hear That Music* the next day, just because of that."

Furay kept an eye on the young musician from afar. In April 1969, Glad was playing a Senior Ball at the Senator Hotel in Sacramento when the band noticed a couple of shadowy figures at the back of the room. Guitarist Tom Phillips recalls, "We were playing and all of a sudden you look in the back, and there's Richie and one of the road managers for the Buffalo Springfield standing in the back of the room. And we were kinda spooked because you know it was kind of intimidating having one of the Buffalo Springfield watching you play unannounced in Sacramento. And we were done and they were gone! Nothing was said. As far as I can remember, I don't think Tim talked to them. But then there was a phone call a few weeks later and they called Tim and said, 'Do you want to come down to L.A.? Randy's not working out. Why don't you just come down and hang out for awhile and see what happens?' So Tim went down there...and never came back."

Up until the sudden appearance of Furay in Sacramento, Schmit was doubtful that Poco would ever be interested in him again. Even after hearing of Meisner's exit, Schmit says, "I thought, fat chance, they'd already turned me down." So when Furay invited him to come to Los Angeles shortly after his surprise appearance in Sacramento, Schmit was ecstatic. Schmit arrived in Los Angeles, and Furay offered him the opportunity to play with Poco in a rehearsal setting and see what developed. "We rehearsed some with Tim," Grantham recalled. "Richie was really sold on Tim, real quick. He liked his singing, of course. Richie was definitely sold on Tim. I think it took a little bit longer for the whole band to be quite as sold on him. Richie saw it immediately. Looking back at Tim, he was a real chameleon. He can play with anybody and sound good. He's got a great voice." The band's reluctance to have him join didn't bother Schmit initially. He reveals, "I used to make 50 bucks a week for rehearsing with them. It blew me away that they'd pay me that much for doing that." But that's all Schmit did for most of the summer - rehearse and follow the band on the road.

While Poco used Schmit during rehearsals throughout the summer, there was no firm job offer from them. Furay was frustrated that his band wasn't anxious to have Schmit become part of the band. "I had to do a lot of talking to get Tim into Poco," Furay confirms. "I liked Tim and as it turned out I probably was closest to Tim of anyone in the band. I liked the way we sang together. I liked him personally; he brought a more youthful image to the band even though we were all still pretty young guys. I don't think his talents were altogether appreciated by everyone the way I looked at it." Rusty Young was not happy that his friend from Colorado had left the band and did not like the idea of Schmit joining the group. "Until Tim came into the band, Jimmy played bass," explains Young. "He's a brilliant bass player, but Tim's not. He's adequate. As an instrumentalist, I really missed having that bottom. Everything came off of that, and when it wasn't there anymore, it really bothered me and I let him know it." The tension between the pair never really dissipated, but as professionals, they continued to work together.

In the wake of his sudden departure, there was the usual bitterness among Schmit's friends in Glad. Ron Floegel was so upset at the way that Schmit had left the group that he visited Los Angeles during the summer of 1969 to confront him face to face. But Poco had left its mark on Glad aside from just luring away their bass player. The day before Schmit left Sacramento, the band took on guitarist Andy Samuels from the Nate Shiner Blues Band. They had one thrilling rehearsal as a five-man band that had Floegel and Phillips excited about the possibilities, but the following day, Schmit abruptly left town. Floegel took over on bass, and they gave themselves a new name - a name Phillips had overheard Furay and Messina considering before calling themselves Pogo - Redwing. That was Glad's subtle jab at the band that had "stolen" their bassist and best friend. Despite any hard feelings, the four remained friends. Tom Phillips remembers hearing from Schmit shortly after he left. "I remember him calling and say, 'Hey, I'm gonna be in Santa Clara. Poco's opening for Jimi Hendrix at the fairgrounds. Why don't you come down?' So I went down there and Poco'd be playing, but Tim wasn't in the band yet. He'd just be hanging out."

The summer tour continued with Poco as a quartet. As the summer waned, Schmit felt that the writing was on the wall. No firm commitment on the band's part had come, and he felt he had to move on. Disappointed, he decided to leave L.A. and head back home to Sacramento. He called the band's office and requested passes to their show at the Golden Bear in Huntington Beach to say goodbye.

Schmit recently recalled, "After we arrived, I went backstage to the tiny dressing rooms to say hello. Everyone was very cordial, as I had expected, but to my surprise, Richie (Furay) asked me if I wanted to come up during the set and do my song with them. As you can imagine, I was pleasantly shocked...I mean, mentally I had the wind knocked out of me. Of course I said, yes, then proceeded to take my seat in the audience. Well, all kinds of scenarios were playing out in my head, and I was very nervous, but I managed to keep from floating out of my chair as I watched, listened, and waited. The time finally came and they called me up on stage. Jim Messina handed me his bass, he switched over to guitar, and we performed the song, *Hear That Music*...and I was the guest performer. I think I leapt right on over to Cloud 10. Before I knew it, it was over...I went back to my seat and enjoyed the rest of the show. When the performance ended, I went backstage again to thank them and to say goodbye. Richie sat me down and surprised me once again. He asked me if I would not go back to Sacramento as planned, and could I stay and start rehearsing to be a full member of the band."

Poco was now back up to full strength as Messina moved back to lead guitar and Schmit took over bass. While the instrumental vitality returned with the trade-off lead lines of Messina and Young, the vocal quality improved as well. The addition of Schmit transformed the vocal sound of Poco because of the similarity in Furay's, and Schmit's voices. George Grantham recalled when he first became aware of the coincidence, "When Tim first joined the group, he was over at this house I had, and we were practicing vocals. My wife and I were in the kitchen and we heard this guy singin.' We looked at each other and said, 'Isn't that Richie?' It was Tim, you know, but it sounded exactly like Richie." This similarity allowed Poco to take advantage of unison lead vocals, best exemplified by their work on their new album. Meisner's departure also allowed Grantham to return to his familiar role of providing high harmonies to the vocal blend.

With Poco whole again, Furay wanted the band to try to do some recording. With the lack of success on the singles chart, Poco returned to the studio in August to cut a couple of tracks to consider as their next single. Wanting to avoid the more country-tinged songs on the first album, Furay had the band record another of his unreleased Buffalo Springfield songs, *My Kind of Love*, for the A-side. *My Kind of Love* was one of Furay's first songwriting attempts, and a version of it was originally scheduled for inclusion on Buffalo Springfield's debut album. The Springfield's arrangement was very pop oriented. True to Furay's intention, the country influence was downplayed in Poco's version. The arrangement featured some subtle steel touches, and Messina's guitar riffing was impressive. Messina believes that lack of a single from the first album led to Poco going back into the studio so quickly. "A couple of things were occurring that point in time," explains Messina. "First, I don't believe we had a single. We were struggling with the fact that Randy had left and the group had basically broken up before the LP was even released, which was a very shameful position to be in." From Messina's standpoint, it was important for Poco to show Epic that it was still a viable entity. "The goal was to give Epic a single and, with Tim Schmit now in the band, it was to put some of his effort and energy into this piece *Hard Luck*. I think it was an effort to get a single and introduce our new bass player."

The B-side of the single was written and performed by Tim Schmit. *Hard Luck* fit perfectly into the Poco scheme of things with an arrangement that featured a lot of Grantham's and Furay's high register harmonies. The strongly country oriented tune soon became a concert staple of Poco's acoustic set. Epic released the single in November with a picture sleeve on West Coast shipments. *My Kind of Love/Hard Luck* did not make the charts. It is the rarest of Poco singles since neither song was included on Poco's following album and Epic deleted the single almost immediately. It is interesting to note that many years later, both Furay and Messina recalled that *Hard Luck* was the A-side of the single. Epic chose to promote the single with a photograph of a naked child blowing soap bubbles beneath the printed title of the song. The incredibly bad taste, even by late '60's standards, certainly did nothing to help the single. The promotion piece understandably did not receive widespread distribution.

Poco began serious work on their follow-up album a month later. On September 16, Poco also recorded versions of *I Guess You Made It* and *Do You Feel it Too* at Columbia Studio. The latter song was recently included in the CD release of the first album as a bonus track. Since it was reportedly discovered on the end of the master reel of the first album, it was assumed to be an outtake. However, studio documentation makes it clear the track was recorded after Schmit joined the band and was intended for Poco's second album.

With Schmit now an official member and Messina back on guitar, Poco hit the road for a short tour of the Southwest between sessions. Among the shows Poco played were as opening act for Creedence Clearwater Revival in front of 60,000 at the Coliseum in Phoenix, a headline gig at the University of Arizona in Tucson, a club date at the Vulcan Gas Company in Austin, and they joined the bill at the Sam Houston Coliseum in Houston with the Byrds, Jefferson Airplane, and the Grateful Dead on October 5. These shows drew some solid reviews for the band and began to solidify them as a touring unit.

Upon their return to California, Poco continued to work in the studio on their new album beginning on October 15 at Columbia Studio in Hollywood. By year's end, Furay told the *Long Beach Free Press* that Poco had five songs in the can with three others in various stages of completion. Poco was hoping to have the album completed and ready for release in early spring. Songs cut during the October sessions included the Rusty Young instrumental *Last Call*, Furay's *Hurry Up*, and Messina's *You Better Think Twice*.

But just as it appeared that Poco was gaining momentum, everything came to a halt. Dickie Davis had enraged Epic one too many times. Clive Davis refused to allow Poco back into the studio. No matter what the group did or what Dickie Davis said, Clive Davis steadfastly refused to budge. It was clear to Furay that Dickie Davis had reached the end of his effectiveness with the label. Furay felt he had no choice. "Dickie was a very well meaning man who loved and believed in the band, but had limitations as a manager went," Furay says. "He knew more than any of us but only enough to get him and us in trouble with the record company, and so I've been told, he turned down what probably would have been a life changing booking at Woodstock." Reluctantly, Furay made the decision to let him go. Messina would sadly recall years later that "he managed to offend just about everybody he met." Grantham's assessment of Davis is fairly positive. "Well, you know, he was a personal friend of Richie's, and Jimmy had worked with him before. I'm not sure it was the best thing to have him manage us. Dickie had a way of doing business that I'm not sure was in our best interests. I think he offended a lot of people. At least that's what we heard. But he got us the [record] deal and I've got to give him that." Davis was given a financial settlement and left by mutual consent.

Unsure if they even still had a record deal with the label, the band was anxious to resolve the situation. Furay shared his frustration at not getting time in one of Columbia's studios to David Geffen. Geffen picked up the phone and resolved the problem immediately. This show of power and influence with Clive Davis impressed Furay. He remembers, "David Geffen was extremely fond of Poco too, and in our time of need, he rose to the challenge. I remember sitting in his office while he called Clive to talk about our predicament, and I was completely astonished by the conversation – although 'conversation' is probably too polite a word for what actually happened. I don't know whether David acted as he did for my benefit, but there was yelling and screaming going on that made Dickie look like a rank amateur." Within a week, Poco was back in the studio and working on their album. When Poco's second album was eventually released, Geffen was thanked in the liner notes for "pickin' up the pieces." This impressive display of influence convinced Furay that Geffen should be their manager. Messina disagreed. "I told Richie that he couldn't manage us," explains Messina. "He was a vice-president of an agency. We needed someone that was going to manage us. I mean, someone who'd find a doctor for us when one of us gets sick on the road or hassle with hotels when our reservations get screwed up. Geffen wasn't going to do that."

Another key fact was that Geffen was a junior vice-president with CMA. For him to manage Poco would have represented a conflict of interest. Unable to secure Geffen's services, Furay asked him for guidance in finding a manager. Geffen supplied the group with a list of managers that they could trust and recommended that they go with CMA as a booking agency. Furay leapt at the suggestion. CMA took over in February 1970 and immediately began putting Poco's house in order. The agency fired the band's accountant, lawyers, and other advisors that Davis had hired. They also began booking better gigs for the band.

Geffen was hardly through with helping Furay's band. "One day he brought Todd [Shiffman] and Larry [Larson] over to the studio and we assumed, although nothing was said, that it was to introduce us to whom he thought would work out pretty good for us," Furay recalls. "One thing led to another and we signed on with them. One of the other guys might remember this completely differently. The desire for a manager was apparent. We needed to get on the road, and we thought we needed a manager with some pull to get us on the national stage - live and on the radio."

Todd Shiffman was a former agent and Larry Larson was a former concert promoter. The pair's strategy was to put Poco out on the road and build their reputation through their live act since the album and singles hadn't been successful. Messina felt that the pair offered the band a solid backing. "Todd Shiffman was a very successful agent, and Larry Larson had been a promoter so they knew that side of the business. They had the ability to reach out and make contacts with the agents and kept us booked. They helped us become a successful performing group in the industry."

Furay admitted, "The thing Todd and Larry were good at was booking. What I mean is they could keep the group working, but they just couldn't create any kind of aura around Poco." That assessment came after years of reflection. In the beginning, having professional management that put Poco in venues above the L.A. club scene was a godsend. Poco had learned the hard way that poor management could stifle a career.

With the roadblock to studio time removed, Poco devoted the early part of 1970 to the follow-up album. The January sessions at Columbia found Poco putting overdubs on *Hurry Up* and cutting two versions of *Honky Tonk Downstairs*, *Don't Let it Pass By*, and versions of *Hear That Music* and *My Kind of Love*. Studio keyboardist Larry Knechtel overdubbed piano on four tunes including *Hard Luck* and *My Kind of Love*, indicating Poco's intention to reissue those songs on their upcoming album using some slightly different arrangements. In February and March, Poco recut *Nobody's Fool* with a long instrumental jam, *Anyway Bye Bye*, and a third version of *Honky Tonk Downstairs*.

Messina again served as producer, but this time he had a recording engineer, Alex Kasanegras, who he felt he could work with.

"Alex really liked music and he understood miking. Alex was so open and willing to work with me. Like when I started developing a new way to record the drums. It just opened up the sound so much, and he would take my ideas and run with them. We developed that trust to a point where I could just sit in the studio with my guitar and be able to play without worrying what was going on in the control room."

In assessing the work in progress, Messina told British journalist Pete Senoff, "Well, this particular album is an experiment with me. Because with 8-track recording brought a change in the recording industry. But I felt that, when it came in, something was strange about it. Everything that was recorded was so isolated. Once you isolate eight different things and put them together, it doesn't sound much like a record. It sounds like a very mechanical situation. Now since 16-track has been introduced into the industry, the situation has become even worse. What I'm trying is going back to the old techniques of the 1950's and experimenting with getting room noise and sound onto the record so that it doesn't feel so mechanical."

In addition to the sonic qualities, Messina began to stretch the band's sound with some inventive arrangements. He also brought to the sessions a batch of new songs for consideration. Messina could only get one of them recorded, however. Furay was still sitting on a bunch of his own, and they were closer to his perception of what direction the band should be taking. This frustrated Messina since their vision had been united during the making of the first album. Now the lack of commercial success, coupled with the notoriety of his ex-bandmates Neil Young and Stephen Stills, had Furay abandoning the country mode where possible. The result was Furay's demands on Messina and Young to arrange songs differently to make Poco's sound a bit more diverse. Often Messina and Young had spent hours on arrangements that Furay rejected out of hand upon hearing them. The sessions for the second album were grueling. Young asserts it took eight studio months to complete it although the evidence indicates it did not take anywhere near that much time. It just felt like it.

"There was an unspoken feeling that we needed to move in a different direction, more into rock," recalls Messina. "Richie had come to the conclusion that he needed to go more towards rock. I was digging that. I was missing the edge that I knew the band had. We needed something that had some energy so that when it hit radio, it would stand out."

Sessions with a new bass player added to the schedule. Schmit had some difficulty fitting into the recording situation.

Messina eventually coached Schmit on certain tunes, telling him what to play. That didn't go over well with the young bassist. Messina muses, "I think I may have intimidated him or pissed him off 'cuz I remember asking him to play his parts a little differently or play it this way or that way. Some people take that well and some people don't. As a producer, it's not something that I'm shy doing. But I can see as an artist, one artist asking another artist to play their instrument differently that it could be a problem." It also re-inforced Young's opinion that Schmit was lacking in abilities on bass.

When the album was finally finished in March, Poco took a short break before hitting the road to put Shiffman and Larson's plan into effect. The affiliation with CMA paid off as they began to play better venues. On April 4, they opened for the Moody Blues and Steve Miller at the Long Beach Arena. At the Berkeley Community Theater, Poco opened for John Sebastian on April 12. A month later they returned to the Bay Area to play the Fillmore West with Spirit and Gypsy. An appearance by the band at The Boston Tea Party in early 1970 reveals an interesting look at the band's live set once Schmit had joined. He took lead vocals on Messina's new song *You Better Think Twice*. Grantham performed *Calico Lady*. Poco also debuted two new songs not on their new release, *C'mon* and *Hear That Music*.

It's surprising, given Messina's later work that he didn't sing that much with Poco. "I think he sang a little," stated Grantham. "The first album had a song called *Oh Yeah* on it. I think we played that some live. That was about the only thing Jimmy sang lead on. As far as *You Better Think Twice*, I just think that Tim was a better vocalist. I think also that there's a lot of guitar work that Jimmy had to concentrate on. The arrangement was pretty complex. There was a lot of stuff for Jimmy to cover."

Epic released Poco's second album in the first week of June 1970 and caught a few fans by surprise. Reports in the press had the album title as POCO'S BACK, but it arrived in record stores titled simply POCO. The cover was patterned after orange crate labels. The back cover had vignette photos of the band with some musician credits. Epic's trade ad marketed the album as "with Schmit added" as opposed to their first album made without him. It also remarked on PICKIN' UP THE PIECES sales of over 100,000 copies.

The album opener *Hurry Up* was a laid back tune that fea-tured Messina and Young on some very hot guitar solos during an ex-tended break. Furay reveals, "This guy came up to court the group. He wanted to use us for something. He took me out to dinner, bought all the wine, really tried to swoon me. And I could see right through him." The second song was Messina's *You'd Better Think Twice*. It was by far his best offering to date, and the group had put together a very tight arrangement. Larry Knechtel added piano to the track. They had even cut an acoustic version that remained in the can. "If you listened to that song, there's a lot put into it," notes Furay. "It's very well crafted and very unique right from that beginning lick. It really showcased Jimmy vocally, instrumentally, and from a technical standpoint." Played with a specialized tuning, Messina's lead work is mesmerizing. Rusty Young, looking back on that track, felt that Jimmy was already planning his departure. "On that track," Young notes, "we all had the feeling Jimmy was ready to move out of the band. He was seeing what he could do by himself." It wasn't until the third track that the acoustic and steel guitars came out for a cover of Dallas Frazier's *Honky Tonk Downstairs*, which had been a hit for George Jones on the country charts. "It was our way of saying that we had no intention of abandoning country entirely," explains Furay. "In fact, we thought that by bringing more of a rock edge to other tunes, we'd draw in the sort of people who never thought they'd like country music and convince them otherwise." New member Tim Schmit was featured as co-writer and vocalist on *Keep On Believin'*. It was a solid, high-energy Poco tune and the closest thing they would ever record to a message song. The side ended with Furay's *Anyway Bye Bye*. Originally sung by Meisner before his departure, *Anyway Bye Bye* is a long blues ballad. "I think Dewey has some relationship to the song. We may have had a discussion about keeping [the Springfield] together. It's kinda like 'Hey, it's all over.'" The song is marked by Young's whining steel guitar played through a Leslie rotating speaker. This process made his steel sound remarkably like a B-3 organ and added a touch of Motown to the band's sound.

The flip side started out well with an outstanding ballad written with Skip Goodwin and sung by Furay called *Don't Let It Pass By*. The second song was a reprise of *Nobody's Fool* from the first album. It was a looser arrangement, and it transitioned into a lengthy instrumental jam entitled *El Tonto De Nadie, Regressa*. As a showcase for the band's instrumental prowess it wasn't bad, but it certainly was self-indulgent since it ran for the remainder of the side! For a band with so much trouble getting airplay, the decision not to include their last single and not release any further material in favor of an 18-minute jam was certainly questionable. Grantham told Robyn Flans about the origins of *El Tonto*, "We were trying to find an identity at one of our rehearsals at the Troubadour, and we just got into this jam. Jimmy Messina was kind of finding himself [on guitar] again through these jams. It just started, and all of a sudden it was, 'this sounds kind of neat.' Richie had a song with a kind of shuffle/country feel called *Nobody's Fool*. We changed it completely and made it into a song that led into the jam." Furay felt the decision to release *El Tonto* reflected the anti-establishment attitude that Poco had during its early days and that many groups were doing the same thing at the time. It is also strange since Poco had recut both sides of their last single with the intent to include them on the album, only to leave them in the can.

According to Grantham, the original version of *El Tonto* ran nearly 27 minutes long. Messina confirms it. *"El Tonto de Nadie*, which was *Nobody's Fool*, was 27 minutes long. That was one side of an album. It was cut live and I had to get it down to 17 minutes. So I had to take a razor blade and the multi-track original and cut some of that stuff down. And the final cut had to be done on a two-track so we wouldn't destroy it. I had to find...they wouldn't let me touch anything, right? I couldn't do it! So I went and found one of the oldest engineers there, in terms of age, who had been there the longest. He had been there during the broadcast days. His name was Charlie. Everyone said, 'Charlie is the king of the scissors.' So I brought Charlie in and said, 'I've got 27 minutes and I need to get down to 17, can you do it?' He said, 'Absolutely!' He comes in with scissors and I said, 'What the hell are you gonna do with those?' He says, 'I'm going to edit with them.' I said, 'Aren't you going to use an Edit-All? Aren't you going to be cutting these somewhere between 30 and 45 degrees?' He stuck out his finger at me. I thought he was giving me the finger. He said, 'Look at my finger. You see this line here and that line there? Well, that's 45 degrees." I said, "You're kidding me!' He said, 'No, I'd rather cut like this with a pair of scissors than a razor blade because I know a razor blade can rip the tape where a pair of scissors will simply slice it. These scissors I have are sharper than a razor.' And by damned, I showed him where to cut and where to scrub, and he'd mark it and cut it and be perfect every time." The song seems dated now, but Rusty Young defends it. "The second album is really hard to pull out of the context of time. It was 1970 and FM radio was such a force in selling albums and selling concert seats. Our goal was not to have a commercial AM hit, but to have something that would be a staple of FM radio and be artistically true to ourselves without selling out. We did that with the extended *Nobody's Fool*. And they played that, all 18 minutes. Instead of three minutes of air time, we got 18."

POCO (more commonly referred to as the Oranges album due to its cover art) was nonetheless well received and sold almost twice as many copies as had their debut album. Epic also released it to European markets, the first Poco album to do so. *Downbeat* said of the album, "In Poco [there is] no spectacular music, no brilliant historical influence, no superstar pretension, but instead an elemental joy from song through song, and a saving grace of uncommon innocence." *Variety* enthused, "Poco's second LP fulfills the promise of the combo's first disc, 'Picking up the Pieces,' and should give the Buffalo Springfield-derived, country-rooted rock outfit a firm foot on the charts. The Springfield influences come from Richie Furay and Jim Messina, two alumni of that quintet. They have instilled within Poco a freshness and vitality, manifested in the vocal harmonies and coherent musicianship." John Koegel in *Fusion* was equally positive. "However much pedal steel guitar Rusty Young may play, Poco refuses to exchange its increasingly popular life style as a rock band for the ephemeral charisma of a fashionable country 'n western group. The band knows its limits, especially with regard to the intensity of its Nashville influence and does not overextend itself into areas it cannot control. Instead Poco uses country harmonies and steel guitar in moderation, and would rather leave the listener wanting more than to have him refuse less."

But it was their continual roadwork, as designed by new managers Shiffman and Larson, that was just as helpful to the group. National tours were now a standard part of Poco's live work. In June, Poco opened shows for Janis Joplin, the Rascals, and headlined small venues and clubs to fill in between major dates. During the summer of 1970, Poco continued to appear at more prestigious concerts. On July 3, they were a late addition to the Atlanta Pop Festival and were recorded live for a Columbia Records album celebrating the event. Poco went on right before Jimi Hendrix, and many observers felt their high energy set far outshined the unusually docile Hendrix set that followed. George Grantham recalls, "It was amazing to hear Hendrix play. That was a great memory." Rusty Young's memories are equally positive, "That night, we played between the Chamber Brothers and Jimi Hendrix – not a slot you'd really want to be in, but the set went well and everyone had a great time." Nevertheless, the wealth of talent at many of these festival shows made the members of Poco feel excited and in awe.

After returning to Los Angeles in July, a series of mysterious recording sessions took place at Columbia Studio. Furay and company booked time and recorded three new songs, *C'mon, You Are the One*, and *Hear That Music*. All of these tracks would never be released. It is unclear why they were recorded so soon after the release of their second album. Perhaps these were sessions to consider another one-off single a la *My Kind of Love/Hard Luck*.

In August, Poco played the Peace Festival at Shea Stadium, New York, and were a huge hit. Although only 20,000 (of an anticipated 60,000) attended the festival, it remained Poco's day. The late arriving crowd had many of the bigger name acts hesitant to go on until more of a crowd showed up. Furay didn't blink. He led his band out in the early morning hours, and as they plugged in, Messina stepped to the mike and told the crowd, "I tell you, we're really glad to be here today, to be able to contribute our talents toward having a peaceful nation and have other nations and other countries join in on creating the same sort of situation. The only thing we can say is we hope you enjoy the music and hope it helps you form an opinion and help make this world a more peaceful place for everybody to live." Poco opened their set with a spirited, joyous *Pickin' Up the Pieces*. The vocals were a bit rough, but Poco's energy instantly drew the crowd to them. Without a word, the band dove into a medley of *Just in Case It Happens, Yes Indeed, Grand Junction*, and *Consequently, So Long*. Furay's lead vocals soared over the stadium as the band cooked behind him. Rusty Young's maniacal steel work on *Grand Junction* kept up the high energy with Messina's sinuous lead lines cascading off Young's steel work. Poco brought the medley to a close with a modest version of *Consequently, So Long*. As Grantham quietly remarked, "It sure is nice bein' here. I think we're gonna close out our portion of the day with the second side of our second album. Slow song, then a slow instrumental." Furay eased into a quiet *Don't Let It Pass By*. Young played a soulful organ part on his steel as Grantham and Schmit crooned in the background. As with the album, Poco ripped into *Nobody's Fool*. The crowd stomped and hollered as it melded into the jam tune *El Tonto De Nadie, Regressa*. Poco left the stage to chants of "Peace Now!"

East Coast critics praised their excellent performance, and many counted them as the sole highlight of the festival. Peter Knobler in *Zygote* wrote, "People were so refreshed by their music, so awakened by their sheer exuberance, that the stands erupted in freaky joy." Knobler would eventually become friends with Furay, and when he took over editorial duties with *Crawdaddy*, he made sure that Poco was often mentioned in columns or articles. Knobler was the one who pointed out to Furay his use of down lyrics with up-sounding music. It was a feature of Poco music until Knobler made a point of it. Now aware of the tendency, Furay avoided it in future songs, trying instead to match the tone of his lyrics with the music.

The Peace Festival also began a New York love affair with the group that continued throughout its lifetime. Regardless of their standings in the charts, Pocomania ruled in New York. In many ways, the Peace Festival was Poco's Woodstock. It was a defining moment in their early career. Grantham noted that New York was a special place for Poco. "That must have been what got it all started for us there because New York was a great town for us. New York and Boston, the whole northeast corner was our best market. I thought we'd be real big in California, the West Coast. We were popular, but nothing like in the Northeast. We always started or ended tours up there, always." Richie Furay agreed, "Playing the Shea Stadium Peace Show really made us happy. The response was great - we were really excited about it. Nobody wanted to go on early since everybody was waiting for a bigger crowd, but we decided to go on anyway. I'm glad we did because they seemed to love us."

August also saw Epic finally break a single out from the POCO album, releasing an edited version of *You Better Think Twice/Anyway Bye Bye*. The single started off slow, failing to break into the Hot 100 until October. It managed to stay on the charts for 11 weeks, but rose no higher than #72. In October, Poco appeared on *American Bandstand* to lip-sync *You Better Think Twice*. They also made an appearance on *Something Else* hosted by John Byner. On the show, Poco lip-synced their single while aboard a boat moored at Newport Beach harbor. Some inventive camera angles and earnest miming by Poco spiced up the clip. Of course, both Furay and Messina were shown playing their acoustic guitars and not electric ones.

POCO's success was yet another stepping stone towards rock stardom, but it was slow in coming. While sales of POCO doubled from their debut disc and a single hit the charts, the band was still not happy that stardom continued to elude them. While they had attracted a greater share of attention in the music press and crowds were increasing at their shows, the band was still not making money. Their weekly allowance had not increased, and several members were now married and thinking about starting families. The lack of a hit and the soaring success of CSNY continued to eat at Furay. His frustration and his unhappiness were obvious to his band mates. As they toured throughout the United States, the tension and stress began to grate on them, creating an uncomfortable atmosphere. The close proximity of sharing hotel rooms and being crammed into vans driving hundreds of miles at a time were taking their toll. Although the summer touring season had provided Poco with a greater visibility and increased critical success, it wasn't enough to keep another member from leaving the band.

5
Consequently, So Long

Angry eyes...whenever Jimmy Messina conversed with his friend and mentor Richie Furay, that's what he came away remembering. Messina had felt a close kinship with Furay ever since meeting him back in 1967, but this new dynamic was disturbing. The increased frustration of failing to come up with a hit single and gain stardom was beginning to tear their friendship apart. The summer tour had not made things any better. From a personal standpoint, Messina felt responsible for Furay's unhappiness at Poco's lack of success on the charts. "I couldn't help taking Richie's unhappiness personally. At the time, I really felt that I was the cause of his being unhappy since it always seemed to come out when I was talking with him. So I decided, if I was making him unhappy, then I should leave." He also struggled with Furay's creative dominance of the band. Once close partners, Messina now felt distant from his friend and increasingly unhappy himself. "I thought that after Richie rejected a couple of songs, the best thing was not to submit any more material," explains Messina. *"Golden Ribbons* was written for Richie to sing, but Richie never liked the song." Furay and Messina had recently had disagreements over Furay's idea that Poco should emulate Creedence Clearwater Revival's energy level, and Messina felt that Furay was too concerned about "hits." Messina explains, "Richie really wanted to be a hard rocker and I'm not really a hard rock musician, but that's where he wanted to go. OK, so we had musical differences, because I wanted to write songs like 'Peace Of

Mind' and 'Same Old Wine' – things like that. Richie wanted to do tunes like John Fogerty – that kind of hard rock – and I wasn't into doing songs like John Fogerty; I didn't want to be a Creedence Clearwater" Messina was very defensive about his position. "When people are afraid to keep changing, it starts to make me very paranoid. *Peace of Mind* was written then. *Same Old Wine, Golden Ribbons*. Most of those tunes they couldn't relate to. My feelings about how they should be produced and arranged were something more than where their...limited heads were."

Messina had also tired of the band politics. Poco was a democracy but Messina felt that was a mistake. "The group was very democratic. Everyone had their equal say. And there were some members who were capable of making equal decisions and some members who I felt were not. People who are willing to spend more time deserve to participate more." Young claims that although Messina received the production credit, all the members had their say in the studio, which probably didn't please Messina. The decision to share the producer royalties among the band also continued to grate on him.

Despite all that, Messina saw himself as a problem-solver and continued to put out his best efforts. But as the summer wore on and the tension mounted out on the road, Messina realized that he couldn't take it anymore. He had married the daughter of actor Barry Sullivan, Jenny, at the beginning of summer. The long tour was already creating a strain, and the band could not afford to have spouses travel with them. In addition, their weekly stipend had not increased, and financial concerns were now more important to the newly married Messina. Coupled with the fact that there was little joy in playing with the band anymore, Messina decided he needed to move on.

In August while the band was in Philadelphia, Messina traveled to New York to inform Columbia President Clive Davis of his decision to quit Poco and ask for a production job with the company. Davis recalled, "Jim was touring with Poco at the time and he had a fairly common musician's dilemma. He was tired of Holiday Inns, and tired of being away from his lovely wife, Jenny, who was studying acting in Los Angeles. He wasn't making much money and he was having disagreements with the group." Feeling that Poco was about to make a breakthrough, Davis tried to change Messina's mind. Davis insisted that he take some more time to think it over. Three or four weeks went by with no change in Messina's attitude. When he contacted Davis again, Messina was adamant about leaving Poco for a production job. He even presented Davis with an itemized budget for his first year. Impressed by Messina's thoughtful consideration of his future, Davis agreed to Messina's request. Of course, Davis had him sign a standard staff producer's contract, calling for Messina to produce six albums per year after he'd finished up with his commitment to Poco.

After the eight-month experience of POCO, the group had decided that a live album could be done much quicker and it might answer critics who praised their live work, but weren't impressed with their records, thus killing two birds with one stone. Grantham recalled, "We'd kept hearing how good we were in concert as compared to our first albums. We were supposedly much more exciting and much better all around live. So we had the idea to do a live album." Epic agreed with Poco's decision and made arrangements for two shows to be recorded live. Poco returned to the studio to work up some material in September. Several songs were cut but remain unreleased. Among the songs were yet another version of *I Guess You Made It, You Better Think Twice, A Man Like Me*, and *Pickin' Up the Pieces*. Jimmy Messina also took the time to record *Lullaby in September*, a musical gift to Furay and his wife Nancy on the impending birth of their first child. Timmy Sue Furay arrived in September. Although a girl, Furay named her after band mate Tim Schmit. Schmit and his girlfriend had a daughter themselves the following day, naming her Jeddrah.

The group made arrangements for remote recording at two East Coast venues and rehearsed some new material. In many respects, Poco wanted the live album to be viewed as a legitimate new release. Naturally, some "older" material would be included, but Poco felt that the new songs should be showcased. Grantham said of the new songs, "They were just things we hadn't gotten around to recording yet. We didn't want to do an album that early in the game that was just our two previous albums live. We wanted to put some new songs on it. They were ready to go."

It was during the rehearsals that Messina let the band know that he planned to leave. "We had been rehearsing for the live album," Grantham confirms. "We had this meeting with Jimmy real soon before doing the live album, and he kind of sprung it on us. We had to accept it. He was producing the live album so we pretty much had to accept his terms. Time was an element. Jimmy kind of sat down and said, 'Here's what I want - I want to produce the album, work with my replacement, etcetera." With no chance to change the dates for recording the live album, Poco went ahead with their plans knowing the album would feature a lead guitarist that wouldn't be around to promote it once it was released.

Furay contends, "I don't remember the timing, but I believe the decision to record DELIVERIN' was made before he announced

to the band he was leaving. Of course, Jimmy's decision was difficult to take, but the band was pretty sound otherwise and we never
looked back." Poco rehearsed diligently for the upcoming shows
and then flew east for the crucial concerts.

Late in September, Poco recorded concerts at the Boston Music Hall and the Felt Forum in New York. It was a gutsy move since
the gigs had them opening for the Moody Blues.   *Circus* magazine
reported that Poco played such a hot set that there were calls from
the audience for more Poco during the Moody's set. Richard Meltzer
commented, "There's something wholly American about [Poco], and
it's their defiance. They defy you to find a single weak point other
than dull cuts." Another review, in *Billboard*, said that Rusty Young
was the real standout of the Felt Forum performance, especially his
contributions to *You Better Think Twice* and the new song *You Are
the One*. *Variety* also singled out *You Are the One* as a fresh new
song. Surprisingly, Poco did not include the latter song on the subsequent live album. Despite the fine reviews, Furay's voice was less
than acceptable on the Felt Forum shows. Instead, the bulk of the
album was taken from the Boston shows. After the shows, Messina
closeted himself with the tapes to assemble the live album. "I was
probably the one to select which songs were the best to include.
And generally with something like that, I'll try to take the performances from the same show, first go there and make sure that everything worked. Unless there is a train wreck somewhere, I'd rather
keep that show together. From there I might edit one performance
from another show in there."

In the meantime, Furay wasted little time in lining up
Messina's replacement. Chicago bassist Pete Cetera was taking steel
guitar lessons from Rusty Young.   When Young mentioned that
Messina had announced he was leaving and Poco was in need of a
guitarist, Cetera flashed on a conversation he'd had a year previous.
Illinois Speed Press guitarist Paul Cotton had shared with Cetera his
admiration for Poco's brand of sprightly country-rock. Cetera told
Young he was sure that Cotton would be interested since the Speed
Press was falling apart with the departure of Kal David. Young
passed along the information to Furay that Cotton might be available. Poco was aware of Cotton's abilities, having shared the bill
with the Illinois Speed Press on a couple of occasions.

Poco's need for a new guitar player coincided with the demise
of the Illinois Speed Press. They were booked to open the fall leg of
Chicago's tour, and Cotton was trying to salvage his commitment to
that tour. "We had worked with Paul," Grantham recalled. "The
Illinois Speed Press had opened one or two shows for us. They were
such a great band and Paul was wonderful. So when it came time to

replace Jimmy, the first guy, and the last, we thought of was Paul Cotton. I mean, we were all slayed by him, by his playing." Cotton explains, "The Speed Press was the house band at a lounge called the White Room in Buena Park for the summer. We were down to a four-piece, very exposed and playing our roots. Poco was reduced to a four-piece too. That's where they got to hear me for the first time ever. I went into their dressing room afterward and introduced myself and hoped." After having seen Pogo at their debut at the Troubadour, Cotton had confided to a companion that "this is the band I would like to be in." The members of Poco could tell Cotton was a kindred spirit.

Furay contacted him about the job and got a surprising response. Cotton explains, "I actually said 'I'll get back to 'ya' because I wanted to talk it over with my guys. And they said, 'Go for it! Paulie, that's your kind of music!'" Cotton had assembled a new version of the Speed Press with hotshot guitarist John Uribe to open for Chicago on their upcoming tour. However after hearing his bandmates, Cotton was convinced it was the right move for him. Remembering Poco's initial shows at the Troubadour, Cotton decided to join up rather than try to pump life into the Speed Press. He toted his guitar up to Furay's house in Laurel Canyon one day and ran through some tunes, including an acoustic version of *Bad Weather*. Before the day was up, Cotton had joined Poco.

Furay still beams at the mention of recruiting Cotton. "When Paul came along there was no looking back!" Furay asserts. "He was exactly what I was looking for to add a little "edge" to the sound – not taking away from the original country aspect of the music, but bringing a little rock and roll to the over all sound. Plus, Paul is a wonderful songwriter and gifted singer. He was a win-win addition."

Rehearsals began with Cotton, and Messina helped acquaint him with the arrangements and chord changes. When Poco hit the road, the two guitarists roomed together so that Messina could continue to help Cotton and the band over the rough transition period. Cotton explains, "I went on tour with them, not playing but rooming with Jimmy. This was just before DELIVERIN' was released. We were on tour in the East along the seaboard, and I was hanging with Jimmy and he was teaching me the songs and the guitar licks. It was an odd situation easing another guy into the band." This arrangement was bound to cause problems so without warning, after a Halloween night concert at the Fillmore West in San Francisco, Furay informed Messina that Cotton could handle things and he was no longer needed. Messina was crest-fallen. Former Buffalo Springfield band mate Neil Young was in attendance, and Messina had wanted to play for him. Instead, Messina joined Young in the audience and watched Poco's set. Messina flew back to Los Angeles the next day as Poco continued to tour. Cotton's first solo performance with the band was captured on tape and shows that his arrangements were virtually copies of Messina's in the beginning. At this early stage, Poco did not perform any of Cotton's material and kept Messina's *You Better Think Twice* in the set.

By all accounts, Cotton fit right in with Poco, both personally and musically. Cotton remembered, "Jimmy had showed me everything about those early songs, which I paid no attention to! I can't play like that, never could. We're total opposites as singers, guitar players, you name it. But that's what they wanted." It's interesting to note that Messina had attempted to convince Cotton to play "his" style of guitar, as well as teach him chord changes and arrangements.

The official reason given for Messina's departure was that having been recently married, Messina wanted to devote more time to his family. The rock press generally understood that Messina would remain Poco's producer in much the same way as Brian Wilson had remained the Beach Boys producer, but quit the road. In fact, Messina never considered staying on as Poco's producer. Furay didn't necessarily follow the official line. He told Pete Fornatale shortly after Messina's departure, "Jimmy left to go out on his own. I'm not sure whether he wants to be a performer or a producer, and I don't think he knows yet. It's going to take him a little time to find out exactly what he wants to do. However he didn't want to be a part of Poco, so he left." Obviously, Furay knew his partner better than expected. Inside of a year, Messina began working with Kenny Loggins and found the perfect compromise - artist and producer.

With their new guitarist in tow, Poco learned to incorporate Cotton's style with their own while on the road. The band played a host of East Coast college dates, including one at Glassboro State College in upstate New York where a rising new star, British pianist Elton John opened the show. In mid-December Poco played the Fillmore East in New York and got a good review in *Billboard*. Fred Kirby asserted, "Poco has reached the promise they've demonstrated from their beginnings." On January 15, 1971, they headlined the Santa Monica Civic and drew rave reviews. The L.A. *Times* wrote, "For good clean, wholesome rock and roll fun, there's simply no beating Poco." A new arrangement of *Kind Woman* and Young's steel acrobatics on *El Tonto De Nadie, Regressa* were cited as highlights of the show. To no one's surprise, Rusty Young remained Poco's virtuoso live performer. While the other members were certainly competent, it was Young who consistently stood out instrumentally. Young also stood out visually to *Times* reviewer John Mendelsohn, who noted "the normally sedate [Young] leaping from his stool to send his instrument into a fit of ecstatic shrieking." It was obvious from the good press that the addition of Cotton didn't slow the movement of Poco's career. Furay was very pleased at how easy Cotton fit into the scheme of things. "I got away with murder," Cotton muses. "They let me be myself. After I ripped off those fingerpicks at the Fillmore, we said, 'OK, let's go!'"

In February 1971, Epic released Poco's third album. DELIVERIN' was not a run-of-the-mill live album. The opener was a rousing song of Furay's called *I Guess You Made It*. Tim Schmit handled the lead vocals. Grantham's insistent use of the cowbell powered the opening riff. Again making use of the Poco trick of turning negative lyrics into a positive song, it proved to be a great new set opener. Furay had written the song back in 1967 as a member of the Springfield under the title *Who's the Next Fool*. Another of Furay's new songs, *C'mon*, followed it. Lyrically, it summed up Furay's philosophy of life with lines like "I believe that you and I as men should love one and another...satisfied, have peace of mind, love your neighbor as your brother." Tim Schmit was responsible for the third new song in a row with *Hear That Music*. It was an upbeat country song, written after seeing Pogo live in 1968. A terrific version of *Kind Woman* followed. Slowed down from the Springfield version, Furay conveys the lyrics with emotion and conviction. Its inclusion was important to Furay, who explained to rock historian John Einarson, "As far as I'm concerned there's a real bad mistake on [the Buffalo Springfield] track from an aesthetic point of view, a 5/4 measure, that bothers me to this day. I rerecorded the song later with Poco and corrected it." Side one ended with a spirited acoustic medley. Opening with Schmit's *Hard Luck*, it segued into Furay's *A Child's Claim To Fame* and ended with *Pickin' Up the Pieces*.

Side two opened with an acoustic version of *You Better Think Twice* using the arrangement of the acoustic studio version that Poco left unreleased from the POCO sessions. Young and Messina's guitar and dobro work was outstanding. Unlike most shows, Messina did the vocals for this recording. Another new song, *A Man Like Me*, followed. It was the album's low point only because it was an average piece of material written by Furay. Things picked right up with an excellent closing medley of country tunes from the first album. The seamless blending of *Just In Case It Happens*, *Yes Indeed*, *Grand Junction*, and *Consequently, So Long* ended the album on a real high note.

DELIVERIN' was a stunning piece of work both in content and performance. It should be noted that including so much new material on a live album was a novelty. Stu Werbin gave DELIVERIN' a glowing review in *Rolling Stone*, saying that "it serves to render the first two [albums] nearly superfluous." The Boston *Phoenix* wrote, "This group should stay out of the studios and stay on stages." The *Phoenix* also noted that Tim Schmit "comes of age on this album." As good as the album sounded, the group wasn't totally satisfied. A staff engineer did the mix, and Rusty Young claims he was one of Columbia's veterans on the verge of retirement. Consequently, very little effort went into the mix. Perhaps the most distracting is that Furay's vocals are buried in the mix. A quadraphonic version was issued years later, and an improved mix was used that had a better balance, more upfront vocals, and more between song chatter. Whatever its flaws, DELIVERIN' still remains Rusty Young's favorite Poco album and probably captured early Poco at its most proficient.

Epic was also pleased when DELIVERIN' began to climb the charts. They decided to release one of the new songs as a single. Epic engineers edited *C'mon*, backed with *I Guess You Made It*. Furay insisted that the studio version be released, however Epic refused. It proved to be a fateful decision. *C'mon* entered the charts in late May and began to climb. However as it started to take off, a radio programmer in the South became convinced that the chorus of "C'mon and love me" actually said "C'mon and <u>suck</u> me." As his incurrect conclusion circulated among radio programmers, the single was dropped from play lists and the single died. *C'mon* stalled at #69 after seven weeks on the charts. Furay bitterly blamed Epic, claiming that if they had released the studio version, the mistake would never have been made

The departure of Messina and the continued inability of Poco to hit the big-time crushed Furay's spirit. Filled with self-doubt and uncertain of his future, he began an affair with a secretary to one of the Columbia Record executives. Furay's recent biography, *Pickin' up the Pieces* with Michael Roberts, details the struggles that he went through domestically. The dual life weighed heavily on the usually upbeat leader, and he began to withdraw from the rest of the group.

Poco continued its relentless road work and played some headline gigs. After some dates in California, Poco played Carnegie Hall on February 12. Grantham felt playing Carnegie Hall was a special moment in Poco's early career. "I think that was one of the peaks, definitely. Getting to play Carnegie Hall. I mean, what an honor. What an accomplishment! Incredible to play, especially for a rock band." Poco then headlined the Fillmore West from March

11-14. In April, Poco joined a tour with Leon Russell, Badfinger, and Lee Michaels for several dates in Texas. Poco played an excellent set at the Music Hall in Boston. In May, they headlined the Fillmore East with Linda Ronstadt opening for them. They also shared the bill with the British progressive band Emerson, Lake, and Palmer for a few shows in May, including a sold out show at Cleveland Public Hall on May 14. The long tour ended with an appearance in Furay's hometown of Yellow Springs, Ohio, where Poco played a 90-minute set at Antioch College. Furay thanked his bandmates from the stage for sacrificing a day off to make the concert happen.

The tour was successful as Poco's profile was improving. One aspect of their live show that needed improving was their equipment. Rusty Young observed, "In some of the concerts we've been doing we'd get up against some blues group who had about 20 Marshall's for each of them. All three of them. And we'd get up and play our music and sometimes wonder if we were loud enough, that factor kind of stumped us in the beginning but I think we're into the right thing now." With the move to a more rock sound, they upgraded their amps and sound system, and Poco shows from 1971 on generally were noted, not always positively, for their volume. One key was Furay's intention upon Cotton's arrival to take Poco in more of a rock and roll direction. Furay would later say, "I had a vision of [Poco] being more of a rock and roll band than a country band. But I have to tell you that [Messina] was the one responsible for Poco's country format. Jimmy's not really a rock n' roll guitar player."

Wanting to take advantage of DELIVERIN's chart performance, Clive Davis assigned Poco to work with Steve Cropper, who had recently signed a production deal with Columbia. Epic wanted a new studio album on the streets as soon as the band could produce one. Cropper had an excellent reputation as a guitarist and songwriter. As a member of Booker T's MG's, Cropper had made quite a name for himself. His co-writing credit for the classic *Knock On Wood* was a sterling example of his songwriting talents. However record production was something fairly new for Cropper. Furay recalled, "We needed a new producer and Columbia pushed very hard for Steve Cropper, they'd just signed a deal with him and thought he'd be perfect...but it didn't work out." Columbia, of course, had high hopes for Cropper. Although his rock credentials were in order, Cropper had virtually no experience as a producer.

Aside from the fact that Cropper had production aspirations, the deal was more acceptable from Columbia's perspective because Cropper was in the process of building his own studio, Trans Maximus, in Memphis. While this looked good on Columbia's balance sheets, it had unforeseen effects on the first project. Poco came off their long tour with no break and arrived in Memphis as the first group to use Cropper's new studio. Unfortunately, Trans Maximus wasn't ready when Poco arrived. Cropper only had an eight-track machine when the industry standard was changing to 16-track. In fact, Poco had recorded their second album on a 16-track machine. Poco was forced to make their album on antiquated equipment. Not surprisingly, the sessions did not go well. The group felt no rapport with Cropper, and he wasn't able to do the technical things to get the sound the band was looking for. Cropper was more of an arranger but Poco didn't need that as much as they needed a good solid technical man, according to Rusty Young.

Young maintains, "As it ended up, Steve did a lot of sitting in the control room and drinking, and we did a lot of working donw with his little eight track machine." Furay complained that they had been on the road for a long time and had gone straight to Memphis instead of going home. Having to record away from home after such a prolonged absence didn't help their performance. Furay remembered, "We wrote eight of the songs right there; we rehearsed the songs in the afternoon and record them in the evening...I really feel you should perform a song before recording it but now were in the same predicament when we've finished this tour they want us to go into the studio and start cranking it out again, and I'm really not in favor of this." Young concurs, "We toured for six months, had six weeks to make the record, and then we had another six month tour. So we weren't in a position to do anything else. Clive Davis told us we had to do the record now; management was saying 'Can't you make it work on sixteen tracks?' The whole thing was a mess. That was a really disappointing experience. We weren't happy and we were tired at that point."

Poco's dissatisfaction with Cropper was interesting given the fact that it was the first time they had to use an outside producer. Some of Cropper's lack of involvement may be attributed to the extra attention that Messina had always lavished on the production. Much of Poco's criticism of Cropper was that he offered them the same kind of thing as Messina: arranging their material. Obviously, Furay and company expected Cropper to offer more technical elements, which he failed to do. From Cropper's standpoint, it seems pretty clear that Poco's expectations were misplaced. If Cropper had anything to offer another act, it would be the benefit of his arranging skills. After all, Cropper was a musician, not a technician.

Still, Poco's criticisms are not that far off base. Cropper did not become a producer of any note and soon returned to performing. Ultimately, it is Cropper's failure as a producer that pervades the album's sound. Whatever his inability to relate to Poco's music, professionalism demanded Cropper either offer more effort or get help. Furay confirms, "Steve sort of gave up halfway through." Poco eventually re-cut two tracks in Columbia's studio in San Francisco because they were unhappy with how they had turned out in Memphis. Young told Jerry Gilbert after the record was complete, "I'm not sure the album sounds exactly like it would have sounded if we'd done it entirely ourselves - but Steve didn't influence us at all. It's a really honest sounding album - a real live sounding album because we only did one or two overdubs on the entire album." What Young fails to add is that the studio's limitations dictated the lack of overdubs. Furay was almost apologetic in interviews. "It's not a Memphis blues album. It's very definitely Poco. Steve left most of it up to us; he just got it down on tape for us."

Years later, Young complained, "The reason that we weren't happy with Steve Cropper, more than the album itself, was that he really didn't participate in the production but still received credit and money. A producer makes a lot of money out of a record, in this case made more money than we did, and we all felt that was really unfair for us to work as hard as we did and have some guy be given production credit. And we're all real opinionated, all of us in the band, it's real difficult, I'm sure. Steve was frustrated by the fact that we wouldn't listen to his opinions and that's why he pulled out." Cropper agreed that the experience had been frustrating. He had told the band that there were no commercial tunes on the album and to write something else, however they ignored him. After it was clear that the band was going to proceed without heeding his advice, Cropper quickly lost interest in the project.

Despite the disappointment with Cropper, Schmit felt that the production was an improvement over previous Poco efforts. Frustrated by what he perceived as a controlling Jim Messina, Schmit liked the atmosphere under Cropper. He explains, "When I came in, everything was pasted. The bass and the drums would record, then somebody else and it would be put together. The record becomes too perfect; too sterile; there's nothing human about it when you overdub every instrument."

Paul Cotton's introduction to Poco in the studio was a challenge. "We were at Trans Maximus for six long weeks, and the studio had a major breakdown right in the middle. I was trying to stay positive; it was my first album with these guys. I think it really forced us to hang out together away from our family and friends. Tim and I were roommates for six weeks during the recording." Still, the addition of Paul Cotton was viewed as a positive step for the band. Tim Schmit observed, "Paul's made it better. He's made it more concrete. He's made it more fun. He's a good person to be around. It was work to James [Messina]. It's still that, but it's not like going to the office or something. It's more fun."

However Cotton couldn't help noticing that Poco's leader wasn't himself. "Richie was going through a tough patch in his life," observes Cotton. "[It] scared the heck out of me. His mood was more introspective at that point." As outlined in his recent biography, Furay had separated from his wife Nancy to pursue his affair, and his mood remained rather dark and distant during the sessions. Thankfully, the separation did not last long, and Furay broke off the affair and invited his wife to go on the road with him to ensure he wouldn't stray.

After a brief break, Poco hit the road again for the summer concert season. Miles Thomas, needing to fill a slot in Poco's road crew before the tour, turned to a friend from his days with the Turtles. Denny Jones had served as a roadie during the last turbulent days of Turtles and for the past year had been working for the band Bush until they broke up. "My first show was in June 1971 in San Diego. We had the big red truck, and right after San Diego, Miles and I drove non-stop all the way to Seattle. We were supposed to do two shows up there and in Portland with Brewer and Shipley. And the shows were canceled. I said to myself, 'So this is the way it's going to be like, eh?' That trip was crazy – Miles was smoking every five minutes, drinking Cokes, and talking non-stop." They also had a show at Red Rocks in Denver canceled when rock shows were abruptly banned at the venue. In July, Poco played the Schaeffer Music Festival in New York's Central Park. It would prove to be a popular venue for them for years to come. The reaction was incredible. Cotton would later recall, "I first noticed it in New York. We introduced this western thing to the city and it was Pocomania from then on." It was also obvious that Cotton was the perfect replacement for Messina in concert. It remained until late in September for fans to find out how well he sounded on record.

The rest of July was spent playing rock festivals in Montreal, Rochester, Michigan, Minneapolis, and Milwaukee. At the Place des Nations in Montreal, Poco played the Man and His World event. The Montreal *Star* reviewer John P. Hardy noted, "Poco has played to bigger and better crowds at SRO concerts in Shea Stadium and Madison Square Garden, and here at the Place des Nations, they often echoed the complaint of numerous other performers, who resent that the audience is fenced off and kept in a security quarantine some 15 yards away. 'It's hard to relate to an audience that's so far away,' said Poco's rhythm guitarist Richie Furay." During Poco's set at Milwaukee's Summerfest, a rowdy crowd pelted the band with debris. When Grantham was hit in the leg by a bottle, Poco bolted from the stage in self-defense.

FROM THE INSIDE appeared in September, and it opened with a country sing-along *Hoedown*. Written by Furay and Young, it was a fairly simple song but perfectly cast in the Poco mold. The second track introduced Cotton as a songwriter to Poco fans. *Bad Weather* has become a Poco classic among loyalists, however what few fans realize is that Cotton originally recorded the song with the Illinois Speed Press. Poco had heard him perform it live when they shared the same bill with the Speed Press and were anxious to record it themselves. Apparently it went through several arrangements before they settled on this one cut in San Francisco after the original sessions. Furay contributed the memorable 12-string lead guitar riff to it. The third song, Furay's *What Am I Gonna Do*, sounded the first sour note. It is a depressing song and it is nothing like any previous Furay effort. Lyrically, it revealed the dark side of Furay's personal life. Furay has admitted that this song resulted from a time when he fell in love with another woman. Although he remained with his wife Nancy, the torment over this relationship colored his contributions to FROM THE INSIDE. Furay explains, "I was in a very dark place during the FROM THE INSIDE sessions except for *Just For Me and You* which is one of the best songs I've ever written, and *Hoe Down*. Nancy and I were going through a difficult time in our lives and you write about those things in your life too." *You Are the One* had been recorded for the live album but wasn't used. Tim Schmit does the lead vocals, however the band plays like they were half asleep. It would seem this track in particular is the perfect indictment of Cropper as producer. A more sympathetic producer would have had the group re-cut the tune with more energy and life. Cotton's rocking *Railroad Days* showcased his talents and hinted at Poco's more rocking style.

Tim Schmit's only songwriting contribution opened side two. *From The Inside* is a fine effort that tells of his impending fatherhood. Cotton offers, "Tim's [song] I still think is a classic." The next song, Furay's *Do You Feel It Too*, dated back to the group's earliest days. Furay had written it in 1965 before the formation of the Buffalo Springfield when it was called *Can't Keep Me Down*. This arrangement is similar in feel to *Nobody's Fool*, but more depressing. Cotton added a filler tune about his dog called *Ol' Forgiver*. The album ends promisingly with Furay's two best efforts. *What If I Should Say I Love You*, another strong ballad, was one of those songs re-recorded in San Francisco after the original sessions ended. The final track, *Just For Me And You*, was the only spirited Poco song on the album and ends it on just the right note.

FROM THE INSIDE remains Rusty Young's least favorite Poco album. He remarked recently, "In those days we weren't the kind of act that could go in and say 'we're not releasing this record!' They would have nailed us to the wall." For years Furay also considered it the poorest, although his most recent appraisal is not nearly as harsh. The *Rolling Stone* review concentrated on the depressing tone of the album and the marked difference in the live versus studio versions of *You Are the One*. *Fusion* magazine pointed out the acoustic feel of the album and gave it a solid good review. "There are really no throwaways on this record," wrote John Koegel, "an accomplishment few groups realize." *Billboard* raved, "Poco remains one of the most original groups around today and they should win much favor with their fans with this latest outing." One also has to wonder about Cotton's peculiar vocal style that had him sound as if he had a chew in his front lip. This tendency was still noticeable on their next album before disappearing. The arrangements on FROM THE INSIDE weren't as tight as previous songs, indicating that Cotton and Young hadn't quite meshed. There was a distinct lack of the kind of guitar interplay that marked Young and Messina's work in the past. Partly to blame was the fact that they had to learn to play with each other's guitar styles while on the road.

FROM THE INSIDE rose quickly to #52 on the charts, however it was still a disappointment after the fine showing of DELIVERIN'. The high hopes the band had for greater sales faded rather quickly. With the release of the album, trade papers announced that Cotton's *Railroad Days* would be the first single. However, Epic chose to hold off and instead released *Just For Me And You/Ol' Forgiver* as an edited single late in October. It made a brief appearance on the charts at #110 before disappearing.

On September 30, 1971, Poco went into Columbia Studio in Los Angeles for a live radio concert broadcast in Los Angeles over KMET. Performing in front of family and friends, Poco put on an excellent performance. This concert, widely bootlegged as COUNTRY BUMP, showed that while Furay still dominated the group's material, Cotton managed to have all three of his songs from FROM THE INSIDE performed. It also showed that most of the first album's material had finally been retired from the set list after being the staple of their set for so long. Furay had complained that Poco's set had grown a bit stale with trying to teach new players the old songs and stay on the road. "It does get old playing the same songs," Furay told *Rolling Stone*. "Every time we would lose a member, the band would spend time redoing our old songs with the new guy." It also showed that Furay had learned a lesson after losing Messina. Never again would he dominate a Poco album simply by virtue of the sheer number of songs on it. He would, however, continue to dominate them by the quality of his material.

Cotton's arrival signaled a major change within the band. From the day of his arrival, Cotton was encouraged to provide material for the group. Furay explains the reason for the change, "I did most of the writing and it sort of drained me, you know? I really think it's good that we do have more than one writer in the group because Paul writes and Tim's starting to write. I'm really glad that we have three writers – even Rusty's starting to write songs with lyrics, which is really great." Indeed, while Young was experimenting with songs with lyrics, it would still be several years before Poco would perform them

Cotton was ultimately surprised at Messina's attitude about not being able to get songs recorded with Poco. "You'd think he'd have been satisfied with being able to produce this band," he said wistfully. However there was no doubt that Furay gave him room as a songwriter, although that wasn't the plan in the beginning. "I think I was recruited as a guitarist. But I had that song *Bad Weather* that seemed to fit the band, and that was a strong point. They wanted to re-record it again and again and again...There are about five recordings of it...and I'm still not satisfied with it." Although having Cotton's songs on the new album may have been a sort of "welcome to the band" gesture, the band never considered excluding his material from upcoming releases when he brought a new batch of songs to rehearsals.

Meanwhile, the lure of Los Angeles had grown dim for Furay. The smog was proving hard on his throat, and with a baby daughter now a part of the family, he decided to move away from the L.A. crazies to Colorado. Cotton explains, "Actually that came from Richie and I talking because we both had familes. I had a small son and we realized it was time to get out of Hollywood. Time to get out of L.A. and the insane atmosphere." Grantham relates that Poco's destination wasn't originally his home state. "We first talked about moving up north to the Bay Area. I was up there with my wife at the time. We had found a house and bought appliances. We were painting the house and rented it. We went back down to LA 'cuz we were in the studio down there. We got to LA and found that plans had changed and we were going to Colorado! Here we had rented a house in Woodside, I believe. It really caught me off-guard and we had to change all our plans. It was a mess. But it was fine with me too because Colorado was home."

Being home turf for Young and Grantham, Poco decided to move its base of operation there in late August. The effect of this move on Poco's profile in the music business is immeasurable. The band went from being right at the heart of the music business to about as far away as possible. Cotton and Schmit were also thrust into entirely new surroundings. Colorado proved to be quite an adjustment. Tim Schmit was totally out of his element. Gone were the club social scene and the easy interaction with other bands and musicians. Already a popular studio singer, Schmit was no longer just a phone call away from appearing on someone's album, and that made him unhappy. Denny Jones reveals, "That move created a lot of friction. Richie lived up in Nederland so he rarely socialized with us down in Boulder. We also had to cancel dates in the early 70's because Richie was snowed in up at Nederland. So that created some bad feelings, as you can expect." Although Cotton adjusted to the move, the surprise to many was the ease at which Furay took to his new home. "From my perspective it brought me 'home,'" explains Furay. "It was finally a place I wanted to settle down in and bring up my family! As for the group – I don't think any of them really liked it even though Rusty and George were from here." The isolation didn't help Poco's profile in the music business, however Cotton claimed it did wonders for his songwriting.

When Poco returned to the road, they found themselves at the peak of their drawing power. They sold out a two-night stay at Carnegie Hall three weeks in advance of the shows on December 7 and 8. This sort of response prompted Epic to do something they had never done before - release a second single off a Poco album. This time they edited Cotton's *Railroad Days* backed with *You Are the One* and released it late in December. However the single didn't even chart. It shouldn't have surprised anyone, since singing about "blown up railroads" isn't normally Top 40 fare. Still, Cotton and Furay were sure it would be a hit, and when it wasn't, both took it very hard. A foreign pressing of this single contains an unreleased studio version of *You Are the One*, using the acoustic arrangement featured during the live concert used for COUNTRY BUMP.

Frustrated by the failure of the collaboration with Steve Cropper, Furay decided to take a bolder step. Poco entered the studio with producer Richie Podolor shortly after Christmas. They cut two new tracks intended for single release. Poco cut studio versions of the new songs on their live album: *C'mon* and *A Man Like Me*. "Richie had worked with Steppenwolf and Three Dog Night," recalls Furay. "We were thinking, 'This is the guy that can do it!' Jimmy was gone, and we were searching for a producer because we didn't feel we had the capability to do it on our own and we wanted someone with a track record."

The Podolor session should have been a warning. Without Messina to lead the way, the group was totally in Podolor's hands.

While the results were vibrant and exciting - Cotton's later assessment was that the results were some "very hot rock and roll" -
drummer George Grantham thought the process was rather strange.
"When it came time to mix the record," Grantham sighed, "he had
a way of taking three or four vocals and pushing up a word of that
take or <u>that</u> take. I don't know, it kind of drove me crazy. I think it
got to everybody. Not that he wasn't great at what he did, it's just
that the way he did it was very strange." The tracks were very
good, however, and Furay was excited about getting them out as
soon as possible. "We recorded two or three songs at American Recorders with Richie and his partner Bill [Cooper], and we were ecstatic with the results. We were sure CBS would agree to him
producing the next record and were anxious to go to NYC to play it
for the execs." Furay hurried off to New York to meet with officials
with Epic Records, sure that he soon would be hearingr their big hit
single hit the radio waves. The silence was deafening.

6
A Good Feeling to Know

The officials at Epic Records shook their heads at this latest attempt by Poco to make a hit record. In fact, they didn't even agree to pay for the sessions. One problem was the group had worked with an outside producer not affiliated with Columbia, which violated Poco's recording contract. According to Grantham another problem was that "they just didn't agree that [the songs] were the product they wanted to put out." Epic officials told Furay, "You sound too much like Steppenwolf." Furay sighs, "We went to CBS and were so excited about presenting these songs to them that they'd be floored that we could sound like this in the studio. And they turned it down. They said 'no.' There was a lot of politics being played at this time. It was a blow to me that made me start to think that if CBS was going to stand in our way after giving them this kind of a commercial sound, we either had to get off the label or it just wasn't going to happen." Epic insisted that Poco work only with someone connected with the label. Those who have heard these outtakes call them stunning. Furay's vision for the future had been temporarily clouded by corporate politics.

Furay remains bitter at the turn of events. "Well, we never got the opportunity to use Richie Podolor, which in my opinion was a devastating blow to us as a band. I almost felt sabotaged. I don't remember how or why they came to the decision to reject Richie – but they blew it, plain and simple. Poco wasn't a big money maker for Epic, but we had the potential and the possibilities were unbelievable – but they refused to go with him. I know there was a lot of politics then (and now) in the music business and to what degree some of that played into it, I don't know, but, musically – record wise, it was a horrendous mistake on the record company's part and the beginning of driving me out of the band. I firmly believe Richie would have made the 'radio friendly' record we so desperately needed at that time in our existence."

The mood shifted as Shiffman and Larson finally booked Poco on their first European tour in January 1972. Furay had anxiously been awaiting a trip to Europe since the Buffalo Springfield days. Poco was originally hired to support Mountain on the tour, however when that group backed out, Poco became the headliner. It was a low overhead affair. Denny Jones, having just joined the Poco road crew six months before recalls, "I was the only guy that they took from the crew because I was more rounded. They took Tommy Walsh from the sound company. I did the monitors. We both did all the driving and all the stage set-up ourselves, the two of us. I had never done the monitors before. We drove the equipment truck on the other side of the road, a 24-foot truck! We landed at Heathrow, got the stuff loaded – we drove all the way to Cannes in the south of France. The two of us! And the truck broke down in the middle of nowhere. Then we got there and had to put the entire sound system together ourselves. And putting Rusty's pedal steel together was no easy task! I had to put together the Leslie cabinet too. I learned it from the schematics."

Poco opened the tour with a special performance at the MIDEM music conference in Cannes, France, on January 20, 1972. The Byrds, also touring Europe at the time, shared the bill. Poco's set was rescued after an electrical failure fried their equipment. Thankfully, Byrds soundman Dinky Dawson loaned them some of the Byrds equipment, and their set went off perfectly. "It was brutal," Jones moans. "No one spoke English. There were 5,000 people under this huge tent and the power goes out. I had never set up the monitors for them before and I was sweating." After a couple of gigs in Switzerland, the band played Paris on the 22nd. While in France, Poco also appeared on French television's Pop 2 show. The show used footage shot at Poco's Paris show with Poco performing *What If I Should Say I Love You, Just For Me and You, What a Day, Hear That Music*, and *C'mon*. Poco crossed into Brussells, Belgium, and played a couple of dates in Germany. They taped an appearance on the West German TV show *Beat Club*, performing *C'mon* on January 29. Poco followed that with a show at the club Zoom in Frankfurt the next day.

Their show at the Trivolis Concert Hall in Copenhagen, Denmark, on January 28, 1972, was politely received however the crowd was strangely quiet. A British reviewer noted that Poco "concentrated mainly on material from the 1st two albums such as the medley from DELIVERIN' and *You Are the One* from FROM THE INSIDE. But they really came into their own at the end of the performance, during a 20-minute jam in the encore with drummer George Grantham shifting the tempo around and Young creating an amazing solo, putting the steel through his Leslie to give it a chattering organ sound." A portion of the show survives on a collector's tape and shows the band in similar form to their recently released live album DELIVERIN', playing nearly the same set.

Poco crossed the English Channel and began their British tour with an appearance on BBC-TV's *Old Grey Whistle Test*. The band recorded the backing tracks earlier in the day and was filmed singing live vocals to the backing track on *Just For Me and You* and *Railroad Days*. They followed with shows at Loughborough University. Things changed a bit in London where Poco finally played before their British fans at the Rainbow. Surprisingly, only their opening act, Billy Preston, was pictured on the program. Writers in *Zigzag* later revealed that Poco did not draw well, forcing promoter Johnny Morris to offer incredible incentives to get the crowds to pack the Rainbow. Still, the Rainbow gigs on February 4 and 5 were later accorded legendary status by English Poco fans. Jones agrees, "The highlight was playing the Rainbow in London. It was a great old venue." *Melody Maker* raved about their performance. The set was essentially the same as the one performed during the radio concert except Poco eliminated the acoustic medley. They performed a new arrangement of *A Man Like Me* and closed with a high-energy version of *Grand Junction*. In all, Poco played four dates while in England. George Grantham explained Poco's experience on their first trip in Europe: "We'd finished playing to some audiences that we're not used to like up north, Germany and whatever. The audience response is not what we're used to in the States. They sit there through the set...they appreciate it, but we don't know it until the end of the set. And we're used to, right from the beginning, the audience responding. I remember when we played the Rainbow, it was like it was in the States."

Another reminder of the States was waiting for them backstage. Tim Schmit recalls, "I also remember Don [Henley] and Glenn [Frey] coming to a Poco concert in London when we played at the Rainbow. That was probably '72 or something. They came over and I said, 'What are you doing here?' 'Oh, we've started a band and we're making a record.' Which turned out to be the Eagles' first record."

Poco finished their British tour with a club appearance at Barbarella's in Birmingham and the Brighton Dome. The band returned to the continent for a sold out three-date Dutch tour with Fairport Convention. They opened at Eindhoven on February 11, followed by concerts at Groningen, and ended with a performance at the Concertgebown in Amsterdam. Local reviews were positive, "Poco as a live performance surpasses their record album. The sound of the group is more than unique."

The European experience was not an altogether positive one for all of Poco. George Grantham has mixed memories. "It was like *'Stranger in a Strange Land.'* I thought I'd gone to Mars or something. It was so weird. At the time I was having some difficulty with my marriage so I felt real isolated, kind of alone. It was so hard. I never felt so far from home in my life, and of course there was no one to talk about it except the band." To ease his homesickness, Grantham recalled playing the newly released HARVEST album by Neil Young. "I remember playing the heck out of it. It kept me sane."

The group returned to the States however Young's Leslie cabinet took a detour. Jones recalls, "We had a special case built for it. A big white case with Poco stenciled on it. We shipped it over to Europe but it never made it back. It ended up in Bogata, Colombia. A month later, it was delivered at Schmit's house in Boulder." During their off time in February, Furay went to the Troubadour to check out Jimmy Messina's new venture. The Kenny Loggins Band featuring Jimmy Messina drew large crowds and generated tremendous excitement during their engagement. Messina graciously asked Furay to join the band during their encore. Although it was the band's first live shows, it was already clear that the band was well rehearsed and that Messina's presence was important to the overall sound. Still, it wasn't clear how well Messina's new venture would pay off that February night. Within days, there was no doubt about the impact Loggins and Messina had on the crowds. Word got around quickly about the exciting new act at the Troubadour, and the remainder of the band's stay was sold out.

After a couple weeks of relaxation and rehearsals, Poco went out on the road again. Poco hit the Northeast, playing Boston, Vermont, and several New York dates at the Capitol Theater in Port Chester and in Passaic, New Jersey. Poco also played college dates at Princeton and Hofstra University. Their set had been shuffled to include a couple of new tunes. One was a Rusty Young instrumental entitled *Skunk Kreek*, after a local Colorado eatery that allowed the band to rehearse there. The other song, *Good Feelin' to Know* was a new Richie Furay tune that many felt held Poco's future.

The band's return to the States signaled a change. They were all depressed at their lack of chart success, and they did a lot of finger pointing in the press at their record company. "Our record company is behind us," Rusty Young joked to *Crawdaddy* editor Peter Knobler, "way behind us." The band claimed all they needed was that one big hit single. Furay observed, "Singles are so much fun. You go crazy over those things. We'll keep throwing them to the lions. One day they'll bite. Right?"

Their best bet for a hit seemed to be a new song of Furay's that they were including in their live set. Many people in the radio business told them it was a sure fire smash. Written in December, *Good Feelin' to Know* seemed to have all the elements for an accessible pop tune. Buoyed by this enthusiasm, Poco decided to go right into the studio and cut the tune.

Before recording, Furay had briefly considered asking Jimmy Messina if he would produce the band again. He also tried to interest Epic in allowing Richie Podolor to produce them, however neither option panned out. The experience with Steve Cropper had been devastating, and Furay was looking for a comfortable situation. However he also desperately wanted that hit single and decided instead to hire Jack Richardson. "We went with Jack Richardson because of Jack's track record with the Guess Who," explains Furay. "We were desperately wanting to tap into the commercial radio airplay situation. We had the songs, I thought, and our motive was to have a producer who was in touch with commercial music and certainly Jack had that."

Contacted by Shiffman and Larson, Richardson agreed to take on the job. "The band was living in Boulder, Colorado, at that time," explains Richardson. "I went out there initially and spent about 10 days with them up there at Richie's place in the mountains. We were doing my version of pre-production, which was putting the material together. First thing that hit me was that they were excellent musicians, good singers. I had always been one to lean towards the vocal aspects of a project. There was a certain amount of competitiveness involved, especially between Richie and Paul Cotton." Poco was also using the Skunk Creek Inn as their rehearsal spot. It was a non-descript restaurant in a strip mall in southern Boulder. Richardson joined the group and listened to their songs to get a feel for what they had to offer.

It was clear to Richardson that *Good Feelin' to Know* was an obvious choice for the single and a potential hit. "*Good Feelin' to Know* was designed to be a single. I've had any number of people over the years say, 'Gee, we can't understand why it didn't make it.'" Richardson wasted little time, booking a session at RCA Studio in Chicago. Poco cut versions of both *Good Feelin' to Know* and Cotton's *Early Times* as the B-side of the single. Poco persuaded Epic to release it as a single even though there was no new album to promote. *Good Feelin' to Know* was a quintessential Richie Furay song. Its three-chord chorus, joyous vocals, and upbeat tempo should have been perfect radio fare. Lyrically, Furay expressed the newfound peace of living in the Rockies.

Good Feelin' to Know/Early Times was released in June 1972. Incredibly, it didn't chart at all. The effect of yet another failed single was far reaching. Epic began pushing other acts, feeling that Poco had peaked. The band itself was discouraged, and this latest disappointment began to affect each member's songwriting output. In interviews both Furay and Cotton expressed their frustration at the lack of success and claimed it was affecting their ability to produce new songs. Furay admits, "It was a blow to me that *Good Feelin'* wasn't a hit. I thought it was a smash all the way." The rollicking, upbeat song seemed perfect summer radio fare. The version released by Epic used a fade ending and backing vocals that had Grantham's voice prominent in the mix.

In fact, Furay was so discouraged by the single's inability to make the charts that he considered recording a solo album. When David Geffen found that Furay had been considering a solo album in May 1972, Geffen attempted to sign him to his Asylum label. Furay had told *Crawdaddy* in June 1972 that a solo album appealed to him. "I've been writing songs and thinking about harmonies for the group for a long time," Furay told editor Peter Knobler. "Now maybe I'll write some things for one voice and a guitar." Geffen was scouting name talent for his label, having already signed Joni Mitchell, Jackson Browne, and the Eagles. Although the offer was not made public, Geffen pressed hard to get Furay into his Asylum artist stable. It is doubtful that Furay was serious about leaving Poco, however he confirmed to *Rolling Stone* a year later, "The rumors were true. I <u>was</u> gonna do [a solo album]. Now I've backed off a bit." Furay put Geffen's offer on the back burner and instead convinced Geffen to take on Poco's management. While Geffen was unable to assume the managerial duties immediately, Furay had him advise the band on several issues, including choosing some material for their upcoming album.

Despite their disappointment, Poco continued to play live on a regular basis. On July 25, they played the Ohio Theater in Columbus with J.J. Cale, followed by an appearance the following day at the Blossom Music Festival outside Cleveland. Poco also made their annual appearance at the Schaeffer Music Festival on August 25-26 in

Central Park in New York City. The band was excited about the performance since they had planned to record the shows for another
live album. However, union difficulties and bad weather forced
them to abandon the idea of recording the shows, however they
were still notable performances. *Variety* noted of their opening
night, "A Poco audience is an exuberant crowd, but on their own
enjoyment accompanying the happy American rock quintet. Before
an SRO crowd in Central Park, the sameness of much of the combo's
material failed to stay their wild fans." Poco's final show was
broadcast live in the New York area. The performance was a little
ragged as the band debuted several new songs. Tim Schmit's *Restrain* and Furay's *And Settlin' Down* both reflected more of the
rock style that Furay now wanted Poco to follow. But the frustration with the band's lack of success was also evident when Furay introduced *Good Feelin' to Know* by telling the audience they were
going to play their latest smash hit record because radio stations
wouldn't. As it was, rain briefly halted their show, and after attempting to resume their set with acoustic instruments, Poco canceled the show when electrical problems disabled the sound system.

During their frustration, Poco was a fun band on the road.
Denny Jones contents, "There was no golf in the morning. They recovered from hangovers or went to bed. I remember people in the
lobby telling them, 'You're such a well-behaved group, all dressed
and ready to go!' They hadn't been to bed yet! [Laughs.]"

During their summer touring schedule, Poco resumed recording a new album in RCA Studio, Chicago. Jack Richardson and
Jim Mason served as producers for the project. Furay observed at
the time, "We're still looking for the outside interpreter to help
while we're in the studio and objectively look at our music because
we're so involved in it that sometimes we can't see past it, and
even though we create it and we know more about it, I think we
still need that outside person to objectively look at us and help us
along the paths." The band huddled in Chicago amid the mounting
pressure of coming up with a hit single, a new producer, and a
leader whose frustration was visibly growing. The sessions were
completed rather quickly, and the band ultimately did overdubs in
New York while on tour. The resulting album Poco produced was a
marvel.

GOOD FEELIN' TO KNOW opened with Furay's rocking *And Settlin' Down*. After the depressing tone of his work on the previous
album, this track was a refreshing change. The lyrics dealt with
Furay's frustration at the constant tour grid that kept Poco on the
road to survive. *Ride the Country* was an outstanding Paul Cotton
song that found him beginning to hit his stride musically despite

some ridiculous lyrics. Schmit contributed a delightful track, *I Can See Everything*. It featured acoustic guitars and plenty of Poco harmonies. With the failure of the title track as a single, David Geffen urged the group to record a Buffalo Springfield song. He and Furay decided on *Go and Say Goodbye*. This version uses a bit more of the classic *Salt Creek* bluegrass lick that the song was based on, however lacks the guitar interplay that marked the original Springfield version as a classic. The side ended with Cotton's *Keeper of the Fire*. Musically it is excellent and somewhat reminiscent of the Eagles recent hit *Witchy Woman*. Cotton croons his vocal over an ominous rhythm track. However, the song again showed Cotton's lyrical limitations. Cotton now says the *Keeper of the Fire* was Richie Furay. "We saw him as a catalyst," Cotton says. "He was it."

The album continued with Cotton's *Early Times*. The tune had been part of Poco's live set for some time in the jam portion of *C'mon*. Like many of Cotton's early Poco tunes, one can only feel that it was a simple filler tune to add to Cotton's allotment for the album. Lyrically, it too was about his former band, the Illinois Speed Press. The title track brings the quality back considerably. This version differs from the single. It is slightly longer, and Grantham's harmonies are buried in the mix. *Restrain* was Schmit's second contribution to the album, and it was a forceful rock track. The album ends with Furay's delightful *Sweet Lovin'*, a song about his daughter. Poco makes use of a heavy organ and chorale effects on the long ballad.

In contrast to the experience in Memphis, recording this album was significantly better. Grantham told *Dark Star*, "That was a lot of fun to record. We did that with Jack Richardson in Chicago. We kept trying to do [our albums] away from LA, go find some hot place somewhere else with a hot producer."

The album, although not a huge success at #69 on the charts, did spend 20 weeks there. Reviews were quite positive. *Rolling Stone* pointed out, "It's Furay who make the biggest plays and gives the album its primary reference points." *Crawdaddy's* review claimed, "The album is strong, virile, and at the same time lyrical and touching." Reviewer Peter Knobler noted that the album "is the up, hard-driving album that perhaps should have followed their live album. It fairly rocks with power, due in great part to the emergence of lead guitar player, Paul Cotton." *Zigzag* focused on the group's recent move to Colorado. "This latest album is a paradox. The group has found what it wanted. The words of their title song underscore their satisfaction. But, and it is a definite but, instead of the music slowing down it has moved up. The tempo is quicker: the joy, more apparent. Poco has come back with its "up" spirit. They are happy. There is something else about the music. Timothy B. Schmit has written a piece he calls *Restrain*. It is like nothing the group has ever done before. When you hear it, it will boggle your mind."

Cotton, more than any other member of Poco, was extremely upbeat about the album. "This one is so much better. It's got polish, better production, depth. It's hot, and sounds right up front in places." Without a doubt, Poco's effort was much better on GOOD FEELIN' TO KNOW. Perhaps their smartest move was to take some time off from touring and rehearse their material. They also road tested several tunes before recording them. Unlike their Memphis experience where they often wrote songs in the morning and recorded them that evening, Poco had sufficient time to smooth out the rough spots before entering the studio. Enough cannot be said for the work of Jack Richardson and Jim Mason. Richardson managed to give the band the sound they were looking for. If there was any drawback, many feel the mix was flawed. Cotton explained to *Dark Star*, "I'm opposed to a lot of midrange and that studio happened to be very midrange. I mean the speakers didn't represent it when we mixed the album. They were midrange shy and we added midrange and that probably made it sound harder." The result wasn't a bad sound but the usual sparkling highs are missing. Richardson disagrees, "It was the same studio where I did *American Woman* and *No Time* so I don't think it was the studio. I was intimately familiar with the facilities. I think you're always in a situation where everybody has their own vision of how the sound spectrum should sound like from their standpoint."

Poco even worked hard on the album package. A booklet was included that dedicated a page for each member to design and put together, as well as lyrics and album credits. Grantham chose a picture of himself feeding a small bird on his lawn. Cotton did a collage of images including pictures of himself as a child and a George Harrison autograph signed, "To Norm (King) Cotton." Tim Schmit included several photos of himself, his wife, and daughter. Rusty Young had photos of everyone in the band, including Jimmy Messina, as well as some of himself as a youngster. Furay's page had a framed cross-stitch sampler with the phrase "Hotel Ain't Home" over photos of his daughter, his wife and himself, and his home. Despite all the quality work, GOOD FEELIN' TO KNOW did not garner the sales that the band had hoped.

As always, it was back on the road for Poco. In September, Poco was booked to open a series of shows for Jefferson Airplane. Although at many of the shows Furay claimed Poco made it difficult for the Airplane to follow them, the critical reaction didn't bear that out. The show at the Hollywood Bowl was reviewed by Stan Findelle of the Los Angeles *Free Press*, who noted, "Poco has now languished as a journeyman band for over three years, avoiding fads and conquering several musical idioms handily. Yet they've never kept the superstar promise. Though their country hybrids do not especially thrive in the Bowl's atomized sound systems, there were some crisp changes delivered by the group. And yet, coincidentally, they appeared to be straining to escape the perfunctory relative to earlier performances they've given. There's still a grand following for Poco, especially among critics, but if much more time passes and Poco is still the warm-up act, we will have to begin to take their name's meaning seriously."

A few days later in San Diego, Poco again stumbled. *Union* reviewer Barry Fitzsimmons observed, "They were booked as the warm-up group, and rightly so, as they seemed to have their problems. Poco spent many years developing a fine country-rock sound in *Pickin' Up the Pieces* style. But they've lost it and there's a great need to put all the pieces back together again." Later shows in Phoenix and Tucson followed the same pattern, however by later in September, Poco seemed to right itself. They opened for John Mayall at the Hollywood Palladium. Leonard Brown of the L.A. *Free Press* wrote, "It's not hard at all to imagine a sect of self-flagellating penitents getting off on an average weekend's boogy on the L.A. music scene. For their ecstasy, they have only to jam up against the stage apron and let Poco wash away their sins with the love and joy which creates that band's juicy spate of sound."

The fall tour kept Poco busy, playing venues across the country. They played some makeup dates in Albany and Flushing, New York, from their spring tour. They toured the West, playing at Winterland in San Francisco and the Santa Barbara Bowl in mid-October. From there they played colleges on the East Coast and down through Florida. Jack Richardson came out to record Poco live during their show at Winterland. "I did a live album with them in San Francisco, at Winterland. We were sandwiched between T. Rex and a Canadian band called Lighthouse. And we had to use the stage people from the promoters there. They set the thing up, and we had the steel guitar coming up in bass drum mikes. Things of this nature. And the band played absolutely atrociously that night. It was scrubbed entirely. It never even made the mixing stage. The tapes were not even usable."

On November 2, Poco appeared with eight other bands at Hofstra University for the filming of a new ABC-TV show entitled *In Concert*. Produced jointly by Don Kirchner and Dick Clark, the endeavor was ambitious. Poco's booking was a nod to the fact that the band still had an excellent reputation as a live act and a TV show showing live rock acts had to include them. The plan was to film enough groups for the first two shows of the series. The production immediately ran into technical difficulties that led to enormous delays. As these problems mounted, it became clear that some bands wouldn't get on stage until the very early morning hours. Poco volunteered to return to their hotel, get some rest, and return to film their segment. It was frustrating and Furay sarcastically told *Rolling Stone*, "We're such nice guys it drives me crazy. We're such good kids that Donnie Kirshner should make cartoons out of us like the Archies. Or maybe if we can't make it back [to the concert hall] tonight he can get the Archies to do our set."

Poco did manage to return to Hofstra and mounted the stage at 5:30 a.m. They slugged through their set before the cameras and an exhausted audience. From their less than stellar performance, ABC-TV eventually used three songs. When Poco's segment aired on the second broadcast of *In Concert* on December 2, they opened with *Good Feelin' to Know*. It was rough with Grantham's off-key harmonies grating through the first part of the song. Furay adlibbed some additional lyrics as Cotton cranked up with an extended guitar solo that ended the song. Poco next played *And Settlin' Down*. The performance lacked any real energy from the rhythm section. Again the vocals were ragged as Furay tried to pump life into what was a tired, scattered performance. Rusty Young did use the drawn out ending to do some nice solos on steel guitar. The show ended with Poco's *Go and Say Goodbye* being played over the closing credits. Ironically, Poco's performance of this tune was the strongest of the three and yet it was aired incomplete as the credits ended long before the song was finished. Larry Yeland of *The Express* attended the long day of music and felt Poco came off well. "Playing their style of good-time music soothing music, they left the audience in a happy trance-like sleep. Poco has gone through many changes and perhaps its last change has been for the best, for even at 5:30 a.m. after an entire night of kick-ass music, they really got to everyone. Total involvement on the audience's part, and the band really dug it."

Poco had little time to consider its TV experience. They had tour dates scheduled throughout November and December, playing the Midwest at venues in Milwaukee, Madison, St. Louis, Laramie, Denver, Louisville, Dallas, Houston, and San Antonio. Poco returned to their stronghold of New York City for a date at the Felt Forum on December 2. Abigail Lewis of *Billboard* reviewed their show and noted, "Richie Furay's voice never wavers, nor do his fingers, and it is his spirit which both binds and highlights the group effort." How-

ever Lewis also revealed, "Their familiar repertoire was well performed, it was barely augmented by any new material." Almost in
response to the jab, Poco began revamping their set for the remainder of the tour.

In the aftermath of GOOD FEELIN' TO KNOW's modest success
as both single and album, Poco felt quite bitter about the lot that
had been dealt them. They pointed fingers at Epic, radio programmers, and their management. Shiffman and Larson's strategy of
constant roadwork had succeeded in raising Poco's profile out of the
L.A. club scene. However they had been unable to reach the level
that everyone had hoped. Despite their profile in the concert business, neither Shiffman nor Larson seemed able to influence Epic to
provide more promotional support or think creatively to promote
the band beyond the unending string of concerts and the rare TV
appearance. After reaching a plateau, Poco's audience didn't seem
to be growing. Denny Jones explains, "Everybody had had it with
Larson. Poco was making good money, $10,000 a show. We played
a lot in New England. But Larson played it safe so they could pocket
the money, which they did. But that pissed everyone off because
then we'd go into Kansas City and couldn't draw flies. He focused
on markets that Poco was already strong in, but it wasn't expanding. We could have lived in St. Louis, they were huge there. They
were huge in New York, but Texas, that was another story. They
couldn't draw flies. So the band wanted someone new." In addition, the constant road work was also creating a strain on both family and group relationships. Furay made a pivotal decision at the
end of the year and let Shiffman and Larson go. He turned instead
to the man he had long wanted to charter Poco's course, however
to many in the Poco camp, their new manager was soon navigating
the group into troubled waters.

7
Here We Go Again

Poco was headed for a gig in Connecticut when Furay was busy punching the buttons on the car radio hunting for their latest single. Instead he heard the strains of the Eagles' debut hit *Take It Easy* wafting over the airwaves. A sinking feeling rose in his stomach. "I suppose I should have viewed *Take It Easy* as a good sign – proof that D.J.'s who'd scorned country rock were now willing to give it a try. Instead, I was devastated. Poco was the musical dream and passion of my life, but all of a sudden I saw it as a dead end."

Furay chose to internalize the revelation for the remainder of the year, however he knew that he needed a new path. When he visited Los Angeles to conduct some business, he paid a visit to David Geffen and sought his counsel. They met at Geffen's home, and Furay immediately felt at ease and unloaded his burden. Furay recalls, "David listened attentively before presenting me with an option that I hadn't known existed." The option was the first country-rock supergroup with John David Souther and Chris Hillman. Geffen knew that both musicians were looking for other projects and felt that a group composed of the trio would be a sure-fire success. Furay was convinced by Geffen's enthusiasm, and before the afternoon was out, Furay had not only agreed to the new group concept, but also agreed to transition Poco's management over to Geffen's management company.

The highly successful Geffen-Roberts firm took over Poco's management in January 1973. The other members of Poco, un-

aware of Furay's previous dealings with Geffen, were initially excited about the deal. Rusty Young recalled, "[Geffen] wanted acts
for his record company that were selling records. And Poco has always sold records - we sell a lot of records. So he wanted us on his
label, which is one thing, because it was a brand new label and
needed established acts. The second thing was that he figured he
could be the hero of all heroes if he could make Poco the success
everyone said it should be. So he took us on those grounds or for
those reasons, I guess I should say."

To some observers, Rusty Young among them, Geffen saw
himself as Poco's savior. Many in the music industry had sung
Poco's praises for years, however the band had yet to reach the
heights of stardom. Geffen was sure he could turn the tide and lead
them to the success they deserved. Ned Doheny, an artist in the
Asylum Records stable, insists, "David had this knight-in-shining-
armor syndrome. He particularly liked it if he could rescue you
from a compromising situation. He really liked to rescue." Geffen
once again met with the band and advised them to record more
than just the 10 or 11 songs needed to complete their next album.
He told them to cut a batch of material, including outside material,
and then select the best group of songs for their next album. It was
a daunting task. Epic had always insisted on a quick turnaround on
Poco albums. Geffen had enough of a relationship with Clive Davis
at Columbia to be able to convince them to allow Poco some additional studio time to put Geffen's plan in action. Despite Geffen's
positive attitude, he also offered himself an out. Schmit explained,
"Geffen told us that if we aren't busted right open by December,
it's probably never gonna happen. But he believes it is gonna happen. And so do we. We're not ready to quit yet."

With Geffen at the helm, Poco felt the band would get the attention that they deserved. With such a high profile management
company behind them, the band felt energized and thought of nothing more than finishing the remaining four albums they owed Epic so
they could sign with Geffen's Asylum Record label. The first item
of business for Geffen was to drop CMA as Poco's booking agents and
sign them with Premier Talent. He also established a new joint
publishing company, Poco Publishing, for the group's songs.

In February, Poco began rehearsing for their next album. During the band's rehearsals, Gram Parsons and the Fallen Angels were
kicking off a tour at the Edison Electric, a small club in Boulder.
Furay and several other Poco members attended the opening show
and it was terrible. Parsons muddled his way through an under-
rehearsed set with a band that while talented, wasn't ready for the
road. Furay still felt obligated to go backstage to pay his respects.

He found Parsons busy getting high and oblivious to the poor performance of himself and his band. Dismayed at how far his friend
had fallen, Furay left quickly. Rusty Young and a few others hung
out to party with Parsons, which Young would later recall was not
the best idea at the time. Not surprisingly, when rehearsals resumed, Furay brought out an old tune he'd written about Parsons
during the early days of the band and had the band learn it again.
Crazy Eyes would eventually become the centerpiece for the new
album.

     A few weeks later, Poco began sessions for their next album
at Studio A, RCA Studios in Hollywood. Again, the team of Richardson and Mason was behind the boards to produce. Strangely, Mason
did not receive credit for his work on the album. Although there was
some talk of attempting a double album, Poco instead decided to
follow Geffen's advice and record more than they needed. Furay
also invited outside musicians such as Stephen Stills, Chris Hillman,
George Frayne, Billy Graham, and Paul Harris of Manassas and percussionist Aynsley Dunbar to participate. Cotton explains, "He
wanted these ultimate players on those songs. I don't blame him,
really. *Crazy Eyes* is a masterpiece. The song, itself, I mean. He'd
been holding off on recording it for four years and it finally came
time." Furay was somewhat reluctant to record the tune, however
Jack Richardson pressed him. "When I suggested he do it, his comment then was, 'Gee, I really don't think it's ready.' But I finally
convinced him to do it. On the session we did all the bed tracks,
then I took them to New York and we did the sweetening on them.
In the meantime, Steve Cropper, I think it was, did a version of it.
We had just come back from New York with the final overdubs on
that one, and Steve came in and told Richie, 'Oh hey, I did your
Crazy Eyes!' And of course, my ass just about fell off at that point
in time, thinking 'Oh Jesus, what a time to do that' because Richie
was not sure how he was going to do it. So Steve played his – it was
about three minutes, 20 seconds long, and it sounded like about
seven minutes long. So I said, 'Well guys, do you want to hear what
I did with yours?' And it was about nine minutes long, but it felt like
about three and a half minutes long. Richie kind of smiled at the
end of it, and I kind of came out on top of it."

     Based on Geffen's information, Furay and neighbor Chris Hill-
man were talking about working on the group project together. The
time was right for Hillman, whose situation with Manassas was winding down. Towards the end of Manassas, Hillman was so bored that
after shows he and Paul Harris would laughingly tell themselves,
"There's another doorknob for the RV." When it became obvious
that Stephen Stills was looking elsewhere for inspiration, Hillman let

it be known that he was interested in a new gig. Although nothing was set in stone, Furay felt having Hillman work with him on the Poco album would be a good way to see if the pair could work together.

The sessions found Poco exploring a number of songs that were later determined not strong enough to make the cut for the album. The sessions were upbeat and loose. Furay recalls an incident with fiddler Billy Graham. "We were cutting *Fool's Gold*, a real hoedown of a song written by Rusty, and as the rest of us watched from the control booth, Graham raised his bow and started sawing away in the totally wrong key. Everyone broke up laughing." Commander Cody was in an adjacent studio during these sessions, and George Frayne offered to contribute some keyboards. However, he drove everyone nuts during take after take when he refused to play an F-sharp chord, telling Furay, "That's a really good steel-guitar chord so I laid out." His contributions were left unreleased.

Also in March, Geffen's first attempt at putting Poco over the top came when he convinced Epic to release *Go and Say Goodbye/I Can See Everything* as a single from their previous album. The version released sounds slightly speeded up with Cotton's guitar mixed lower and Schmit's bass boosted. Unfortunately, the single failed to make the charts. This was a tremendous blow to Geffen's prestige since he had assured the group that it would be a hit. Rusty Young believes that to save face, Geffen intimated to Furay that the rest of the group was the problem. "We put out an album called GOOD FEELIN' TO KNOW in which he even helped select material. When that album didn't sell any better than the other albums, it reflected poorly on him. This is my opinion here, there was nothing for him to do except say, 'Well, it wasn't me, it was the guys.' So he went to Rich and said, 'Listen, you're a star and these other guys are really holding you back. Why don't you sign with my record company and I'll do this and that for you?' That's really what happened." Managers sowing the seeds of discord were something Furay had experienced with Buffalo Springfield and he should have recognized what Geffen was doing. However the sad truth was that Geffen was only telling Furay what he wanted to hear. "I had watched some of my friends, Stephen and Neil go on, Jimmy go on, and Randy go on," recalls Furay sadly. "I was really disappointed with *Good Feelin' to Know*." In his own mind, Furay decided that this would be his final album with Poco.

After their initial recording sessions at RCA, Poco set out to open a month-long tour of the West and Southwest for the English band Yes in April. Geffen had no doubt intended the tour to be somewhat of a showcase for Poco to introduce them to a more pro-gressive audience. It was a curious pairing, and some serious head scratching went on in some quarters. Yes fans were not likely to find Poco that interesting. There was no question that the tour would allow more people to see Poco live, however they were not likely to turn around and purchase their records. Despite the odd coupling, Poco played several outstanding shows with several new tunes being debuted. The tour opened in Los Angeles at the Forum and worked its way through New Mexico, Texas, St. Louis, and At-lanta, and ended with several shows in Florida.

It hardly came as a surprise that critics and fans ready for Yes were less than enthusiastic about Poco. An anonymous critic for *The Great Speckled Bird* groused of Poco's April 19 appearance in Atlanta, "Poco lost their motivating energy somewhere along the line. All that's left is a monotonous, sticky, syrupy sweet, country rock sound. Sufficient for passing the time. What can I say? New shoes wear out quickly when you stomp around in them too much." Robert Blades of the Berkeley *Barb* was equally dismissive. "Poco preceded Yes and were the evening's largest disappointment. They were soooo loud; they couldn't help obscuring their vocals, which are typically their strongest point. All the tricks they used to turn out GOOD FEELIN' TO KNOW were ignored at Winterland. Richie hogged the spotlight, only releasing it once to bassist Timothy Schmit and once to the other guitarist, Paul Cotton. GOOD FEELIN''s only mistake, in inclusion of Steve Stills' *Go and Say Goodbye* was repeated Saturday night, tastelessly deafening 6,000 people."

After the Yes tour, Poco headlined some shows in May before taking the first part of the summer off. They played before 10,000 at Penn State University on May 6. Poco and Frampton's Camel played a free concert at Buffalo State College. They moved on to New Jersey where they played another free show at Farleigh Dickerson University in the afternoon of May 5 and followed it up with an evening concert at the Capitol Theatre in Passaic. Swinging back west, Poco played Kansas City, Chicago, and the University of Illinois before taking a break.

Not content to let an otherwise excellent album die, Poco en-couraged Epic to try again in May 1973 and the label re-released *Good Feelin' to Know* as a single. Again it failed to get on the charts. To date, it remains a mystery why it didn't even break the Hot 100. When he first heard it in concert, critic Bud Scoppa felt sure it would become Poco's signature song. *"Good Feelin' to Know* sounds right now like the best Furay song since he formed this band, and I wouldn't be surprised if it becomes eventually the song most closely identified with Poco." In many ways, Scoppa's initial assessment proved accurate, and yet the single was twice ignored by radio. Jack Richardson was as puzzled as anyone, but conceded that Furay's assessment that its arrival in the radio market was timed too late after the Eagles flurry of hits and Poco got lost in the shuffle.

In late May, Poco returned to RCA Studios to resume work on their latest album. Whether by coincidence or design, these sessions produced much of the material that the band chose to include on their upcoming album. Furay's involvement was less than expected. He offered several cover tunes however only two new songs for consideration. His attention was focused on the title track of the album, spending hours with Richardson and arranger Bob Ezrin. Richardson took the basic tracks to New York and did the orchestral overdubs with Bob Ezrin. Richardson also didn't hear much beyond Furay's *Let's Dance Tonight* for a potential single and recommended the band consider outside material. He got Cotton to agree to cut a version of J.J. Cale's *Magnolia*.

The amount of material that Poco recorded far exceeded previous recording sessions. "That one was supposed to be a double album," confirms Richardson. "Epic decided after we were finished recording, but before the mix, that it was only going to be a single. So we, as a team decided which tracks to use. There were plenty of them, but the ones we chose seemed to go together the best."

As the lucrative summer booking season loomed, Poco was anxious to get back on the road. However, Furay was reluctant to go back on tour, much to the dismay of the others. There were rumors of a Buffalo Springfield reunion that had Furay a bit distracted. The press was filled with news of the Byrds reunion, and many were clamoring for the Springfield to do the same. Furay admitted to *Rolling Stone* that it was a distinct possibility, but that it was up to Neil Young. However Furay did have his reservations. He speculated, "It would have to be better than the way the Byrds did it because they simply didn't spend enough time. You know, some of the people in the Springfield people have memories of how it was and how it should be and sometimes I think it's best to leave well enough alone." That's exactly what happened. Although Neil Young's lengthy HARVEST tour was to spawn the live album TIME FADES AWAY later in the year, the tour also left him shaken and distrustful of many in his inner circle. The idea of reviving Buffalo Springfield proved too intimidating. Furay's summer was free.

When they finally convinced Furay to go back on the road, Premier Talent lined out a late summer tour with Poco playing with Mark-Almond and David Blue. Poco also opened a few East Coast dates for the Beach Boys. Poco debuted some of their new material, adding four new songs to their live set. Poco's summer tour found them again at the short end of critic's praises. Two shows at Winterland found the San Francisco *Phoenix* moaning, "Poco, which closed the show, played a competent but sometimes lethargic set. It's almost as though they're trying to be the first country heavy-metal band." Poco was second billed to Mark-Almond in Albuquerque on August 14 and played to a less than capacity crowd. Ten days later, they opened for the Beach Boys at Dillon Stadium in Hartford, Connecticut.

Still anxious to complete their Epic contract, Poco again turned to their strength. Jack Richardson explains, "I talked with Don Ellis, who was then president of Epic Records. The band wanted to do a live album to fulfill their contract. They had another album to give Epic, according to the contract. We were going to do a live album in Central Park in New York. I had that pretty well all set up, and then Don called me and said, 'You know that if you are going to do this live album, 60 percent of the material has to be new material.' The band had just come off of this double album approach and they were just dry. I talked to them and told them this just wasn't going to work because Epic wanted 60 percent new material. So we scrubbed that."

Poco played two nights at Wollman Rink in Central Park in New York City on August 31 and September 1. Although they weren't recorded live, both shows sold out as New York fans were riotous in their response. Phil Gelormine of *Billboard* reviewed the shows and noted, "If prone to occasional excess at times, Poco can be forgiven, for its sheer vitality served to bring the music higher and carry the musicians along with it. They played extremely well off each other with their bright harmonic sound a valuable asset." John Rockwell in the *Times* tempered his praise. "Poco is now essentially a good-times entertainment ensemble, rockers who play to please, rather than make a particularly cogent artistic statement. But mostly it all sounds pretty much the same." Barry Taylor in *Melody Maker* wrote similar sentiments. "Poco is a case in point and I don't think that they will ever reap the elusive universal success of popdom until some drastic changes are made."

Although Poco fans didn't realize it, that drastic change was about to take place. A hint of what was to come hit the music press right before the summer tour started. In June, *Rolling Stone* reported that Furay was leaving Poco to join former Byrd Chris Hillman and J.D. Souther in a new band. Furay was quick to deny it, and the rest of Poco felt it was just another in a series of rumored departures for their leader. The music magazine dutifully noted the denial, but stated that it would likely happen anyway.

However the truth was Furay, encouraged by David Geffen, had met privately with Hillman and singer-songwriter John David Souther about forming a new group. At first it appears that the project was only a sideline diversion for Furay. He confirmed his impending project to British journalist Jerry Gilbert during the summer saying, "I think it will be fun and I think it will be healthy but this doesn't mean that Poco's breaking up or that I'll leave the group. I think it's fair that each one of us should have that opportunity. It's like Traffic; I'm not sure if they're better now than before but I'd like the situation with us to be improved by what I'm doing rather than be torn apart. I can't deny the rumor that I was going to split. The band has been together for six years and sometimes you just lose perspective playing with the same people over and over. Our combination was great but it just wasn't progressing the way we wanted it to grow - we needed to expand and if one of the group wanted to go out and do a solo album, then the rest of the group shouldn't feel intimidated. That would be a healthy situation after six years." However, by the time Gilbert returned to England to file his story, Furay had changed his mind.

After completing the tour at the Worcester Polytechnic Institute on September 4, Poco returned home. Almost immediately, Furay dropped his bombshell. He called a meeting at the offices of Geffen-Roberts and announced that he was leaving Poco. The other four were stunned at the news. It was obvious that Furay was emotionally torn. He said very little, allowing Elliot Roberts to do most of the talking. Grantham recalls, "It all happened pretty fast. It all happened in one meeting in one day. It just happened and Richie went out of the room; we sat around and decided at that same time that we were going to keep going. There was going to be no delay." Cotton reflected on Furay's decision to leave, "Right up to the day we had no knowledge that he was leaving. It had come up in the past about him leaving because he hadn't wanted to tour, but never thought that he would leave. Richie had some other music in his head, and I just thought he was going to do an album with Chris and J.D. They are closer to being in his dream than we are because he doesn't want to leave that mountain in Colorado." When Furay returned to the room, they told him that they were going to remain as Poco.

In the same manner as Jimmy Messina, Furay had no intention of leaving Poco in a bind. They had a booking at the brand new Roxy nightclub in Los Angeles for five nights, October 3-7. He offered to play that engagement before officially leaving Poco, however the others would have none of it. The sting of Furay's rejection of them was much too strong. They ordered Roberts to cancel the dates instead. Schmit explains, "We decided it was a waste of time. We've known Richie was leaving for some time and there's no reason to prolong the old group. We're very excited about the new Poco, which is the four of us. We're a dynamite group and we're concentrating all our efforts on working up our new act."

The decision to leave Poco was not an easy one for Furay. The band was like family to him and he maintained that he would never play in a closer band. However his ego needed to be fed. So many of his former band mates had gone on to superstardom and it grated on him. It was bad enough when Steve Stills and Neil Young had gone on to fame, but when former Poco mates Randy Meisner and Jimmy Messina also ascended into the higher reaches of the charts, it was a terribly humiliating experience. The jump to what would become known as the Souther, Hillman, Furay Band was admittedly an ego trip for Furay. Poco had once been his band, playing only his songs. Now he was limited to three or four songs per album. He talked about wanting to branch out and play some lead guitar. With Cotton and Young there was no room for his lead lines in Poco. An added enticement was Geffen's promise of a six-figure cash payment. Although Furay reportedly never saw the money, the offer was enough to sweeten the deal.

Even before the news of Furay's departure had reached the music press, Epic released Poco's next album, CRAZY EYES. The album opened with an anti-pollution song of Cotton's entitled *Blue Water*. Cotton's acoustic picking and Young's dobro work propelled the tune. The song segued into a spirited Young instrumental, *Fool's Gold*, that featured guest artist Chris Hillman on mandolin. Tim Schmit's lone contribution was an excellent one. *Here We Go Again* is an exceptional song with a creative arrangement.

Furay's first contribution is a cover of Gram Parson's *Brass Buttons*. Parsons had taught the tune to Furay back in 1964 when they were both hanging out in Greenwich Village. Furay explains, "Gram hadn't recorded *Brass Buttons* yet. He taught me that song when we lived across from each other in New York. I stored it away. It was like Neil [Young] teaching me *Clancy*; sometimes you just hear a song and think, 'Wow, this is good.' It was just one of those songs." The side ended with a patented Cotton rocker, *A Right Along*. Cotton and Young trade some memorable lead lines.

The title track opened side two. *Crazy Eyes* had once been part of Pogo's live set in late 1968. During the recording session, Furay offered it to the group once again, this time wanting an arrangement on a grander scale. Grantham recalls, "We used to play it in the first year the group was together. It was completely different. It wasn't geared to orchestration then." Furay explains, "I always saw the tune as a single acoustic guitar and banjo tune." But now Furay and producer Jack Richardson treated the song like a movie theme, and Bob Ezrin arranged it accordingly. Horns and strings were added to the basic track. The song itself was about Furay's impressions of Gram Parsons. Tragically, shortly after the album's release, Parsons died of a drug overdose. Cotton offered a superior cover version of J.J. Cale's *Magnolia*, and the album ended with Furay's bouncy *Let's Dance Tonight*. Young's work on slide was exceptional. The song doesn't quite match the exuberance of previous Furay songs, but it ends the album on just the right note. Furay admits that he had written the tune as a potential single, however his departure ensured that it would not be released.

The material left over from the CRAZY EYES sessions proves that Poco was exploring their past as well as their future. Besides the older songs of *Brass Buttons* and *Crazy Eyes* that made the album, Poco recorded several other older songs for potential inclusion on the album. Paul Cotton rearranged *Get in the Wind* from the first Illinois Speed Press album, and Furay cut a Buffalo Springfield outtake called *So You've Got a Lover*, a cover of Dee Clark's *Your Friends*, and a song he had written with former manager Dickie Davis called *Nothin's Still the Same*. Poco had attempted to record *Nothin's Still the Same* back in 1970 shortly after the song was written. New songs were also attempted. Tim Schmit's *Passin' Through*, Cotton's *Faith in the Families*, and Rusty Young's *Skunk Creek* were all attempted and left in the can.

However the highlight of the songs left uncompleted was Furay's *Believe Me*. The track featured the outstanding piano work of Manassas member Paul Harris, as well as outstanding guitar work by Cotton and Young. Stephen Stills was to have played lead guitar on the track however, according to Cotton, "Stephen was really crazy in those days. Yeah, he came in and attempted to do a solo, and I don't know, something was in the air but it got erased. Then I came in and attempted it the next morning, and Stephen had left town or something." Jack Richardson was more explicit. "We got Stephen to come in and do some solo work on one of the tracks, and Steve came in, shall we say, not in the best of condition. We spent about eight hours getting a 16-bar solo. It was a pretty disastrous kind of thing. He doesn't even remember to this day actually being there. The irony of it all is that after it was all over, there was a spot on there that I had to fix up with some guitars so I told Paul Cotton, 'Why don't you go in there and fix up that one guitar thing.' It was a section that was 12 or 13 bars ahead of the solo that Stephen Stills had done. So we set it all up, and I said to the assistant engineer, 'Let's run through it once.' So we did it, everything was fine. So I said, 'OK, let's do it. Roll tape!' We punched in and we just got groovin'. Paul played a great thing. We kept groovin' and groovin' and all of a sudden I said 'Stop!' because we had gone over and had used the same track that Stills' solo was on, and we had recorded over a goodly portion of the solo that we had spent so long to get. There was a dead hush over the control room. I immediately got up and left, went outside, and walked around the block about four times at the RCA studios in Los Angeles. I went back in and things were still pretty silent, you could hear a pin drop, and I looked at Paul and said, 'You better get out there and play a solo. You'll probably play a better one anyway.'" Stills' contribution was replaced by Cotton's guitar work. Rusty Young had said that *Believe Me* was intended as the centerpiece for Poco's next album. Regardless, it remained in the can as did all the other material.

Released in September, CRAZY EYES wasn't hurt by the news of Furay's departure and got as high as #38 on the album charts. Critical views of the album were somewhat positive. Stephen Holden of *Rolling Stone* wrote, "CRAZY EYES is far and away the most ambitious, musically satisfying album yet to issue from one of the most formidable but still commercially under-appreciated country-rock band." *Fusion*'s review however, cited what they considered the album's weaknesses. "There are a couple of bad eggs on this album," wrote Jacob Wiesel. "The most disastrous of which is the painfully maudlin tearjerker, *Magnolia*." The underground paper *SunRise* featured two reviews of the album. The first review by Bro Moll noted, "The album seems to have been put together rather hastily, so the group is fulfilling its three album obligation with Epic so they can get out of their contract. Nevertheless, the group seems to have grown a great deal, and come up with an album that is quite different." J. Sanford Bahler's review was less charitable. "I may be wrong but this LP just doesn't seem to be well thought out or put together. I'd say that sure as hell it's the producers that are now responsible for Poco's sound and that's not good."

Blaming Jack Richardson doesn't fly with Rusty Young. He believes strongly that the albums Richardson produced were among the best sounding records Poco made. If CRAZY EYES had any failing it was it was light on high-energy Poco music and heavy on the ballads. In fact, Richardson did a very commendable thing after the sessions were over. Poco was extremely paranoid that Epic would do something with all the outtakes they had submitted for the CRAZY EYES project once the band left the label. To ensure that Epic could not subsequently release the tunes, Richardson quietly went back into the studio and wiped the vocals from the multi-tracks.

8
You've Got Your Reasons

Sitting in the plush office of manager David Geffen, the shocked and confused members of Poco awaited the arrival of their patron. Geffen entered the room somewhat distracted and faced the quartet. Young's recollection is still vivid. "Tim, Paul, George and I were sitting in a room. David Geffen came in and he went right down the line. He pointed at Paul and said, 'Now you write and sing don't you? Ok, you're going to be alright.' He went to Tim, 'You write and sing songs too. You're going to be alright.' Then he went to George and me and said, 'You don't write and you don't sing, do you? You guys are in trouble.' The light bulb over your head does 'Ding!' and that was real motivation. True motivation."

Aghast at Geffen's backstabbing, the band was uncertain about their future. In the interim, staff managers John Hartmann and Harlan Goodman their own management firm. John Hartmann was a veteran of the William Morris Agency and had trained under Colonel Tom Parker. He was responsible for signing Buffalo Springfield to William Morris in 1966 for bookings. In 1967, Hartmann and partners opened the Kaleidoscope ballroom in Los Angeles and enjoyed a brief run. He subsequently joined Geffen-Roberts and took over management of several clients on their expanding roster. However as the Geffen-Roberts partnership was disintegrating, Hartmann began looking for an out. He talked with fellow colleague Harlan Goodman about forming their own management company.

Harlan Goodman joined the Geffen-Roberts management firm and soon found himself bearing the load of ensuring that the clients were working. Between the pair, Geffen and Roberts could focus on their primary clients while Hartmann and Goodman managed the rest.

Hartmann and Goodman pitched their services to Poco, and the quartet agreed to sign with them and their fledgling firm. The group informed Geffen-Roberts that their services were no longer required. Young recalls how the pair made their pitch, "They came to us and said, 'Listen, let's go off and start on our own. This is crazy, there's got to be a better way.' We said, 'Great, let's do it. They can have Richie.'" Hartmann claims that he left the firm of Geffen-Roberts the same day that Richie left Poco. The new firm set up shop in Hartmann's apartment.

Elliot Roberts' perspective on the separation with Hartmann and Goodman was radically at odds with this version. He claims that the added stress of dealing with CSNY eventually caused him to insist that the various associates of the Geffen-Roberts firm divide up the clients and go their separate ways. One thing is certain. Regardless of how he remembers it now, Roberts' response at the time was swift and brutal. Intent on driving Poco from existence, Roberts called the band's booking agency, Premier Talent, and threatened to pull all Geffen-Roberts clients, including Neil Young and Joni Mitchell, from Premier's roster if they continued to book Poco. President Frank Barcelona refused to take the calls and kept Poco on his talent roster. Roberts carried out his threat, and Premier did suffer in the short term. Hartmann and Goodman were grateful for Barcelona's steadfast support and urged the band to get back on the road and take advantage of Premier's show of faith.

Rusty Young felt that many in the music industry felt Poco should have died with the departure of Furay and that belief added incentive for Poco to continue on without him. Poco felt Geffen was behind many of these threats in an attempt to ensure that their audience would follow Furay to his new band. Such a bold move was not beyond him, given Geffen's power in the record industry. Young observed, "It really separated the people who were our friends and believed in us from the people who were there just for the ride." Young felt Chris Hillman's attitude towards Poco also helped. Hillman told reporter Todd Everett of the LA *Free Press*, "It was Richie's band and they all played - more or less - around what Richie had." To Young that statement alone was enough to make the band angry and provided them with the urge to prove Hillman and all the others wrong. "Poco was always more than just Richie," Young explains.

After Furay's departure, Poco had to re-think their situation both from a business and a musical perspective. Having dealt with the business end of things, the band got down to assessing where the group was musically. Grantham, Cotton, and Young were initially upset and angry at the perceived abandonment of their founder and leader, especially when it became clear that their management company wasn't interested in them after Furay left. Schmit's reaction was less angry than his band mates. He told British journalists, "I know the feeling but I haven't felt any bitterness about what's gone down. It was something to learn from. The result is that we have become closer as people and tighter as musicians." Grantham felt lost after Furay left, "Oh man, I didn't know what to think. I didn't know if we could do it without Richie in the group at all. It was really hard for me. It was kind of scary." Cotton also was initially intimidated, "Whew! Those were some major tracks to fill there. I think it forced me to become more of a writer in terms of output."

As the band worked up their new live set, they also came up with some new material. Several songs dealt with the departure of their leader, as one could expect. Poco decided to try out some of their new tunes in the studio before resuming their roadwork. As with CRAZY EYES, the band used RCA Studios in Hollywood with Jack Richardson on the board. Only a couple tracks were completed before the newly booked tour dates forced them to abandon the effort and hit the road.

Despite Cotton's enthusiasm, he remained worried. He had pushed to recruit another guitarist to replace Furay. "I did," assured Cotton, "because my natural background is playing with another guitarist." However his suggestion was ignored. The rest of the band was intent on proving something to their detractors by making it without Furay or replacing him. His colleagues finally convinced Cotton that the talent was already there. Cotton began listening to a number of British bands like the Who to get a feeling for creating more sound on stage with a smaller group. "I had a lot more guitar parts to play," he shrugged. "I had a White Falcon plugged into a stack of Marshall amps and just blasted. We made it work!"

Poco set aside an intense six-week period for rehearsing for their upcoming live dates. The band's intention was to eliminate as much Furay material as they could. That was easier said than done, so the group rearranged tunes to lengthen them with long instrumental jams. Schmit was excited about the new direction. "I think since we have become a four-man band we have gotten into jamming more and it does my heart good...mostly with Poco, during rehearsals, we [used to] work on our strict song structure." This shift to a more free-form approach would be road-tested before trying it in the studio. The changes Poco were forced to make also made them re-evaluate Poco. It wasn't all that bad. Paul Cotton observed, "We became quite the little four-piece. I think we were awesome actually. That thing just became awesome – Rusty, George, Tim, and I just full out every night – I really enjoyed that."

Although their attention was focused on Poco, Young and Grantham did step into the studio in Boulder to play on a session for former Burrito Brother Rick Roberts' second solo album, SHE IS A SONG. Roberts had Chris Hillman producing, so the sessions were likely to have been a bit strained. Young recalls, "Rick and George were doing some stuff together and George, I think, called me and said, 'Why don't you come down and play dobro on a tune?'" Young's appearance was more for Grantham's benefit than anything else.

The new Poco returned to the concert stage in November. This first round of touring concentrated on the East Coast. Schmit explains, "When we first started touring [without Furay] it was before we had the record out and we had to show people that in spite of everything we were strong. I mean, there were all sorts of rumors going around that we were breaking up but in fact we all centered around the same idea when Richie left – let's keep going." Their fans were in for a surprise as Poco virtually abandoned their country-rock sound for a more hard rock format. They made up for the lack of a second guitarist by using more volume. During this eastern swing, Poco appeared at New York's Palace Theatre for *Don Kirchner's Rock Concert*, a new syndicated concert TV program. They were also recorded live for the *King Biscuit Flower Hour*, a syndicated radio show. Both appearances showed the confidence that the quartet had in themselves. The *King Biscuit* recording took place on only their second live appearance without Furay.

On Thanksgiving (November 22), Poco opened for Loggins and Messina for the first time. Although Loggins and Messina were clearly headliners, ticket sales for the Madison Square Garden show had lagged until Poco was added to the bill. Pumped up by the opportunity to play in front of Messina for the first time since he quit the band, Poco's set was terrific. They had the crowd rocking and silenced the "We want Richie" chants.   Of course, Loggins and Messina quickly took the crowd back, but after their set Jerry Gilbert of *Sounds* reported that Grantham and Young were the first to congratulate the duo as they came off-stage. Poco stayed on the East Coast through November before winding their way west. On their way back, they played an unusual bill at the Kiel Auditorium in St. Louis when the thundering Bachman-Turner-Overdrive opened for Poco. Decades later, it would still be cited by local media as one of the strangest concert bills the city had ever seen. Dick Richmond of the *Post-Dispatch* commented, "Poco had to follow this hypnotic act (BTO) and it was rough right from the start. The members of the band were not together on the first two numbers. When they finally did mesh, the soft rock for which the band is noted was all right, but far from super." A series of dates opening for the Guess Who followed.

Public and critical perception of Poco changed with Furay's absence despite their efforts. While the band was sure they could survive without Richie, they didn't consider one important distinction. In the eyes of the public and the critics, Poco was identified with Furay. Without him, Poco became another faceless rock band when none of the other members stepped forward with the charisma of a front man or exhibited a dynamic personality. Denny Jones contends, "Who was going to step up and be the Richie? Who's going to be the front man? It had to be Schmit! The women loved him and he had that elegant voice. It couldn't be Rusty, he's sitting down. Now years later he did become the leader, but that was later." Indeed, most press items dating from this period quoted Schmit more often than his colleagues. However he didn't have the passion or energy that Furay had displayed and rarely made a memorable impression in the press. Another contributor to the relatively anonymous profile was the band's decision to rarely feature photos of themselves on their next few album covers, solidifying the anonymous image.

With Poco back on the concert trail, Epic chose to release the first single from CRAZY EYES. Although the label chose Schmit's excellent track *Here We Go Again*, *Billboard* reviewed the B-side, the instrumental *Fool's Gold*. Another Poco single missed the mark.

After six weeks of touring, the new Poco finally made up the Roxy dates in Los Angeles on December 13-14. These were high profile shows and the band was ready. The band rocked the large club and got an excellent review in *Rolling Stone*. "Poco is in fine shape as they displayed for all to see. It was abundantly clear here that Furay was not what held Poco together." It was exactly the effect the band had been trying to achieve. Young explained afterward, "Everyone put so much stock in Richie and how much Richie meant to Poco and we're all determined to show that Poco was made up of five guys and all the tunes and all the things that were Poco weren't just one person or any two persons. We're all really committed to proving Poco can happen and be a supergroup."

As anxious as the band was for everyone to forget Furay, they were equally anxious to rid themselves of their onerous Epic contract and find greener pastures. Although the prospect of signing with Asylum Records evaporated after separating from the Geffen roster, Poco resumed their recording on the new album in February in RCA Studios in Hollywood. With so much of the band's affairs in upheaval, they decided to stick with Jack Richardson as producer. His restrictive schedule, however, forced Poco to work under hurried conditions. Many times Young and Cotton found themselves hurriedly cutting solos before Richardson would leave to produce his star client Alice Cooper. Young complained, "We always thought that our music suffered because of his schedule so we cut him loose." As much as Poco respected Richardson's abilities, they could no longer tolerate being so low on his priority list. Despite this problem, Richardson remains in high esteem within the band. Young boasts, "Jack really did get us the best sounds on record. CRAZY EYES, for example, is one of my favorite records. I think the sound on disc on that particular record is excellent."

While at RCA Studio, Poco passed the time between the sessions playing ping-pong with Ringo Starr and Harry Nilsson, who were working in an adjacent studio on Nilsson's SON OF DRACULA soundtrack. Young also was a witness to some of John Lennon's antics during his "Lost Weekend" period. Incredibly, Jack Richardson also asserts that Poco rehearsed right next door to the fledgling Souther-Hillman-Furay Band as they were putting together their first recorded work in Los Angeles. "It was not a particularly pleasant time," Richardson noted.

The band surveyed what was left over from the CRAZY EYES sessions and they rescued two songs from the can. Rusty Young provided a tune that featured some lyrics for the first time. However the band struggled to come up with enough material to fill an album in such a short span of time. They obviously didn't want to use any of Furay's left over songs, and they were adamant that they did not want to use any outside material. The band eventually lengthened the arrangements of several songs and left the studio with eight completed tunes for the new album.

For Richardson, it was disheartening to see that there was no potential single among the tunes. The material they presented to Richardson was not the most accessible in terms of potential chart success. Richardson had tried in years past to find outside material for the band, however he didn't even bother this time. Having turned their backs on Richardson's proposal to use outside material a year earlier, they were even less inclined to entertain the notion now. "They were not in the singles mood at that point in time," Richardson explains.

Richardson feels the album was a reflection of the down mood the band was mired in immediately after Furay's departure. "The record was heavier. They wanted to be a little bit heavier. They were, to be quite honest with you, somewhat disturbed at the fact that Richie had decided to leave and go with Souther and Hillman. It was a very dark sounding album with a little undercurrent of anger from the group. I think they felt they were kind of hung out to dry."

"It was a really dark album," Richardson asserts. "In fact, when I mastered that album, over at Doug Sax's Mastering Lab, I was a little late. When I got over there, Doug said, 'Boy, it's a pretty dark sounding album...but I fixed it.' So he played back the first cut he'd processed, and it sounded like the Hardy Boys. I said, 'No, no, no, Doug, you've missed the point. This is to be a very dark sounding album. I don't want a lot of top end. It's not supposed to be there.'"

Epic was less than confident with the group, however they held fast and waited to see how this first post-Furay album would do on the charts and in the record stores. With another album in the can, Epic tried another single off CRAZY EYES in March. They edited *Magnolia* and backed it with *Blue Water* and released it. The cover of the J.J. Cale ballad was an interesting choice for a single, but admittedly, Poco hadn't given Epic too many options this time out, especially when they would not let *Let's Dance Tonight* be considered.

Poco went back on tour while awaiting the release of their new album. In February, Poco headlined the Santa Monica Civic Auditorium in front of a riotous crowd. The set opened with a unique intro arrangement into *Keeper of the Fire*. Schmit followed with a rare live version of *Here We Go Again*. Poco dusted off *I Guess You Made It* and debuted *Drivin' Wheel* from their forthcoming album. The band encored with a song "by a good friend of ours" and cooked through *Good Feelin' to Know*. The reviews didn't reflect the reaction they received on these West Coast dates. Richard Cromelin of the LA *Times* wrote, "The music's inability to truly touch or move is furthered by an indifferent demeanor on the part of the quartet which, rather than reaching out to the audience, makes it feel as if it's peeking in on an efficient rehearsal. Even the peppiness that sprang up at the end of the set had an obligatory feel to it. Poco isn't good at pretending and that's part of what being on stage is all about." The Seattle *Times*' Patrick MacDonald stated, "After [Robin] Trower, Poco's country rhythms were hard to get into. Much of the audience left and those who stayed didn't seem to be taken with the set. The band's new tunes are retreads of old Poco material. Country-rock never seemed so dated."

As the tour criss-crossed the country playing small theatres and colleges, Poco found itself overshadowed by a relatively obscure opening act. Playing the fairgrounds in Birmingham, Alabama on May 11, 1974, Poco found a sellout crowd waiting to cheer Buckingham Nicks. The duo of Lindsey Buckingham and Stevie Nicks played a workman-like set and then announced to the stunned crowd that they were breaking up to join Fleetwood Mac. Many in the crowd didn't bother to stick around to listen to Poco's set.

Despite the critics and the odd crowd, Tim Schmit found most audiences to be on Poco's side. "During the first part of the tour a lot of kids didn't know Richie had left the band; POCO SEVEN wasn't out yet. So, people would start shouting "where's Richie" and all kinds of stuff like that. We chose to ignore it for the most part - figuring that as long as the music was good, things would be cool. Usually by the end of the show when they were all dancing in the aisles, everyone knew Poco was still Poco-even without Richie."

Epic released the new album, POCO SEVEN in May while the band was on the road. The album's green cover was adorned with a stylish logo using the band's name across a horseshoe. The logo was designed by Phil Hartmann, talented brother of Poco's co-manager John Hartmann. The album opened with Cotton's *Drivin' Wheel*, which featured Cotton, Schmit, and Grantham taking vocal solos during the introduction. The arrangement sounded as if they were seeking to re-establish their vocal identity. As often happened with Poco, extant live versions of this song are far superior to this version, which drags a bit despite some outstanding drum work by Grantham, especially right before the solo section. The next track featured a reunion of sorts as Jimmy Messina added some mandolin licks to Young's spunky *Rocky Mountain Breakdown*. LOGGINS AND MESSINA sideman Al Garth contributes some notable fiddle lines as well. Although lyrically simple, the tune did show that Young was starting to branch out in his compositions. The thundering *Just Call My Name* was the first indication of Poco's new direction, however it wasn't a promising one. One difficulty with Poco's attempts at a harder edged sound was that Schmit's voice was not well suited to it. The arrangement is also razor-thin, without any obvious contribution by Young until several verses into the song. Schmit's *Skatin'* finished the side on a higher note. The arrangement was innovative even if it was more rock than normal for Poco. The sound is filled out more with Young laying down filler on the steel filtered through a Leslie speaker and Cotton's chunky guitar riffs driving the verses. Grantham contributes some nice vocals, as well.

Side two opened with a recut version of Cotton's *Faith in the Families*. The song had been partially recorded for CRAZY EYES but left unfinished. The bossa nova beat was interesting and provided a unique contrast to usual Poco fare. Cotton's lyrics addressed Poco's move back to LA from Colorado. However, the backing track recorded for the CRAZY EYES album was superior to this version. Schmit's *Krikket's Song (Passing Through)* was a fairly undistinguished love song also left over from the CRAZY EYES sessions. The song's only notable change was the addition of a string arrangement. The Cotton tune *Angel* was an interesting track, but the take sounds stiff and under rehearsed. It was a dark, moody tune that worked well in the live set when electric guitars replaced the acoustics and dobro of this version. *You Got Your Reasons* was a Paul Cotton ballad with the lyrics aimed at Furay's decision to leave Poco. Young's steel work is perfectly suited to the song's mood. Cotton slips in some angry guitar riffs, and Schmit blows some harmonica accents.

Overall, POCO SEVEN proved to be a fairly ambiguous effort. Only eight songs were offered, two from the previous album's outtakes. Three songs exceed five minutes in duration, with another two within seconds of five minutes. It seemed obvious, despite their protestations to the contrary, that Poco missed Richie Furay as a songwriter and vocalist. SEVEN, however, proved that the group could still produce listenable music. SEVEN got to #68 on the *Billboard* album charts, one notch better than its predecessor. Critical reception was lukewarm. The LA *Times* wrote, "The recent departure of co-founder Richie Furay has been coincidental with increasingly larger dose of metallic alloy in their sound mix. As usual, stratospheric harmonies remain the group's premier feature." Joe Bugno of the *Distant Drummer* remarked, "Although there isn't a lengthy classic production number like *Crazy Eyes* on this album, the songwriting of both Timmy Schmit and Paul Cotton has been in the same category in terms of quality as that of Furay. Cotton's material seems to be the stronger of the two." Ellen Mandell of *Hit Parader* agreed. "The major emerging songwriting force seems to be Paul Cotton, whose classic *Bad Weather* still remains one of the finest tracks they've ever recorded. POCO SEVEN, their first effort in their third stage of development confirms what many of their followers have suspected all along: that Furay was the last country holdout in a band with its eye on a more pure breed of rock."

Paul Cotton explained Poco's new sound. "POCO SEVEN was certainly heavier. I was into a lot of English rock then, anything English. I was miking my amps the way Peter Townsend (of the Who) did. I read what amps he used and how he miked them. We tried everything." Cotton's main concern was the loss of Furay's guitar to fill the middle when he took a solo.

More tour dates followed, as did another single release in June. Epic prepared an edited version of *Faith in the Families/Rocky Mountain Breakdown*, however it went nowhere. A rare promo version exists with *Rocky Mountain Breakdown* the featured cut on both sides of the single. Tour reviews were less than complimentary, but not vicious. The general critical outlook was that Furay was Poco, and without him the group was a mere shadow of its former self. Poco's appearance at Central Park in June found the band off its game. Tired after weeks on the road, Poco sounded sluggish as tunes such as *Fool's Gold*, *Rocky Mountain Breakdown* and *Restrain* did not reflect the energy of their recorded versions. However, *Faith in the Families* and *Drivin' Wheel* were arresting and made the show a cut above the usual concert fare.

By the fall, however, reviews were pointing out the futility of the loud rock avenue that Poco had chosen to travel. Chet Flippo in *Rolling Stone* characterized it as "bordering on sludge-rock" in his review of Poco's show at the Felt Forum in New York. Grantham recalled that Poco was under intense pressure to compensate for Furay's absence during this period. "Everybody was trying to take up the slack left by Richie. That's when Rusty used to go through that smash ending to our show. He never really liked doing it." The smash ending Grantham refers to was Young's tactic of raking the legs of his metal folding chair across his steel guitar. When performing this flashy and impressive feat at Clark University, college reporter Jan Press asked Young afterwards about the change in performance style. Young responded, "I don't think that we've changed really, as a group." Press was not convinced, observing, "What we saw leaned more towards real rock n roll and a change in performance...not much, but enough to notice. Despite Young's observations, there is a 'new' Poco of sorts. Bringing his talents up to the spotlight may be the very element that will lift them from their rut." The lackluster results were often due more to over-reaching than to lack of inspiration. No one seemed to have questioned the band's decision to continue as a quartet.

Poco's summer leg of the tour was supported by acts such as Robin Trower, Procol Harum, and Golden Earring. In the Pacific Northwest, Trower outshined Poco in the critics' eyes. At the Paramount NW in Seattle, nearly half the crowd left after Trower's set. Nevertheless, Poco put on a great show for those who stayed and came out for an encore as the crowd cheered and stomped their approval, much to the critics' consternation.

With the end of their recording contract with Epic in sight, Poco returned quickly to the studio, this time choosing the Record Plant in Los Angeles. They began recording in late August and con-

tinued into early September. The sessions were extremely productive. Tim Schmit recalls, "We had the whole album rehearsed before we went into the studio. That saves time and money. In the
past we rehearsed in the studio, but that doesn't give you any reference to work from."

Rather than replace Jack Richardson, Poco hired Mark Harman, a recording engineer to co-produce the album with them. After watching Richardson for three albums, the group felt it had
absorbed sufficient technical knowledge to get the sound they
wanted out of their albums. "We were trying to find out just what
a producer was," explained Schmit. "Let's try not having a producer this time." Young explains, "We decided to look for a hotshot engineer and hire him, and produce the records ourselves. So
we met three or four guys and Mark was the one we liked and we
felt could do the best job, because he was so into us and our music." Harman proved to be a mellow addition to the team. Without
the pressure of cramming all their recording into a short space of
time, as they had with Richardson, the band found themselves more
productive in the studio. They averaged recording a song a day.
Harman proved his worth during the mixing of the album.   Tim
Schmit explains, "He just kind of sat in the back and kept on top of
us. If the drums were getting too high or too loud, that meant that
the guitars were getting louder and the voices were getting louder.
Pretty soon the meters were all in the red and he'd say, 'Guys, you
just better start over.' And that's what we did."

The band quickly tidied up the album with overdubs and finished the mix. Without delay, they headed off for the concert trail.
Manager John Hartmann announced that the new album would be
entitled SAGEBRUSH SERENADE, giving fans new hope that Poco had
abandoned their heavy rock sound. The band quickly grew to dislike
the title of the album. Schmit recalls, "I hated that as a title of the
new album. We wanted to get back to the country-rock where we
belong, but SAGEBRUSH SERENADE seemed to me a little too hokey.
So Rusty threw out the idea of calling it CANTAMOS and we all went
'Yeah!' It fits the album and it fits Poco because we're a vocal
group."

The return to a more country-rock sound was due in large part
to the large participation of Rusty Young in songwriting. Grantham
explains, "Rusty, of course, stepped in, and his style was closer to
what we sounded like with Richie than Tim's was. So the more involved Rusty was on an album, the more it took the flavor of the
country-rock thing. Tim's songs were 'out there' a little bit."

In the meantime, the concert business was taking a beating as
the nation's economy took a tumble. The recession of 1974 hit lei-

sure activities hard, with both the price of gas (when you could find it) and tickets beginning to climb. Promoters were reporting business was down by as much as 50 percent in some locations. Many bands were feeling the pinch, including Poco. Washington *Post* reporter Tom Zito noted, "Six months ago the countrified rock of Poco easily sold out the 3,750 seats at Constitution Hall. The group's concert there Monday night, however, filled only a fifth of the house." President of Premiere Talent, Frank Barcelona, surveyed the scene and offered, "[A kid's] got to be much more selective and promoters as well as groups are beginning to realize that they've got to come on with a strong enough package to win the kid's concert dollar. Poco now is willing to go for an opening act that costs, say, $2,500 and will help fill a hall rather than using the local band that costs $500."

Now just one album away from freeing themselves from Epic, Poco chose to record another live album while on their upcoming tour to fulfill their contractual obligation. That close to the end of the contract, Epic did not make any demands for any new material on this live album. After submitting CANTAMOS to Epic, Poco went back on the road in November. The tour got off to a rough start with three canceled college dates. When they got back on track, Poco played shows in Boston on November 3 and November 4 at the Nassau Coliseum where they once again shared the bill with Loggins and Messina. Their appearance in Washington D.C. was lamented by the Washington Post reviewer Larry Rohter who complained, "The new Poco is just spinning its wheels. The original country-rock band is no longer the best." In spite of the less than glowing reviews, Poco recorded their show on November 9 at Yale University in New Haven, Connecticut, and it proved fairly successful. However after reviewing the tapes, it became clear that they needed more material. Consequently, the band also recorded two additional shows in Milwaukee and St. Louis. Both shows were excellent, especially the Ambassador Theatre show in St. Louis. Among the three shows that were recorded, Poco had enough material to compile an live album.

CANTAMOS appeared in stores late in November. The album began with its centerpiece *Sagebrush Serenade*. The song was a dazzling showcase for the band's vocal and instrumental talents. *Sagebrush Serenade* featured a long instrumental break, with Young and Cotton trading lead lines using acoustic and electric guitars, dobro, steel guitar, banjo, and mandolin. Although sung by Schmit, amazed fans were stunned to learn that none other than Rusty Young wrote the song. Cotton's *Suzannah* was an ordinary ballad. Young struck again with the energetic *High and Dry*. It had the sound of a potential single with a sharp three-chord chorus and another long instrumental solo section. Schmit again takes lead vocals and some punchy bass lines. The side ended with Cotton's sterling apocalyptic vision entitled *Western Waterloo*. More than one fan heard the song as a swipe at Richie Furay (the traitor). Cotton had no such intention. "The song had nothing to do with Richie. That's 'trader.' It's a song about how the Indians lost the West."

The quality material continued on the flip side. *One Horse Blue* was another outstanding Cotton tune with excellent electric guitar work and more sparkling banjo and steel guitar backing. Tim Schmit finally checked in with *Bitter Blue*, a strident ballad with top-notch high harmony work by Grantham and Schmit. Cotton's final contribution, *Another Time Around*, was the closest thing to an out and out rock song on the album. Young's screaming steel work drives the tune into the stratosphere. Another Schmit tune, *Whatever Happened to Your Smile*, followed. Rusty Young's third offering *All the Ways* drew the album to a close with another Schmit lead vocal.

CANTAMOS marked the emergence of Rusty Young as the much needed songwriter to replace Furay. His strong, musically mature style certainly gave Poco a boost after the less than stellar effort of SEVEN. Lyrically, Young still had a ways to go, but there was no doubt that his talent for coming up with memorable melodies shined brightly. Young's contributions were a surprise to his bandmates. Grantham explained to *Different Drummer*, "The songwriting responsibilities started to worry us. That's when Rusty really came through. Just when we needed him, he was there." Tim Schmit handled the lead vocals on Young's songs for the album. Despite the strong offering, Epic did not promote the album heavily, and its #76 chart showing was the lowest of any Poco album up to that point. The fact that CANTAMOS was the third Poco album released in barely over a year also contributed to its lackluster chart performance. At any rate, CANTAMOS may well be the forgotten masterpiece in the Poco canon. Bud Scoppa's assessment in *Crawdaddy* noted, "Poco has regained its equilibrium and has turned out an impressive new album, CANTAMOS. In terms of material (an ongoing problem area) Tim Schmit, Paul Cotton and most recently Rusty Young are now turning out unified and appealing batches of work." Gone also was the dark mood that hung over every track of SEVEN. The Poco on CANTAMOS was closer to the classic version, with plenty of upbeat, lively tunes in a comfortable country-rock setting.

While CANTAMOS hit the shelves, Poco wound down its latest tour with a series of dates in the Southwest and California opening once again for Loggins and Messina. Young remarked, "That was something that we would have never done while Richie was in the band. We would never have shared a bill with Jimmy." Although Young took swipes at Messina in the press following his departure, it was clear that fences had been mended by 1974 and that the pair was beginning to talk about working together sometime in the future.

After the tour, Poco took a needed break. They appeared on the NBC-TV late night rock show *Midnight Special* on January 24, 1975, garnering some needed exposure. Using a set piece based on the cover of CANTAMOS, Poco played five songs including a hot *Sagebrush Serenade* and an acoustic *Bad Weather*, where Paul finally revealed that he'd written the song about the breakup of the original Illinois Speed Press.

A week after this appearance, Epic finally released a single off CANTAMOS. They edited *High and Dry* down to eliminate the song's long instrumental passage, shortening the song to just over two minutes long. Backed by *Bitter Blue*, the single also missed making the charts.

Poco took a short break before tackling the arduous task of sorting through the live tapes from their previous tour. They spent the early part of 1975 making choices of tracks and performances. Having finally completed that task, the band along with Mark Harman mixed the final selection in mid-March. They turned over the tapes to Epic in May and didn't look back. "What we did was to go out on a tour and record a bunch of live gigs," Tim Schmit explained shortly after completing the mix. "We put together an album and took it into the studio and mixed it. We then handed it over to the record company - and they still have it. We didn't have a title for it, but if they are going to release it I hope that they consult us."

With a live album in the can that they used to satisfy their Epic contract, Poco began negotiations on a new recording contract. For the first time since their creation, Poco had a track record to use in the negotiations for a contract, and they were anxious to see if they would hit the jackpot.

9
Sittin' On a Fence

Poco opened negotiations for a new recording contract in the spring of 1975. Not surprisingly, Epic made a lucrative offer to retain them, however Poco wasn't about to stay for any amount of money. The last several years had been spent trying to find a way to rid them of the contract as quickly as they could. Epic, in turn, had failed to support the band in many meaningful ways and had made things more difficult as the years past. The last straw had been the debacle over the cover of CANTAMOS. Poco wanted a deluxe cover with a die-cut window in it. Epic balked at the cost and flatly told the band that if they wanted it, the band would have to pay for it themselves, roughly a nickel per album. Poco did exactly that for domestic copies of the album, however overseas copies were shipped without the deluxe cover. Young was furious and let Epic know that their stinginess would be taken into consideration. When Poco's management received Epic's offer, Poco dismissed it out of hand.

Instead, they seriously entertained an offer by ABC Records. Many of the label's employees were friends of the group, and it seemed a natural choice. Former road manager Vince Marchiolo was one such friend. "I was recruited by ABC to do Artist Relations," Marchiolo relates. "I think the execs got sick of my constant talk about 'why not sign Poco?' I felt ABC could do a better job at finally getting the group recognition they truly deserved." A personal approach seemed to be a welcome approach to the band. "Talk is cheap," Young explains. "ABC was the only one who believed in us strongly enough to put their money where their mouth was." Jerry Rubenstein, president of ABC Records, had made a personal pitch to them. Rubenstein was Poco's former business manager and had a fond place in his heart for Poco. "The president of ABC is a real close friend of ours," Young states. "He's been in our corner for years and when he is personally committed we know he means it. He's not some guy we just met from New York whom we see once every six months or a year, and who doesn't know us at all. Half of the people at ABC are personal friends we have known for years and when they back this up with financial commitment how can we lose?" Schmit agreed. "The newly appointed director of the record company had been our business manager for two years previously, plus our old publicist is one of the executives. Even a guy who used to road manage us works for the company, and really it's kind of like lots of friends."

This personal approach meant quite a bit to the group after the poor treatment they had received at the hands of Epic label officials. ABC Records was not in a position to match Epic's offer however it didn't matter. Poco inked a deal with ABC for less upfront money on April 15 and looked forward to a new relationship.

Epic Records did not take the defection well. Despite the warnings, executives at Epic were upset by Poco's decision to leave the label. According to Young, Epic's president vowed that Epic would fight by releasing Poco albums to coincide with their new ABC releases in an effort to split the market and blunt the selling potential of the new Poco releases. Threats of Poco's demise were nothing new to the band, who ignored them.

Undaunted, Poco entered the Record Plant in Los Angeles again with Mark Harman behind the boards and came away with what they considered their finest work. Released in July 1975, HEAD OVER HEELS was even more interesting and varied than their previous album. After using CANTAMOS to re-establish their country-rock identity, the band's songwriters began examining different musical styles. When Poco assembled at the Record Plant, they were excited about the new material and sure that they could produce the hit for ABC that they all wanted.

Keep on Tryin' quickly established another Poco classic with its simple acoustic backing and high harmonies. Grantham gushes, "It's one of my favorite studio memories. As it developed, [Tim] got excited, then we got excited." Schmit explains, "It was something I've always wanted to do, to show off Poco's vocal quality to its full. It's a song that just came through me. In it, I'm talking to my wife and myself. It's a love song." The tune was cut after Rusty Young had left the studio, and no effort was made to add his talents to the song. Young proved that his CANTAMOS contributions were no fluke with *Lovin' Arms*. Former Loggins and Messina sideman Al Garth added violin and viola to the track, along with a hearty laugh at the end. Cotton continued his string of consistent tunes with *Let Me Turn Back to You*. Young's *Makin' Love*, with Band member Garth Hudson guesting on piano, sounded like another potential hit. Schmit recalls exitedly, "Getting a hold of Garth Hudson was a complete thrill for me because I am a Band freak. We got him because Mark Harman, our engineer, is good friends with those people." Cotton's excellent *Down in the Quarter* rounded out the first side, using a swelling string arrangement to power the song.

The album's second side didn't pack quite as much punch. Young's Latin-flavored *Sittin' on a Fence* was a strong rhythm piece with some attempts at relevant lyrics. Cotton's *Georgia, Bind My Ties* featured some quality lead guitar work that drives the track. The third song *Us* is a fairly simple ballad, except that it features the lead vocal debut of Rusty Young. "It was a real personal tune," explains Young. "Some of the other guys sang it; we worked it out in three-part harmony and it didn't sound right and then they each sang it in turn and it didn't sound right, so I did it. I had a great time and it was a learning experience." Co-producer Mark Harman added some pipe organ and piano to the song. Schmit cut another tune without Rusty Young's involvement, *Flyin' Solo*. Grantham recalls that the tune came together in the studio at a session towards the end of the day. After playing it for Young the next day, they decided against adding to it at Schmit's request. "He liked things real sparse," explains Grantham. Poco roadie and guitarist John Brennan co-wrote the tune. Poco next covered an obscure Steely Dan track called *Dallas*. Cotton explains how Poco came to cover a Steely Dan song. "Tim had been doing sessions with Steely Dan singing backgrounds. They offered him this tape of unused songs. Tim presented it to me and we kind of sat on it for about a year and there's still some things I want to do from that tape and one was *Dallas*." Schmit observed, "I called Donald Fagen and asked him if he had any tunes floating around and he said he had. I asked him to send me a tape and *Dallas* was on it. Rusty wasn't that keen on doing it though, but the rest of us were really into it." Although several of the band wanted the song to be the single, ABC had other ideas. The album ended with Schmit's punchy *I'll Be Back Again*.

Grantham, for one, felt Poco dropped the ball by not releasing *Dallas* as a single. "It was supposed to be [a single]. That's why we did it. I really thought that should have been a big record for us, but I couldn't get much support from management or the guys in the band. I don't think the effort was put into taking that song somewhere it could have been. See, when you work with a lot of writers, I think it's normal for them to believe in their stuff. Where I wasn't involved in a lot of writing, I thought it was a great song. I thought, 'Man, we need to be open to songs like this.'" Ironically, it turned out to be one of the last songs written by an outside writer and recorded by Poco for nearly a decade.

The major music press largely ignored HEAD OVER HEELS despite ABC's push, including a full-page ad in *Rolling Stone*. Timothy White in *Crawdaddy* had little positive to say about HEAD OVER HEELS. "The band has been sadly left in the dust by their descendants, principally the Eagles. The album is characterized by much indelicate flexing of vocal cords, the band still favoring second-wind chorales on the end of phrases; Poco's buckaroo contatas continue to be dominated either by the one-dimensional angry-at-love posturings of Timothy Schmit or Paul Cotton's heavy-handed yarnings. Schmit's timid bass playing has never equaled Randy Meisner's, who left the band in 1969. Cotton still appears to be doing a guest shot from the defunct Illinois Speed Press. His voice is Michael Murphy in need of Neo-Synephrine and detracts from the uptempo playfulness that is Poco's trademark and chief asset." *Rolling Stone* didn't even bother to review the album.

The underground press was less brutal, but no less uncertain about Poco's future. Roger Hooper of the *Iconoclast* noted, "Their material or lack of it, might be the group's obstacle to success." The *Boston Phoenix* remarked, "Unfortunately, the Poco that lives on doesn't necessarily know what Poco was all about either. Poco was never particularly original and rarely wrote better than sophomoric lyrics but they conveyed a joy in playing that was singular in West Coast bands. But they are in a rather nasty bind. Their new material is more laid back than the old, and if it is to grab our attention, it will need a more arresting lead voice." The *Bugle-American*, generally a supportive voice in the underground press, noted, "What is needed is a new inspiration, some new blood. You can't rely on Rusty Young's talents, no matter how substantial, to hold up the entire foundation. HEAD OVER HEELS still works as a fine album, but the signs of repetition could kill them if they try to stretch this material any further." Jerry Gilbert's review in *Zigzag* was solidly behind the band. "Poco have come up with some real gems. This ranks alongside any thing the band did whilst Furay was around."

Although the critical outlook on the album was less than stellar, ABC's promotional efforts did have some positive impacts. HEAD OVER HEELS peaked at #43 on the charts, Poco's strongest showing in years. To do their part to promote their album, Poco rehearsed a new set, adding a number of songs from the new album. They were excited about the energy that ABC showed towards them, and they wanted to showcase the new album in their live show. Grantham's perspective on the HEAD OVER HEELS tour emphasized Poco's expansive approach to their music. "It was a little risky," Grantham affirms. "We did take more chances. We did try to get away from the way people might have seen us musically. As I remember, we just tried stuff we really had not tried before." Schmit was equally positive at the time of the album's release. "I think we have grown incredibly musically, so HEAD OVER HEELS is a better album all the way around. It's a big step between albums and it's coupled with our excitement with the new record company."

Poco went out on the road and debuted the new material. They opened for Dave Mason at the Place de Nations in Montreal, Canada, on July 26. The Montreal *Star* remarked, "Poco played a brand of country rock music that created an intimate rapport with the audience and produced a sort of 'sittin' 'round the campfire' atmosphere." They played Central Park twice that summer to adoring crowds. During their first appearance on July 30 Poco received a roaring ovation. They opened their set with *Keep on Tryin'*. Three other new songs from the album were performed: *Georgia, Bind My Ties, Makin' Love*, and *Sittin' on a Fence*. The only other surprise was a spirited version of *Good Feelin' to Know*. Poco sounded much more in control than during their previous post-Furay outings. Poco also played a festival at the New Jersey State Fairgrounds in Trenton with Aerosmith, Kingfish, Slade, Mahogany Rush, and Nils Lofgrin on August 24. The tour hit a high point a week later as Poco opened four shows for guitar legend Eric Clapton. At the Scope in Norfolk, Virginia, Clapton brought Poco out during his encore to have they help him sing *Let It Rain*. Sharing the stage with Eric Clapton was quite an experience for the band. "God, I was blown away," Grantham explained. "That was a lot of fun. Clapton is just so incredible. He was a major idol to all of us and to get to play with him, what a pleasure that was."

Poco's career did appear to be on the upswing. Rusty Young told British journalist Paul Kendall, "On this last tour we did we got a better reception than we've had since the first year of Poco. The momentum is building. It's really exciting and I have to put it down to the record company because ABC is doing a real good job." Perhaps seeing the renewed interest in Poco, Epic put its punitive plan in motion and released a double album of previously released material entitled THE VERY BEST OF POCO. The package aptly represented their work for the label and boasted some entertaining liner notes by New York DJ Pete Fornatale. Disappointingly, Epic did not include any rare tracks or unreleased material. THE VERY BEST OF POCO was often reviewed at the same time as HEAD OVER HEELS and received positive reviews. THE VERY BEST OF POCO charted at #90 although its stay on the charts was brief.

In September, ABC released the first single *Keep on Tryin'/Georgia, Bind My Ties*. It slowly climbed the charts, peaking at #50. Still, *Keep on Tryin'* became the most successful Poco single to date. "To this day I think that thing should have been a smash," Grantham reflects. "I just thought it was a wonderful song and a great performance. I just don't understand why we didn't get a single like most other groups. My all-time favorite Poco song is *Keep on Tryin'*."

As their single climbed the charts, Hartmann and Goodman booked a tour of Europe for their two most successful clients, America and Poco. The tour proved to be successful and well received. Most nights after opening the show, Poco would return to the stage to join America and perform *Don't Cross the River* together. Poco's performance at the New Victoria Theatre in London drew uniformly good reviews. The *New Musical Express* wrote, "Poco's stage set is a gradual buildup from *Keep on Tryin'* through soft country-rock to full-bodied rock and roll. Poco in truth were definitely hot poop." *Melody Maker* noted, "Poco are a gutsier outfit than America and they're also more countrified in their approach to rock. The band played for fun – and fun is what you got. Young produced some unusual guitar with a fret board angled for easier slide playing and his work was justly rewarded with an encore." In Paris, Poco performed to a spirited crowd, bringing an end to their second European tour. Some fans were disappointed at Poco's short sets. They played barely an hour at each show.

In press interviews during the tour, Young revealed that if things went well with the album, Poco was considering adding a couple of members to Poco. He was especially anxious to have former Loggins and Messina sideman Al Garth join the band. "He played with us in L.A. when we did shows there recently," explained Young. "He plays fiddle and saxophone. In those concerts we did *Magnolia* and he played the sax solo on the end of that. Boy, it gave you shivers up and down your spine it's so good." The overall feeling was that Poco easily outshined America throughout the entire tour.

The band flew home and took a short break. Late in October, Poco returned to the road on tour with the Doobie Brothers and the Outlaws. They began in the Northeast with shows in Buffalo and Madison Square Garden in New York. The *New York Times'* Ian Dove noted, "Poco attempted a certain amount of delicacy that often turned into blandness and fell on indifferent ears." *Variety* observed, "Poco's local popularity was in evidence as the ABC Records quartet was able to stir the crowd with a subpar performance." Poco began a southern swing a week later in Atlanta and stayed on the East Coast for shows in Passaic, New Jersey, Boston, and Long Island. The group closed out the year with shows in the West, playing UCLA and the University of Utah with Stephen Stills, Paramount Theatres in Portland and Seattle, and a New Year's Eve show at the Cow Palace in San Francisco. D.P. Bond of the *Post-Intelligencer* wrote of the Seattle show, "The first half-dozen tunes played indicated that this band has got as much going for it live as it always has had on records, which is to say Poco's an exciting competent equally by very few." At Pauly Pavilion at UCLA, the campus paper complained, "Poco likewise performed well, sticking to their older, tried and true material and was well received by the audience. Unfortunately, their portion of the show ended just when they were seeming adventurous."

Hartmann and Goodman investigated the potential of a Poco tour to Japan, Australia, and New Zealand in early 1976; however, it fell by the wayside due to high costs. Cotton noted, "We have a huge Japanese following. In fact, the first band I saw who were doing our music almost completely was a Japanese band!" Sadly, the economics didn't work out, and the band instead focused on the States.

In January, ABC released another single, *Makin' Love/Flyin' Solo*, however it proved a disappointment after the modest success of *Keep on Tryin'*. Rusty Young recalled that *Makin' Love* and *Keep on Tryin'* had received breakout airplay when HEAD OVER HEELS was released. Young had magnanimously told ABC to back off pushing his song and urged them to release *Keep on Tryin'*. They did and kept *Makin' Love* in reserve. Their decision to wait until after the tour's end, four months after their previous single had fallen off the charts, to release the follow-up single didn't help its chances.

Poco returned to television in January with a return visit to NBC-TV's *Midnight Special*. However the performance was not up to their usual high standards. Painfully off-key vocals marred the appearance. Poco opened their segment with a decent sounding version of *Keep on Tryin'*. The camera work occasionally focused on a live chicken wandering around the hay bales where Rusty Young strummed acoustic guitar. Cotton, Schmit and Grantham huddled in front of microphones and harmonized. The set's backdrop was the POCO SEVEN logo. A speedy bluegrass arrangement of *Sagebrush Serenade* followed, with the studio audience stomping and whistling during the solo section. Poco finished up with *Makin' Love* with both Schmit and Grantham wailing off-key. The whole performance sounded under-rehearsed and lacked the polish of their summer shows.

The preparation for Poco's next album took most of the early part of 1976. Hoping to expand their sound and approach some new material with new instruments, the group invited former Loggins and Messina sideman Al Garth to participate in the album. Garth was proficient in the fiddle and sax. Garth recalls how he got involved with Poco. "They said, 'Hey, there's a good chance that maybe we could work together on an equal basis. If it works out then you would become a Poco just like the rest of us.' Still, I was worried. They'd lost Richie Furay, all those changes, new record company. So I said, 'Let's go out on the basis that I'll be a sideman for a while. Let's see how it will work out." Grantham agrees, "We were going to have him as a member, but I think at first on the first tour he was going to be a sideman."

As the sessions progressed at the Record Plant, Garth found the group to be uncommonly open and friendly, quite a change from his previous gig with Loggins and Messina. Garth had clashed with what he considered a tyrannical Jimmy Messina. "He wanted to be Captain Kirk," explained Garth. "Well, there can only be one Captain Kirk." Garth found Poco often asking him for ideas and asked him to contribute to the arrangements. "I got a little bit creative on ROSE OF CIMARRON," Garth said. "I'm thinking of *Too Many Nights Too Long*. I got a chance to write a little part on the end, which they preserved on record." This willingness to share the creative process opened the door for Garth to join Poco.

ABC had provided Poco with a big push during their first year with the label. Poco wanted to repay their confidence with an album that the label could sell to various markets. During the sessions, the band continued to exhibit their creativity and willingness to experiment in the studio. Arrangements were more intricate and complicated. To that end, the band included studio musicians Milt Holland on percussion, Steve Ferguson and Tom Sellers on keyboards, and Sid Sharp on the Concert Master. Poco soundman John Logan also contributed some banjo on a track. Grantham explains the band's mood during the sessions. "I think it was more exciting than anything else. I think the other writers stepped up in terms of their output and their approaches and styles. It was more exciting just trying to say, 'Hey, this is our sound now. We're into different areas of music now.' I mean, it was a natural kind of thing with Richie being gone."

With news that Poco was back in the studio, Epic Records beat them into the stores with another Poco album from their vaults. In March, Epic finally released the live album submitted to them back in 1974 as Poco's final obligation to the label. POCO LIVE hit store shelves featuring a painting of a horse's rear flank with the album title "branded" on it. Not missing the horse's ass insinuation, Poco's road crew sent the label a bale of hay in mock appreciation. The band complained in the press of Epic's tactic of sabotaging their ABC efforts by releasing old material. Whatever Epic's marketing strategy, sales of their Poco albums lagged well behind any new ABC product.

POCO LIVE featured performances from concerts in November 1974. The album opened with an acoustic medley of *Blue Water, Fool's Gold*, and *Rocky Mountain Breakdown*. While the performances were spirited, the sound was understandably thin. Reproducing Young's multi-layered instrumentals live with only a four-piece band was virtually impossible. Cotton performed a solid, shorter version of *Bad Weather*. It was interesting to hear Cotton's lead guitar instead of the familiar Furay lead lines. Poco included a truly superior rendition of Cotton's *Ride the Country* to end side one. This soulful performance showcases a brisker pace than the studio version and stretches out more than seven minutes.

Side two showed some of the hard-rock style that had worried so many hard-core Poco fans in 1974. Cotton does an improved reading of *Angel* to start things off. Cotton's electric guitar and Young's scorching slide work drive the tune in the early stages. Young switches to his steel and using an echoplex gives the illusion of a string backing before returning to the slide. Young's *High and Dry* was done with gusto. Schmit's bass work helps pump this version up, although it still pales next to its studio counterpart. Tim Schmit checked in with *Restrain*, and the album ends with a ragged version of *Good Feelin' to Know* with Schmit on lead vocals.

The album itself barely clocked in at 38 minutes in length. Epic's packaging was minimal with a few small pictures of the band on the back cover with the obligatory song information. Not surprisingly given its limited promotion, POCO LIVE lasted only four weeks on the album charts. The public didn't seem interested in two-year-old Poco. Surprisingly, some of the group were quite pleased with the album and the performances it contained. Grantham even considered it superior to DELIVERIN'.

The critical view of the POCO LIVE was dismissive. Most music reviewers ignored the album altogether. Howie Blumenthal of *Good Times* noted, "Poco is a fantastic live group whose character has miraculously been captured on what might have been a throwaway al-

bum made to fulfill old contractual commitments for Epic. This album is the most spirited piece of plastic I've run up against in
weeks, and, unfortunately, its timing may force a burial in the $1.99
bins like their almost year-old debut album for ABC." Scott Garside
of the *Free Aquarian* held the more common viewpoint. "LIVE, the
usual title tacked onto live recordings these days is about a stale as
the music itself. This recording unfortunately does not capture
Poco at its peak. Anyone permitting the release of such an item of
mediocrity would be destroying an image of a band which has undoubtedly seen better days. A more appropriate title would be
DEAD or BURIED."

Two months later, Poco's second ABC album was released.
ROSE OF CIMARRON was their big play at a major breakthrough. The
title track opened the album. Rusty Young had created a real gem
that used strings in a creative arrangement with Cotton and Schmit
trading lead vocals on the verses. Young explained, "I wanted to
create a song that was a sort of updated Sons of the Desert song."
Richie Furay paid Young a compliment upon the album's release.
"After we did *Rose of Cimarron*, Richie called and said, 'Boy, I
really like that song.' That really was a great feeling to have Richie
tell me that, it was the ultimate compliment." The song has also
earned him more royalties than any other song in his repertoire.
Both Slim Whitman and Emmy Lou Harris covered the tune. *Steala-
way* was another strong offering by Young sung by Schmit. A typical
Schmit ballad *Just Like Me* followed. Young continued his contributions with a medley of *Company's Comin'* and *Slowpoke*. The former was a jingle-sounding ditty with handclaps by Young's girlfriend
Annie Emery, Grantham's wife Jenny, and Schmit's wife Noreen and
6-year old daughter Jeddrah. The latter song was a fiery bluegrass
instrumental that harkened back to the early Poco days.

Cotton songs dominated the flip side. The first was *Too Many
Nights Too Long*. Grantham explains, "Paul's going through a lot of
changes and his songs seem almost classical due to some new influences." This song was a piece of Latin prison drama that used
some Spanish lyrics sung by Schmit (provided by his maid!). Cotton
then revived *PNS (When You Come Around)* from the first Illinois
Speed Press album. He offered a new arrangement radically different from the previous version. For those who have long puzzled
over what PNS stood for, Cotton reveals it stood for *Paul's New
Song*, its working title. Schmit weighed in with his best offering
since CRAZY EYES. *Starin' at the Sky* was co-written by John Logan,
who contributed banjo to the track. Young's sparkling mandolin
play and Al Garth's stunning sax solo made this recording stand out.
Cotton rounded out the album with two rather unremarkable coun-

try songs, *All Alone Together* and *Tulsa Turnaround*. "I wanted to do some authentic country music," explains Cotton. "I wanted to get on the country charts, not like the Eagles did with a crossover, but I wanted to start there and come back. And I found out that it was a very bad idea. The country charts are very unrealistic and very unrewarding." Cotton also probably didn't realize that ABC wasn't exactly a force in the country market.

ROSE OF CIMARRON has grown over time to become one of Poco's most highly rated albums by fans. However, the reaction to it at the time was lukewarm at best. Without even a mid-chart single, the sales of ROSE OF CIMARRON were sluggish, reflected ultimately in its poor #89 chart showing. ABC didn't release an edited version of the title track as a single until August and it barely charted at #94.

The critical reception was generally positive. *Zigzag* snagged a high school buddy of Rusty Young's Lomax Gold to write their review. Not surprisingly, he bestowed a glowing review, although he was perceptive enough to notice the lack of a potential breakthrough single. "I'm a little worried," wrote Gold, "These ears don't hear an obvious hit single that would blaze a trail for the album's rise up the LP charts." Barry Patton of the *Bugle-American* stated, "Poco comes back to life on this effort thanks to the continued songwriting strength of Rusty Young and the revived interests and talents of Paul Cotton and Tim Schmit. Poco has come back sounding fresh and alive once again." The *Aquarian's* reviewer Scott Garside, who had just panned their POCO LIVE two months before, claimed, "Poco has completed its best album in years. The title track is easily the finest individual track the group has written since Paul Cotton's classic *Bad Weather*. All these positive changes have resulted in the best Poco album since CRAZY EYES and also a prime contender for Best of the Year."

Co-producer Mark Harman continued to praise the band. "One of the amazing things about this band is their dynamics - how they fit together personality wise," he told *Sounds*. "Actually, they're incredibly diverse personalities, but it's that pressure that glues it together, and the tension that motivates it keeps it spinning. Poco is like a blowfish at 40,000 feet."

With Al Garth aboard, Poco debuted its new five-man lineup on a tour of the South to coincide with the album's release. The tour package had Poco opening for Willie Nelson and a reformed Flying Burrito Brothers on the bill. Denny Jones has fond memories of certain aspects of the tour. "We played all over the South, Memphis, Savannah, Atlanta. But Willie hadn't quite made it yet so the shows weren't selling out. So Willie had all kinds of guest stars:

Waylon Jennings, Faron Young, Jeannie Riley. Six months later, Willie was a superstar, but every stop on this tour was losing money." The tour routing was fast paced and demanding and finally Poco decided that they needed to be able to keep up. "That's when we got our first tour bus," explains Jones. "We decided we had to do it to keep up. We didn't make the schedule. We got Curly Jones...we went with Stagecoach VIP out of Nashville. Curly owned the company and he was our driver. All the buses looked the same, they weren't tricked out like they are now. And most of the drivers they recruited were old truck drivers who were speed freaks."

Although lined out for nearly a month, Poco left the tour after a show at the Fox Theater in Atlanta on May 21. The reason given was that the band was disturbed by the lack of professionalism exhibited by Nelson's backup band, which often would show up at the hall only moments before they were scheduled to go on. Randy Locke of Nelson's band recalled, "After Atlanta, they quit the tour. Their road manager told us, 'Hey we like you guys, but we can't work with you because you ain't professional.'" Jones also adds, "The guys decided that since the shows were losing money and we were playing to the wrong audience...women in beehive hairdos and cowboys. It would be half a house, we'd open to a handful of Poco fans and a bunch of cowboys. And with Schmit with the long hair, it wasn't translating." An even more compelling reason was that Hartmann and Goodman has taken a chance and signed Poco up as the opening act for the much hyped Stills-Young Band summer tour. Dates were booked from June through September. It was risky since the profits were likely to be slim because the overhead was so high and the tour skipped about from place to place. But no one disagreed that the exposure would be tremendous and that the band needed something to try to boost ROSE OF CIMARRON'S sales.

Poco managed a couple of warm-up gigs prior to the onset of the Stills-Young Band tour. One gig was an obscure outdoor show in Angels Camp, California. Famous for Mark Twain's story of the jumping frog, Angels Camp had only recently begun hosting a summer concert and air show entitled Mountain Aire. Although second-billed, Poco was the hit of the show, performing many songs from ROSE OF CIMARRON including the title track, *PNS (When You Come Around)*, and *Starin' at the Sky* with Al Garth wailing on the sax. Garth's role in the live act was understandably limited. "I jumped into the band," Garth explains. "They said, 'Quick, learn these songs, we have to go out on tour!' So basically I've been playing little background parts. They've got me playing piano now too. I'm not much of a keyboard player, but this is the problem. If Paul wants to take a guitar solo then the middle part of the music falls out. So piano can fill that hole. I don't have to be that good."

The Stills-Young Band tour opened in late June at the Pine Knob Theatre outside of Detroit, Michigan. Despite the intention that Poco would be gaining more expose, the tour proved to be disappointing in the beginning as reviewers and critics routinely ignored Poco to spend their reviews on the unspirited performances of Stills and Young. There were some reviews that did mention Poco, however. John Taylor of the *Pittsburgh Times* wrote, "Much of Poco's material was off its latest album ROSE OF CIMARRON and was unfamiliar to much of the audience, but fans were still carried away by the band's smooth performance and enthusiasm. Poco wavered a bit when it tried to play hard rock and roll but the weak points were seldom noticeable for long. Poco has never received the credit it deserves and this concert was probably no exception. Most of the crowd went to see Stills and Young and expected Poco to be little more than an afterthought. Yet Poco showed that a big name is not a prerequisite for performing good music." After the July 18 show in Charlotte, Richard Maschel of the *Observer* complained, "They sounded like about 10,000 other such groups, nowhere near the Charlie Daniels Band and somewhere behind even the Amazing Rhythm Aces. The crowd, however, loved it, gave them a standing ovation."

The dream pairing of Stills and Young came crashing to an end after a show in South Carolina. When the tour pulled into Atlanta, Neil Young was nowhere to be found. He'd left a telegram behind to his partner telling him, "Funny how things start spontaneous and end spontaneous. Eat a peach, Neil." The show that night was canceled. Stephen Stills tried desperately to keep going. Three shows in Florida were salvaged as he recruited Chris Hillman and George Perry to join his band. Local favorites Lynyrd Skynyrd were added to the bill. In Miami, Stills drew praise for pulling off an entertaining show. Poco held its own. *Variety* remarked that Poco was "tight, spirited and brandished better songs than in recent memory, the country-rock ensemble managed to outshine Lynyrd Skynyrd." Despite Stills' attempts, promoters around the country canceled the remainder of the tour. While Stills bemoaned his fate, Poco was in even worse shape. They were unable to book anywhere near the number of shows lost by the tour's cancellation. The financial blow was tremendous, and the band retreated to Los Angeles to ponder their future.

Late in the summer, Poco appeared at the Santa Monica Civic Auditorium with a surprise for the crowd. At the point in the set where they played *Rose of Cimarron* and *Magnolia*, the curtains behind the band parted, revealing the string section behind a sheer curtain. Both songs were spectacular using the accompaniment. After the show, the band was thrilled with how the songs had turned out. Cotton explained, "We were thinking of ways of presenting [Crazy Eyes] onstage with strings and everything when Richie left."

In mid-October, Poco returned to Europe for a third time. The tour had been arranged before the summer tour fiasco, and the band considered canceling the European tour. Grantham explains, "When you come over here from America, unless you're a big name band and you can make big bucks, you are losing money, and we weren't in a position to come over here and spend a lot of money and lose money. We almost booked a tour over [in America] and tried to promote over there, but then this tour came together and we prefer to do this." Poco served as the headliner for the tour and hoped to recoup some of their losses. ABC sent Elaine Corlett over to Europe to assist with the arrangements.

The tour opened in Scandinavia and Poco received good reviews. The *Swedish Daily News* wrote, "Poco delivers a genuine zest with their music that is healing. No funny stuff, no tricks, pure wonderful music. This is music that makes you happy." Dates in Norway, Holland, and Belgium followed. Poco's tour passed through Cologne, Germany, playing before 1,500 fans at the Sartory Saele. *NME* reviewer Tony Stewart observed, "The particularly favourable reviews their European tour has so far received have filled Young and the band with more confidence and optimism. They want to kill you dead." The addition of Al Garth was considered a benefit. "Once comfortable with their material, it's the front four who give the music so much of its melodic strength and character. Garth's fiddle (although he's not quite so hot on sax) is seldom less than superb, and perfectly compliments the gentle precision of Young's imaginative steel work." After a couple more shows in Germany, Poco headed across the channel for England.

While in England, Poco appeared on the *Old Grey Whistle Test*, performing *Too Many Nights Too Long* and *Rose of Cimarron*. It was a memorable performance, especially since they shared the stage with a superstar. Young explains, "I remember doing a TV show with Elton John in England during the ROSE OF CIMARRON era. The movie studio was like one of those vaudeville theatres, it had lots of chairs and there was no one in the audience, just the cameras. I remember sitting in the front row and watching Elton from five feet away, and he was such a sad little creature, I don't know what was going on in his life – he was there all by himself, no security, managers, and he sat down at the piano and played (sings)

What have I got to do to make you love me? It was just heartbreaking."

Although they headlined this particular tour, Poco didn't bring out big crowds. Poco's show at York University drew only 800, but had them dancing despite a restriction on it. The *Yorkshire Evening Press* noted, "Inevitably, they all came back for an encore with the audience itching to dance in the aisles. Even that wasn't enough. More hand-clapping and foot-stomping brought them on again for another ten minutes. Al Garth again winning the admiration of both band and audience with a stunning sax solo." An anonymous review claimed, "Poco's British tour was a modest triumph for a band which had seemed to be over the hill. After having achieved a brilliant sound on the *Old Grey Whistle Test*, they consolidated things by playing several well-received gigs around Britain. At Wolverhampton they drew an excellent response with many young fans rushing the stage waving posters. Their mix on some gigs left something to be desired and at Hammersmith our correspondent felt that they were at times out of tune and hard on the ear. But there was no denying a generally enthusiastic reception for favorites such as *Rose of Cimarron, Good Feelin' to Know* and *Hoedown*."

The experience was more positive for the band than the previous year's tour if only because there was no doubt that the crowds were there to see them. Jones recalls, "That was a great tour. Poco was very big over there. We did news conferences, drew good crowds, a very successful run." The Cate Brothers opened the British shows and were given short shrift in the music press. The highlight of the band's European set was a new song written by Rusty Young called *When the Dance is Over*. At least one reviewer felt that the song had all the ingredients to be the long-awaited hit single.

But the British music press also got a glimpse of what was going on behind the scenes with Poco. Tim Schmit admitted, "We are all very different. Sometimes I don't like the other members of the band. We don't hang out together when we're not recording or playing. It's like a marriage. The initial spark that brings a couple, or a band together, can never be the same as time goes on. It takes some time to attain something better. When I first joined the band, there were three or four times when I didn't know whether we were going to stay together or not." Schmit also offered his opinion on their new record, "We've always been better on stage than on album. I mean, ROSE OF CIMARRON is really well produced - we're beginning to bridge that gap now - but to be frank I don't think it's anything special."

After the jaunt in Europe, the band spent some time analyzing their year. They quickly realized that after nearly a year of promoting ROSE, they had failed to expand their base audience yet again. In response, they decided to jettison a member and lighten the load.

10
Livin' in the Band

Say what you want about tensions within the group and musical differences, by and large the four members of Poco managed to get along without much psychodrama. But 1976 had proved to be more of a challenge. Al Garth's presence upset the delicate balance within the group so upon their return to the States, Poco decided to let him go. It was a sudden move, especially since the critical view was that he had added so much to the band's live act. Hartmann and Goodman would only cite personality conflicts as the reason for Garth being let go. Grantham offers, "I think the thing with Al could have been just incredible. Such a player. But it just didn't gel right. No one to blame. It just didn't work like we thought it might." Cotton explains, "There were some internal issues with him, especially in Europe. He got really out of hand. He's since improved. He had some other issues as well." Others close to the band point out that Garth tended to be confrontational and occasionally embarrassed the group with public outbursts. Although his personality didn't fit in with the rest of the group, his musicianship played a big role in expanding Poco's musical options. However, since the year he'd spent with them had not resulted in an expansion of their audience, the group saw no reason to replace him.

In fact, the lull in the group's career led to widespread rumors late in 1976 that founder Richie Furay was about to rejoin Poco. When informed of the rumor by British journalist David Procktor, Paul Cotton was speechless. He stammered for a few seconds before making a rather weak statement, "Well, that's what it is, I guess, a rumor." Schmit's dumbfounded response was denial. "We haven't really talked to Richie," Schmit told *Crawdaddy*. "We never really considered it. I don't think any of us would really love to do that at this point." Tim Schmit later admitted that Furay's manager, Larry Larson, had contacted him to sound him out about Furay rejoining. Grantham was of a different mind, "Oh, I think it would have been wonderful. The other guys were more involved. That would have just meant there was more material to choose from and styles. I think the hard feelings had subsided."

Furay admitted at the time that a move was underway to have him rejoin. Poco manager John Hartmann had been in contact with Richie to determine his interest in coming back. "It happens about once a year," he confirmed in 1977. However, Furay insisted that Hartmann's offer was given without the band's knowledge while Furay considered it. When the offer came in 1976, Furay spent some time mulling it over. Furay was coming off a couple of tough years. The SHF Band had collapsed, his marriage was in trouble, he had converted to Christianity, and his first solo album, which celebrated that conversion, was trashed in the music press and ignored by fans. The thought of returning to the comfort of Poco was appealing. He even consulted Jimmy Messina about the offer. In the end, Furay realized that he could not go back. He called Hartmann and declined the offer. When news got to the group of their manager's offer to Furay, the band's confidence in their managers had been severely shaken.

Poco prepared for their next album desperate to give ABC a commercial record. Prior to leaving for Europe, Poco and ABC executives discussed their upcoming project, and the label requested that they consider working with new staff producer Roy Halee. Halee had made a name for himself working with Simon and Garfunkel. Halee was anxious to work with Poco and try to achieve their first big commercial success. While in Europe, Cotton explained to *Dark Star*, "ABC is submitting some more [outside material] to us. Roy Halee, who we intend to work with, has submitted some tunes. We want to make a very commercial album, something like five singles, no doubt about it." Poco took a two-week break after returning from England and then began rehearsals for the new album.

Among the new songs was a piece that Young was referring to in the press as a mini-Opry. "It'll be about 10 or 12 minutes long, and it's going to go through a lot of different changes, instrumental and other country things." Obviously not a potential single, the tune did indicate that creativity was not a problem for the band.

However, as Poco booked studio time, Halee proved to be un-available. Unwilling to postpone their recording sessions, Poco en-tered Burbank Studios with Harman again in December 1976. Because of the summer tour debacle and the lack of tour income, Poco was feeling the pressure to finish the album and get back on the road. "We're not the richest band in the world," explained Schmit. "We have to go out and work to keep our payments up."

From all accounts, these recording sessions were the most turbulent and unproductive in Poco's career. After three weeks it was clear that the album was not coming together. An atmosphere of tension and frustration forced the band to take a hiatus, hoping to forestall a breakup. A change in musical direction seemed to be the main issue as members tried to find a way to push Poco over the top. If ABC did submit any outside material to the band, it was not recorded. The band felt it had enough material to fill the album. Finally, after a considerable amount of soul searching, the group decided to get back to work. Discussion had been held about break-ing up. Schmit confirmed, "Because of a certain chain of events, we seriously talked it over." Instead, Poco returned to Burbank Studios in February 1977 and was finally able to complete the al-bum. The delay forced some live dates booked in March to be can-celed.

There was speculation over what caused the band to consider such a drastic move. It is clear that Young and Cotton were trying to stretch Poco's sound by trying a variety of musical style and ap-proaches. They openly talked of working on a project together out-side of Poco and even started writing for it. The pair copyrighted a piece of work called *Outlaw Blues, Parts 1 and 2*, in 1976. Tim Schmit's more traditional approach did not sit too well with his partners. Rusty Young makes it clear that he and Schmit were not on the best of terms. "Tim and I never got along. Tim never really was one of us. Whenever we'd tour, he'd hang out with the guys in the other band on the bill, like America." Cotton would later deri-sively comment that all Schmit wanted to do was write his Beach Boys songs and hang out. Still, there was enough of a commitment to try to push Poco into the top ranks of rock stardom. Schmit ex-plained shortly after the album's completion, "I know we're tal-ented enough to do other things but we'd like to 'make it' in the context of Poco." Grantham, intensely aware of the uncomfortable sessions that they had just completed, stated thoughtfully, "We have two albums left on our ABC contract. After that the four of us will sit down and take a long, friendly look at the situation. We've grown so close in 10 years together that I'd like to think we can come to an amicable agreement."

After delivering their new album to ABC, Poco went back on tour, focusing mainly in the East where their strength lay. During some extensive rehearsals, Poco added some of the new songs from their recently completed album to their live set. Unaware of the problems behind the scenes, Poco fans were thrilled by the new material, especially Cotton's tribute to Poco. Reviews were scarce, however, as the major media outlets barely acknowledged Poco's shows.

In May, ABC released INDIAN SUMMER. The title song opened the album. It was a mid-tempo Cotton cut with some special production and synthesizer effects with Steely Dan member Donald Fagen on ARP synthesizer and string ensemble. *Twenty Years* was also a Cotton song that featured some good guitar work and producer Mark Harman's piano work. The first Schmit song *Me and You* was pretty average stuff. Rusty Young's first contribution *Downfall* highlighted some wicked guitar lines and Young's increasingly confident lead vocals. Cotton's *Win or Lose*, a flat R & B piece rounded out the first side. Donald Fagen added some ARP string ensemble to the track.

The second side opened with Cotton's stirring tribute to Poco entitled *Living in the Band*. No one knew at the time how prophetic the last line would be. "*Living in the Band* is about my standing outside of that band and looking back," muses Cotton. "Fond memories and a lot of respect for those guys who have come and gone. I was allowed my 15 minutes and they gave me 27 years." Schmit's *Stay (Night Until Noon)* was co-written by his wife Noreen. *Find Out in Time* was Schmit's finest moment on the album, written with neighbor Robbin Thompson. All of these songs set the stage for the album's centerpiece. *The Dance* was Rusty Young's mini-Opry: a trilogy of songs, *When the Dance is Over, Go On and Dance*, and *Never Gonna Stop*, with a reprise of *When the Dance is Over*. The third segment was in a disco style with horns and a lead vocal by George Grantham. Grantham voiced some of the band's reaction to the song. "That was really out there. Very different. At first that seemed a little too far outside but I think we accepted it." But when Young announced he wanted Grantham to sing lead on the disco portion, Grantham's heart sank. "It worked pretty good for me because it was high and I was pretty comfortable singing in that range. But I hated it." Jimmie Haskell did the arrangement, and Sid Sharp played the Concert Master as the song built to a symphonic climax.

Cotton explains why INDIAN SUMMER's material was so inventive for Poco. "We had the hard rock, orchestra, disco, R 'n' B, changed producers, but no more or less than the Eagles at the time.

They had that pop door open, and we wanted to rock on in with the rest of them. The Eagles had gotten rockier and it was inevitable. We knew there was only so much you can do with country and it was bound to happen, especially after seven or eight albums."The band had high hopes for INDIAN SUMMER, but sales fell well below expectations. Despite some better chart action, INDIAN SUMMER did not better its predecessor in terms of records sold. So Hartmann and Goodman booked one leg of a summer tour with Poco opening for Dickie Betts and another leg opening for America. The return to opening act status was frustrating, but at least it kept the band in the public eye.

Poco opened for Dickie Betts in June before Hartmann and Goodman booked a summer long tour with their key clients on the bill. The double bill of Poco and America proved popular and gained Poco some complimentary reviews. Barry Patton of the *Bugle-American* bemoaned Poco having to open for the bland trio of America at the Summerfest in Milwaukee. "In a solid set [Poco] managed to touch material from eight of their eleven LPs. It was by far the most impressive set this reviewer has heard from the group." As the tour moved west, the band decided to start another live album. With their ABC contract nearing its end, another live album in the can would come in handy. They recorded shows at Red Rocks in Denver and at the Santa Monica Civic Auditorium on July 22. The Santa Monica Civic show was planned to be an event. A string section was hired again to play, and the band invited former leader Richie Furay to attend. Poco performed admirably, and when they swung into *Hoedown* for an encore, they called Furay out of the wings to join them. Frank Gavin in *Record World* wrote, "Pinnacle of the evening was Young's trilogy *The Dance* which threw all previous noted influences into a potpourri resulting in maximum feedback between band and audience, leaving everyone breathless for a well deserved encore." The live tapes were turned in to ABC at the conclusion of the tour.

An edited version of *Indian Summer/Me and You* became Poco's most successful single since 1975 when it was released in August 1977. It rose to #50 on the charts before stalling. Grantham did not agree with the choice for the single. "The obvious single never gets picked," he complained. "I think *Find Out in Time* should be the single now but management picked *Indian Summer*. I also think *Dallas* should have been a single but it never was. So who knows?"

INDIAN SUMMER sold much better than its predecessor and managed to get to #57 on the album charts. Rusty Young was disappointed that ABC wasn't able to provide more support for the album. "The week the album came out, ABC fired their president," sighs Young. "For two months there wasn't anyone to give the orders that could have helped the album. By then, it has lost all of its momentum." Jerry Rubinstein had actually resigned from his position as president at ABC Records over disputes with the company over direction. The label was rapidly losing money, and Rubinstein was not confident about the direction the company wanted to go. Sadly, although Rubinstein was one of Poco's biggest supporters on the label, his decision to leave and its timing hurt the band. Former roadie Vince Marchiolo bemoaned that after Rubinstein's resignation and the poor showing of INDIAN SUMMER, "ABC quickly thought of them as just another band."

The critical outlook on INDIAN SUMMER was not particularly supportive. However, Paul Cotton feels that the album didn't get the attention it deserved. "INDIAN SUMMER...I thought we had a better album than the Eagles' THE LONG RUN. I was so damned confident that we were going to blow them out of the water. But it didn't happen that way. But today, that song is my biggest royalty."

After the steady and successful summer tour and the mid-chart successes of both the single and the album, Poco's situation seemed to have solidified. INDIAN SUMMER appeared to be a return to normalcy in many ways. On the surface, the crisis that had arisen during recording had passed. But to the band, something was clearly happening. "I think the tour went fine," Cotton recalls. "Tim was off in 'Tim World' 'cuz he'd like to hang with the other acts rather than with us. So he would kind of disappear a lot, he'd be late, he wouldn't show up for sound checks. So that was a kind of indication something was up."

The band settled back home for a break with the possibility of a fall tour being negotiated by Hartmann and Goodman. Tim Schmit was busying himself in his music room in August when his phone rang and opportunity came calling.

Industry ad before band is forced to change its name, 1968.

Pogo takes the stage at Troubadour, 1968.

Messina back on bass at Newport Pop Festival, Devonshire Downs, 1969.

The Breed with Tim Schmit, Sacramento, CA, 1967.

Tim Schmit joins Poco, fall 1969.

Tim and Richie, Phoenix, AZ, September 23, 1969.

Paul Cotton (second from left) in Illinois Speed Press, 1970.

Paul Cotton and Poco at Queens College, NY, February 19, 1971.

Poco at Queens College, NY, February 19, 1971.

Poco at Capitol Theatre, Passaic, NJ, April 21, 1972.

Poco in RCA Studio, Hollywood with producer Jack Richardson, during CRAZY EYES sessions, 1973.

Furay consults with Grantham, Young, and Schmit during CRAZY EYES sessions.

Young and Cotton rehearse *Fool's Gold* in the studio.

Rusty Young plays standard guitar, Winterland, San Francisco, CA, March, 1974.

Paul Cotton trades riffs with Eric Clapton, Norfolk, VA, August 30, 1975.

Poco and America take a bow, European Tour, 1975.

Poco with Al Garth in tow, 1976.

Poco at Mountain Aire, Angels Camp, CA, June 13, 1976.

Tim Schmit's final show with Poco, Concord Pavilion, CA, July 31, 1977.

Paul Cotton and Charlie Harrison, LEGEND tour, 1979.

Rusty Young, LEGEND club tour, 1979.

Steve Chapman, LEGEND tour, 1979.

Kim Bullard, UNDER THE GUN tour, 1980.

Poco, UNDER THE GUN tour, 1980.

Rare promo poster for Ghost Town album, 1982.

Examples of the obscure venues during the
Ghost Town tour in 1983

Jeff Steele and Rusty at Kidnapper's, Charlotte, NC, September 1984.

Rick Seratte at Kidnapper's, Charlotte, NC, September 1984.

Jack Sundrud (2nd from left) in Podipto, 1969.

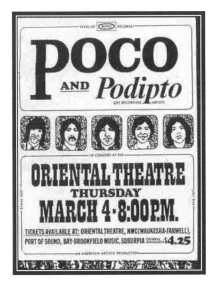

Ad from 1970 show when Podipto
opened for Poco in Milwaukee.

Poco rocks the Palomino with Rusty on Mellobar, May 24, 1985.

A curly-topped Jack Sundrud and Paul Cotton, Pittsburgh, PA, July 4, 1986.

Rusty Young and Steve Chapman, Pittsburgh, PA, July 4, 1986.

Paul and Rusty, Café Bene, NJ, July 25, 1987.

Messina and Young in Pittsburgh, PA, July 21, 1990.

Randy Meisner, Pittsburgh, PA, July 21, 1990.

George Grantham, Pittsburgh, PA, July 21, 1990.

Concert poster from Japan tour 1990.
Paul Cotton was listed and then crossed out.

Poco at Club Bene, NJ, September 24, 1992. Richard Neville on bass.

Poco at EuroDisney, Paris, October 31, 1996.

George Grantham sings harmony with Jack Sundrud in the background, Gulfstream Park, Hallandale, FL, February 24, 2001.

Jack Sundrud and George Grantham.   Rusty on bass.

Both photos taken at Fairfax Park, Commerce City, CO, July 4, 2001.

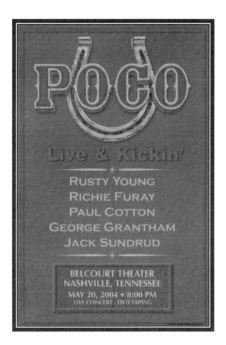

Poster for the DVD concert filming at the Belcourt Theatre, Nashville, 2004.

Poco with Richie Furay at Belcourt Theatre during soundcheck for the DVD filming, May 20, 2004.

Poco at the Fillmore, San Francisco, CA, August 7, 2007. George Lawrence's first show with Poco after George Grantham's stroke.

George Lawrence at Sylvia Theatre, York, SC, October 1, 2007.

The Wildwood Springs Lodge, Steelville, MO, 40th Reunion show, October 2, 2008.

Rusty and Richie harmonize behind Jim Messina vocals.

11
The Last Goodbye

Tim Schmit was in the right place at the right time. He explains, "I got a phone call, and the timing was right for me. I remember I was becoming disillusioned as a member of Poco because we seemed to have stalled out. We weren't in so much demand. Our record sales were going down. We weren't making that much money. I was just starting to open my mind to the possibility of other options when I got a call from Glenn Frey. He said, 'Randy Meisner is quitting.' And I just said, 'If this is an invitation, say no more. I'm in. Where do you want me? What do you want me to do?'"

Frey provided him with the details and Schmit set about telling his band mates. "He told me first," Cotton says. "He called and said, 'Paulie, I'm coming over.' He came over in his Beemer and said the Eagles wanted him in the band. I told him, 'Go for it!' like my guys in the Speed Press had told me. That was it." It was clear that it was an offer too good to pass up. Grantham recalls the moment he heard the news. "I remember one night, in the middle of the night, the phone rang and I picked up the phone, and Tim said, 'George, I've been asked to join the Eagles and I think I'm gonna do it.' I was shocked but I think we'd heard rumors of that anyway." The Eagles' deal was a sweet one for Schmit. They offered him a full partnership in the band, making it incredibly lucrative.

Surprisingly, Poco manager John Hartmann heard the news not from Schmit, but from Eagle manager Irving Azoff. Hartmann met with the remaining members of Poco to determine the band's course of action. With Tim Schmit now a member of the Eagles, Paul Cotton and Rusty Young came to the conclusion that Poco was a dead issue. It was just the excuse they were looking for to move on. They decided to work on a separate project together. The pair abruptly announced their decision to George Grantham, who had no choice but to look for other work. Grantham claims he never saw it coming. "I thought that we'd continue on because we always had. But next thing you know, I was looking for work." Young and Cotton informed Hartmann that they intended to start a new band and put Poco to rest.

Rumors of the move by Schmit started hitting the press in September. In November, Hartmann and Goodman finally made the announcement that confirmed that Schmit had left to join the Eagles. They also announced that with Schmit's departure, Poco was breaking up. To satisfy the remaining two albums left on their ABC contract, Hartmann and Goodman revealed that a final Poco album would be released in early 1978. A double live album entitled THE LAST ROUNDUP was put together from the dates recorded on their last tour. Poco's management promised that among the tracks would be Richie Furay's appearance with Poco at the Santa Monica Civic Auditorium in July.

Young and Cotton helped with the mix of the live tapes in the fall of 1977 and delivered the master tapes to ABC shortly after the announcement of Schmit's departure. Test pressings of THE LAST ROUNDUP were produced and received a limited distribution. The album reveals that Poco was on the verge of finally getting their live act to sound full and textured with only the four of them onstage, due in no small part to the post-production work the band did in the studio. The version of THE LAST ROUNDUP that made it to the test pressing stage opened with *Living in the Band*, followed by *Dallas, Magnolia, Honky Tonk Downstairs, PNS (When You Come Around), Sagebrush Serenade, Indian Summer, Too Many Nights Too Long, Starin' at the Sky, Twenty Years, The Dance, Keep on Tryin'*, and *Rose of Cimarron*. The performances were top-notch, especially the songs that featured the string section.

Hartmann and Goodman's press release also contained a startling revelation. While Poco would cease to exist, a new entity would emerge in 1978, the Cotton-Young Band. No other information was provided since at the time of the announcement there was only Cotton and Young in the band. The concept for the new group was somewhat nebulous at first. Cotton explains, "We thought that we would do what Fleetwood Mac did with the girl singers. We ended up doing some demos with Rosemary Butler, esteemed studio singer, who charged us triple scale! She was a friend of Rusty's. [Laughs.] These were demos, not even a record. We tried her on a couple songs, but we decided that wasn't what we wanted."

With the group now down to just the two of them, Young and Cotton were unsure of the support they had for their new venture. Young recalled, "We went to the label, and we said, 'Listen, do we still have a record deal? It's just Paul and me.' And they said, 'Maybe, bring us some material. Let us hear what you guys are going to do.'" Cotton and Young put out the word that they were looking for musicians and hoped for the best.

The Cotton-Young Band began to hold auditions in December 1977 at the Cat and Dog Rehearsal Studio in Los Angeles. Cotton and Young were looking for musicians that would help them move in a different direction than Poco. The Cotton-Young Band auditions quickly attracted the attention of a pair of energetic Englishmen. Charlie Harrison had played bass with Roger McGuinn's Thunderbyrd the previous year until McGuinn disbanded the group to work with ex-Byrd Gene Clark. Harrison came to Poco through a connection he'd made while in Thunderbyrd. Harrison explains, "The roadie from Poco whose name was Lew Llewellen, he was a Welsh chap, was sharing a house with this guy who was a roadie with Roger named Stan Quantrill. So that's how I knew about the gig. I'd carry on with Lewie, 'Come on, Lewie. Get me in there. Us British lads got to stick together!' 'Oh, I will man but...[mumbles].' Finally, I beat it out of him and called up and it was really cool."

Harrison showed up at the appointed time at Cat and Dog rehearsal studio in Los Angeles. After some quick introductions, Young and Cotton started out by playing a song of Paul Cotton's entitled *Barbados*. Harrison recalls, "That bass line that ended up on the record is the first thing I played. Paul really liked it and I think that sealed the deal." The pair was pleased with the results and turned their attention to a new drummer.

Among those auditioning were two Brits Steve Chapman and Ian Wallace. After both Chapman and Wallace played, Harrison was surprised when Young and Cotton asked him who he thought was better. "Steve and I at that point had been a rhythm section for about 11 years, 12 years," boasts Harrison. "We'd got something pretty good happening. So that was it. I said Steve." Cotton smiled when recalling, "Ah yes, the inseparable Englishmen. We didn't find out until later that they had played together for years."

The pair auditioned a couple of female vocalists including Cecilia Bullard. The main goal was to replace the high harmony vocals of Grantham in the new band, however they weren't sure if this was truly the right solution.　Husband Kim Bullard recalls, "She had auditioned for [the Cotton-Young Band] and they loved her. They were going to go with that, and she was going to be the singer in that band." After several auditions, they decided to defer the decision until after they received a commitment from ABC on the project.

Young and Cotton welcomed their new band mates to the band.　As they began their first rehearsals, Young and Cotton were delighted that both Harrison and Chapman were familiar with Poco music.　The mutual respect was immediate and energizing.　"These guys are real players," Cotton explains, "not singers first, then players, but players all the way."　Young agreed, "They're musicians first, I think, and singers second.　In fact, Steven's not a singer.　For us, that's good, because before the guys were singers first and musicians second.　Paul and I were musicians.　I think that's why this works better for us."　But Cotton notes, "They weren't great singers, which put a lot of pressure on me and Rusty to sing everything."

The quartet rehearsed intently for a few days and went into the Wally Heider studio on December 26, 1977, to cut a three-song demo that included *Barbados*.　Young and Cotton took the demos to ABC and found them somewhat reluctant.　ABC staffers told Young and Cotton that while they liked what they heard, they wanted one last Poco album before committing to a Cotton-Young Band.　It was simply a matter of economics. The label felt it could promote and sell a well-known band like Poco, but launching a new act was risky.　There was also the matter of advances that the company had paid the band but had not recouped.　Rather than take the loss or attempt legal action, ABC hoped that a successful new album could at least get Poco back to even.

Faced with this reality, Young and Cotton reluctantly agreed to give ABC a new Poco album.　They invited Grantham back and placed Chapman on retainer, telling him that he'd have to wait until after they were finished with the album before the Cotton-Young Band would get started.　Grantham returned excited and anxious to continue with Poco.　He settled in to rehearse for a new album.　From a musical perspective, things went fairly well from the outset, but Grantham soon found that the situation within Poco had changed during his brief absence.

According to Grantham, the problem mainly concerned business arrangements and his new standing in relation to Cotton and Young.　Grantham had been a full partner in Poco prior to the breakup. When he returned, Cotton and Young informed him that there were going to be changes. Grantham recalls, "Some changes were being made that were nothing like the way Poco had handled it in the past, and I wasn't too thrilled about it and Paul wasn't thrilled about my not being thrilled about it. One of the things we had in Poco was a group effort publishing thing. So we all shared in the publishing, the whole group. That was really rare. So, at this time for some reason, everyone was sort of going their own way as far as what they wrote...it was theirs. It was not a group thing anymore, and that really upset me and that upset Paul that I was upset. It just turned into a business deal, you know. And unfortunately, I didn't get to do that album with them. I would have loved to have done it."

Unable to resolve the problem to Grantham's satisfaction and unwilling to share their publishing, the trio decided to part company for good. Young and Cotton borrowed money from ABC and purchased Grantham's interest in the Poco name. Now clear of past entanglements, Cotton and Young resumed rehearsals in Los Angeles in an even deeper financial hole than before. While business dealings had fouled the situation, Rusty Young cited other problems for Grantham's not rejoining the band. "George was having personal problems, as I remember," Young said, "He had gone through a divorce. He needed time to himself."

Roughly three days after being told he'd have to wait, Steve Chapman returned to the band. Since ABC didn't seem to be too interested in supporting a Cotton-Young Band anyway, Young and Cotton decided to remain Poco with the new rhythm section. It also made sense from a business perspective since there was a built-in, although limited, audience for Poco and no proven audience at all for a Cotton-Young Band. The decision to remain Poco also put an end to the idea of a female vocalist.

It didn't take the pair long to figure out that working with Harrison and Chapman would take their music into a different direction. Young remarked, "Well, Steven and Charlie, I think, really made the difference in the album and had a great deal to do with its success. That's because I think in the past we've had four or five guys with the same influences and backgrounds. I think the varied background that Steven and Charlie bring to our music is what makes it gel."

The group worked up more new tunes in rehearsal and set up a showcase with their new members to see if ABC was still interested. "We played *Heart of the Night* and *Crazy Love*," Young remembered. "We played four of five new songs for them and said, 'This is what we want to do. This is where we're going.' and they recognized, I think, that *Crazy Love* and *Heart of the Night* were hit records, even in a rehearsal situation and so they said, 'Yeah, go make a record.'"

With Cotton and Young's decision to remain Poco, ABC scrapped the farewell LAST ROUNDUP live album. The new version of Poco would fulfill their contract with two new albums of music. The LAST ROUNDUP remained one of the band's legendary unreleased albums until its debut in 2004. Young has steadfastly distanced himself from the project. "I hope they never find it," he said dismissively. Young's statement was made years later after subsequent events led to his desire to make sure that ABC's successors never had the opportunity to profit from the album. They also scrapped the idea of a female vocalist and informed those that had auditioned that they weren't needed.

After months of rehearsals, Poco entered Crystal Studio in April 1978 to cut their first album with the new lineup. They also used a new producer, Richard Sanford Orshoff, who had produced Jackson Browne's debut album. Cotton and Young gave him unprecedented say in what songs were included on the album. "It was the first time we let a producer choose the material for one of our albums," said Young.

Orshoff had been out of the production business for a few years and had recently decided to get back into it. His agent had contacted ABC Records and they set up a meeting with Poco. Orshoff recalls, "They were rehearsing and I went in and listened to them play two or three of their songs, and they wanted my production ideas for those songs."

He soon realized that he wanted something different from Poco in terms of the recording sessions. "I felt that we had to do something different other than the same mode because that mode seemed to produce 300 to 400 [thousand] sales and we wanted to kick that up." Cotton and Young liked what they heard and agreed to work together. But Orshoff threw the band a curve immediately when he confronted them on their recording schedule. "They were used to recording 12-14 hours a day. So I told them what I was hearing [in their previous albums] and that they were playing, playing, playing, and it was losing feeling. So I told them I wanted to record seven to eight hours a day, five days a week. I wanted not only a musical beauty but a recording polish – something that would grab people's attention. And they thought I was crazy. They said, 'That's not how you make an album!'"

It made for a sometimes difficult process since Young and Cotton had produced themselves for several years and felt that they knew how to make an album. However, it didn't take the band long to realize that the results Orshoff was getting were proving to be worthwhile. Orshoff spent quite a bit of time and effort in working with the band to polish the material before recording. "We sat around and I said, 'Ok, here are some ideas of what I would do here and here and here.' Maybe on one I'd suggest, 'Put a chorus in here instead of waiting for a second verse. It takes too long to get to the hook.' Or 'This section is too busy.' I vividly remember having conversations with them about the music and what to do with it."

Cotton and Young considered including some traditional Poco-sounding material that ultimately remained in the can. "We cut some country tunes but we didn't put 'em on the album," Young recalls. "We cut a lot of tunes and then chose the ones we thought fit the concept we were looking for in an album. We considered over 50 of our own tunes." Chapman claims the material actually sorted itself out. He recalls that the band did consider a cover tune, Little Feat's *It's So Easy to Slip*. "Rusty played some scorching pedal steel on it," raved Chapman. "But we didn't get around to putting vocals on it before abandoning it."

Because Orshoff wanted short days with weekends off, the sessions were long, running until August at Crystal Studio and another month for overdubs at Village Recorders. The slow pace was also dictated by the fact that the band was never sure how committed ABC was to the project. Chapman explains the leisurely pace. "There was no pressure so we took our time. If something wasn't working, we'd just go see a movie!" This lack of drive to finish the album allowed Poco to consider the large amount of material that it did, but the sessions wound up costing a fortune. Still, the band didn't seem too concerned since there was a big question mark in their minds that ABC was all that interested in their new album.

As the sessions progressed, the band used session keyboardists Jai Winding, Tom Stephenson, and Michael Boddicker on many of the tracks, and British saxophonist Phil Kenzie on a couple of tracks. While many considered the additional musicians to be a product of Orshoff's production designs, he recalls differently, "Based on how I produced, which was to try to help the band make the best record of their music, it was their idea." Cotton recalls, "We went to the wall with him on everything. Each one of us. OD'd on vitamins, I think. He was always dipping in this big, brown bag every day. Things got really weird and he ended up teeing every one of us off at some point. But he knew somebody at the record company where he could get whatever it took money-wise to make the album. It probably ended up about $80 grand extra, which was a lot."

Once the recording and mixing were complete, Poco sat back and waited as it took ABC three months to release the album. This

delay further solidified the band's feeling that ABC was not interested in the band any longer.

The album finally appeared in November. LEGEND featured a
stunning and memorable cover by Phil Hartmann. It was a black
line drawing of a horse on a white background. Hartmann explained, "It almost has a Picasso feel to it. I remember that Rusty
Young, the lead singer of the band, said, 'I want you to draw a
horse for the song *Legend*, which is about a phantom spirit horse. I
want you to do it in several lines.' I ended up doing it in 22 lines
and that was as simple as I could make it and still capture the essence I wanted. I drew the image maybe 20 times, until I came up
with the cover that I'm very proud of." The durable design continues to be used by the band.

With regard to promotion, it was curious that ABC included no
photo of the new Poco in the package. That would seem to confirm
the band's feeling that LEGEND was likely to be Poco's final album.
Regarding the title, Young told BBC Radio, "We were looking for a
strong title. Our music has strength now it never did before, and it
conveys that strength."

A strong rhythm-oriented song by Cotton entitled *Boomerang*
opened LEGEND. It was an instant attention-grabber. Trademark
Poco harmonies and acoustic guitars appeared on Young's ballad
Spellbound. Keyboards had never been a consistent feature of the
Poco sound, but Orshoff used them tastefully on this and subsequent
album cuts. More of a departure was Cotton's *Barbados*. This Car-
ibbean-flavored tune had been written several years previously, but
Cotton did not feel it fit Poco. Originally cut as a demo for the Cot-
ton-Young Band, Cotton decided to keep it for this Poco album.
Young's steel guitar added some nice touches. Young's *Little Darlin'*
was a pleasant piece of fluff, and the side ended with *Love Comes,
Love Goes* which featured trade-off lead vocals by Cotton and
Young.

Side two opened with one of Cotton's finest songs, *Heart of
the Night*. It showcased some outstanding sax by British musician
Phil Kenzie and a soaring arrangement. Young added some tasty
steel that made the track. Young told *Omaha Rainbow*, "*Heart of
the Night* is my perfect example. It could easily have been another
Poco country tune, right down that old country road, but Charlie
and Steven picked it up and they made it something else. They
made it contemporary, a musical style that's not so standardized as
the country format we've had for a long time." A nice acoustic
number from Young, *Crazy Love*, followed. More than any other
track, *Crazy Love* showed that those high, ringing harmonies were
still present in the latest version of Poco, thanks in large part to

bassist Charlie Harrison. Orshoff had insisted that this arrangement be used, as opposed to the all acoustic version he'd heard in rehearsals. "*Crazy Love* originally was an acoustic song all the way when they first played it for me – just acoustic guitars and vocals. And I said, 'I think you've got a big record here, but it's not going to fly if it's just acoustic. We need to put the band in there. Let's bring them in at the middle.'" The outstanding *The Last Goodbye* by Young boasted a stirring arrangement and more trade-off lead vocals between Cotton and Young. Poco closed the album with one of their best rockers, *Legend*. The title track was written by Young but sung by Cotton.

Chapman explains that the version of *Legend* on the album went through quite a few arrangements. "We tried a lot of different things. We'd rehearse songs, we'd work on arrangements, and then we might go into the studio and try something completely different. The song *Legend* went through many incarnations before it came out like it did. There were several versions that were actually recorded. Then we'd listen and say, 'Nah, that didn't work.' So we'd take another run at it with a whole different feel and arrangement." Paul Cotton concurs, "There were two or three things we cut but didn't use because they didn't fit the format." It is unclear whether these tracks were subsequently used on later Poco albums or remain unreleased.

Upon delivery of the album, ABC knew it had a good one on its hands and after a month released *Crazy Love/Barbados* as a single. For the first time, a Poco single really took off. It climbed up as high as #17 before falling. Suddenly Poco was news. Young explains why the single was a hit. "We had a lot of friends in the radio industry," Young expounds. "By 1979, these guys were in positions of program directors or music directors and they were happy to play Poco records." Despite the success, Orshoff feels that ABC really dropped the ball for a more prolonged success for Poco by choosing *Crazy Love* as the initial single. "This album barely hit the streets, and FM radio stations all over the country jumped on *Heart of the Night*. By the second week, before a single was released, there was 88 percent FM radio saturation on *Heart of the Night*. But what we didn't know at the time was that ABC Records was in the process of being purchased by MCA, and so I think the A&R department thought their jobs were on the line and they wanted a quick hit. And so I got a call saying that they were going with *Crazy Love*. And I said, 'No, no, no...you've got 88 percent of the FM station in the country on *Heart of the Night*.' 'No, we'll release *Heart of the Night* as the second single.' 'You already have a hit record!' So we argued and they released *Crazy Love*."

Another explanation for the band's newly found success was the new blood that their British members brought to a tired band. Praise for the Brits came at the expense of former Poco members. Young boasted, "They were just the kind of guys I've always wanted to play with - not putting Tim or George down - but you never have to teach Charlie a bass part. Charlie knows how a bass part should be and he comes up with a better bass part than I could think of. Steven comes up with really original drum parts and good dynamic things. George is a great drummer, he's really good and he's not one where you had to show him parts as we did with other musicians who've been in our band."

Despite the glowing accolades heaped on their new rhythm section, it was clear after listening to LEGEND that although ABC insisted on calling the band Poco, it was really the Cotton-Young Band concept at work. Neither Chapman nor Harrison wrote any of the group's material, and they clearly had little to say about the direction of the band. They were more hired hands than members of the band. Neither Cotton nor Young was too concerned about that. They were finally able to produce the music that they wanted to without input from anyone else. When the public responded so well, especially with disco in full swing and punk rock on the horizon, the pair ran with it.

Poco was more than ready to take advantage of the break. As the album began to creep up the charts, manager John Hartmann approached keyboardist Kim Bullard during the CSN tour. Bullard remembers, "I remember we were at Pine Knob with Crosby, Stills and Nash, and John Hartmann said, 'This Poco record looks like it might do something. They need a keyboard player. Are you interested in doing it?' and I said, 'Yeah.'" Initially, Young and Cotton held back from touring until they could see if the album was taking off. When Poco decided to go on the road, Bullard came along and seemed to fit in perfectly. After 10 days of rehearsals in December, Poco went out on a tour of small clubs, booked to reestablish themselves. Having been off the road for nearly a year, Poco needed to re-connect with their fans. "We chose to [play clubs] because we wanted first of all to play together," Young grinned. "This two sets a night, every night, really gives you a chance to play together and learn to play together in front of an audience where it really counts, which is much different than rehearsing. This is a real low-key production, and if we're not good, nothing else is going to carry us."

The new Poco sound was certainly different from past incarnations of the band, and the band struggled how best to capture it live. Chapman observed, "Rusty and Paul wanted to do some from the new record to showcase it, but they also wanted to do some old stuff. But the question was what old stuff worked; were they only going to do their songs? Were they going to do Richie's songs? And with the vocal thing, which was different. I didn't sing. Charlie sang and so did Kim Bullard, who had joined on keyboards by that point. Anyway, the way that Charlie and Kim sang was totally different from how Tim and George sang. George had that amazing high voice. So Rusty and Paul had to figure out what songs worked with this lineup. So the set tended to be somewhat top heavy with newer stuff when we first went out. As we started playing more, they began bringing more songs from way back, starting to play more of them."

Eventually satisfied with the set they had finally worked up, the band was ready to hit the road. Management booked Poco into a couple of small clubs in Colorado for warm-up shows to let the new lineup get its act together. Colorado was still a hotbed of support for the band. Tour manager Denny Jones returned after a year's absence to oversee the road work. "We toured all the way from February 1979 through the summer. We started playing clubs. It was like Poco starting over again." After a week of shows, the new Poco embarked on an eastern swing of club dates in March. After the absence of a year on the tour circuit, critics were both curious and kind. By the time they played the Bottom Line in New York City late in March, *Crazy Love* had hit and Poco sold out both shows. The early part of the tour had been less than enjoyable since the band all fought colds throughout the first three weeks. The dates in Philadelphia had to be cancelled in order for the band to be able to play the prestigious New York dates. Poco fans nearly fainted when the band took the stage and Rusty Young stood at center stage instead of taking his usual place behind his steel guitar. Although Young spent most of the set playing electric and acoustic six-string, he did take up the steel for Cottons *Heart of the Night*. The band's encore was a tune written by Cotton entitled *Two Trains* that the band never recorded. Chapman recalls enthusiastically, "It was a great song. For whatever reason we never recorded...well, we might have tried to record it. Maybe it didn't work well on a pop record, but it was a real good rocking live tune!"

This change in Poco's lineup and performance style was something that Young was excited about. "I really don't enjoy sitting down and playing pedal steel all night long," complained Young, "because it's only one facet of what I do. To me, I play straight ahead country steel guitar on maybe three or four songs in the set...to me that's plenty. As an entertainer, I really enjoy singing and standing upfront, because I never had to do it before." Jones recalls, "Having Kim Bullard on keyboards was unique. Poco never had keyboards before. The sounds had to come from the Leslie. That freed up Rusty, and Rusty basically became the leader of the band. He wasn't playing that much steel. He was playing more guitar and banjo - a lot of that he learned from John Logan, - and stand up more."

Amid Poco's good fortune, corporate upheaval put a damper on their success. MCA purchased ABC Records in March while the band was on their club tour. MCA Records gutted the ABC staff, firing nearly everyone. Although MCA president Steve Miner assured the music press that MCA was committed to ABC acts, the news affected *Crazy Love's* chart performance. "It hurt the single," claims Young. "It stopped the single. It was number one on the MOR charts for seven straight weeks. What happened was that when MCA bought ABC, which it was for the single, because there were hard feelings in a lot of places the way the change came down." The takeover of ABC by MCA had far-reaching effects for the band, of which the single's performance was just the start.

A second single began a similar climb up the charts in May. MCA pulled *Heart Of The Night/The Last Goodbye* off the album, and it soared up to #20 for a strong follow-up. But Richard Orshoff felt it could have been better. "FM stations, when ABC released *Crazy Love*, said, 'Hey, we're already on *Heart of the Night*. If you release *Crazy Love*, we aren't going back on *Heart of the Night* as a second single.' And that's why there wasn't a second hit single on that album. If they had done it the other way 'round, I honestly think *Crazy Love* would have been a number one record. Because *Heart of the Night* would have paved the way with that breakthrough saturation, and then the big hit would have followed it up."

Poco produced promo films for both singles. Each showed the group on stage performing and made use of subtle props and theatrical lighting. Kim Bullard doubled on Phil Kenzie's sax solo, rather than hire someone to portray him in the film. These clips were used for promotional opportunities and the rare TV appearance.

Along with the release of their second single, Poco moved west with their club tour. After a performance in Atlanta, Poco took a short break and began playing gigs on the West Coast. They played the Old Waldorf in San Francisco, the Roxy in Los Angeles, and the Irvine Bowl. Denny Jones contends that *Heart of the Night* was a very strong regional hit. "I remember one of the last shows I did with them was in Caspar, Wyoming. They played it in the set and had people drooling. They made them play it again as an encore. It was one of the biggest selling rock hits in the history of the city. It was number one for 12 weeks. Huge, huge, huge. They made them play it, it was a snowy night, and girls were crying."

But it wasn't long before the opportunities afforded the group thanks to the hit single began to beckon. A tour of Europe was scheduled prior to the release of LEGEND, but Poco canceled it to concentrate on more lucrative bookings in the States. Young explained their reasoning during their stand at the Old Waldorf in San Francisco. "We had the month of June booked over there. Well, this is the end of April now; *Heart of the Night* will be out in May. It will take about three weeks for it to really start charting high. By June I expect it to be in the Top Forty and with a Top Forty single happening here, we want to be here and promote it." On their previous visit to England, Poco had mentioned the increased costs to a band such as theirs and how difficult it was to make any sort of money unless a mega-tour had been booked. Unfortunately for European Poco fans, the tour was never rescheduled.

Crazy Love and *Heart of the Night's* chart performances dictated that the band tour during the lucrative summer season. They performed on a series of package bills with heavy metal bands such as Boston and Van Halen. It was not the best mix of acts. At a performance at the Miami Stadium in Miami, Florida, in May, a rowdy fan threw something on stage that narrowly missed hitting Rusty Young. Disgusted, Young unplugged and left the stage, ending Poco's set that day at three songs. Bullard's memory of the incident still angers him. "That was really a disgusting gig. That was us, the Doobie Brothers, and Boston. The show was running really late so people were getting hot, very hot. It was very muggy and hot down there. We finally got on stage, and people were restless and they wanted to see the other bands. A lot of people wanted to see us, but there were some people had waited all day to see Boston or the Doobie Brothers. So some people were throwing stuff onstage and something came close to hitting Rusty. So instead of being a professional and realizing that you have a lot of fans out there and there's a lot of potential record buyers there and just bite the bullet and keep playing, he decided to walk off after like two songs. 'I can't play!' A real prima donna thing. That was a real morale buster there."

A few days later in Raleigh, North Carolina, a crowd of Marines and fans chanting for Van Halen convinced the band to shorten their set, choosing only their rock and uptempo numbers. Chapman explains, "We did this Raleigh thing. It was really a rock and roll crowd. It wasn't a country-rock crowd, you know what I mean? I can't remember if it was Boston or the Doobie Brothers, but there were a lot of Marines or GI's. We definitely got the sense that it was more of a rock and roll crowd, so we only had to play 30 or 40 minutes so we tailored the set to make it really rock out. I think we did an extended version of *Boomerang*. Really rocked it out."

Billboard's Kip Kirby reviewed their May 31 show at the Tennessee Theatre in Nashville. "The headliners took the stage to a wildly deafening roar and proceeded to unleash some deafening sounds of its own. Its hour-plus set displayed solid, often brilliant musicianship and proved that the legendary magic is still present. Its traditional country-rock sound has evolved into a sort of country-metal energy, occasionally turning into a wall of instrumentation as Cotton and Young exchanged fiery riffs."

The summer did have some challenges. Hartmann and Goodman offered Poco as a free act to the Cotton Carnival in Memphis on June 1. The gig got off on the wrong foot when the crew realized it was a union gig and they hadn't been notified. Denny Jones recalls, "It was a union hall and the costs were prohibitive. We couldn't do this or we couldn't do that. And we didn't know in advance. Remember, this was before faxes and cell phones. Our only contact with management was a pay phone and a land line." Poco's crew created additional problems by tearing down the sponsoring radio station's logo from the front of the stage. After a half hour of angry exchanges, Poco agreed to pay for the sign. According to radio station personnel, Poco's set was sloppy and uninteresting. The next week at the program director's conference call, Poco's attitude was a main topic of discussion, and many program directors followed the lead of the sponsor in banning airplay for subsequent Poco releases.

Despite the few bumps in the road, Poco did do their share of headlining dates in 1979. Jones recalls, "That was a huge tour. It was one of the three biggest touring years for Poco. We had the excitement of the record. Every week I'd call *Billboard* and then report to the guys, 'It's gone to #18, the single is moving up!' It was so exciting!" The venues changed as Poco found themselves more in demand. Small clubs gave way to larger halls. Originally, Poco planned to have McGuinn, Clark and Hillman open up for their summer tour, but changed their minds. The summer tour took Poco to Belmont Park, Giants Stadium, and Kiel Opera House in St. Louis in June. Later in August, they played the Merriweather Post Pavilion in Washington D.C., the Music Inn in Lenox, Massachusetts, as well as the popular Red Rocks in Denver. Poco fans, not having seen the group live since September 1977, were enthusiastic in their response. Mike Joyce of the Washington *Post*, in his review of their show at the Post Pavilion, noted that Young's "boyish tenor blended nicely with Cotton's husky vocals and striking solo work on lead guitar. Later, on the first of two encores, Young delighted the rain-soaked crowd with a flat-out bluegrass breakdown on five-string banjo. It's not the kind of music that will ever make the Top Forty, but it certainly has made a lot of friends for Poco along the way."

Poco opened its fall tour with two shows at the Dr. Pepper Central Park Music Festival on August 3 and 4. Rain threatened their opening show but the remaining crowd was thrilled. *Variety* remarked, "Poco's performance was totally absorbing and multi-faceted. At one moment they would have a pop sound, the next moment a forceful rock sound with Young and Cotton playing dueling guitars." *Good Times* gave them a positive review and stated, "Poco the band will always belong to a large segment of New York's music fans."

At the Garden State Arts Center in Holmdel, New Jersey, Poco had *Aquarian* reviewer Bill Chemerka gushing, "One of the few country-rock groups equally as effective on ballads and uptempo numbers, Poco displayed its chops with style during the unseasonably cool evening. The combination of *Rose of Cimarron* with the current album's title tune, which showcased Rusty Young's incredible talent on steel guitar, was the most powerful part of the show."

On August 25, Poco played familiar territory when they returned to Red Rocks Amphitheatre in Denver. Founder Richie Furay joined the band for their encore. Kim Bullard remarks, "I recall Richie being at Red Rocks at one point and doing *Good Feeling to Know*, and he shook the house down! He has such a powerful voice." After the show, Furay admitted that he was thrilled for Poco and the newfound success. "There was never any doubt that the quality was there all along. I'm glad they've survived in whatever form."

Poco's new record label released an unprecedented third single in September. Having already released a ballad and a midtempo tune for singles, MCA opted for *Legend*, the only true rocker on the album. Unfortunately, the fire beneath Poco had pretty much gone out. *Legend* barely charted at #103.

The fall tour ended in August, and the band went their separate way for a short time. Harrison was headed back to his home in England. Before he left, he voiced his frustrations to Young. "I think I was making $250, $300 a week, and I was getting tired of this hired hand stuff and I said to Rusty, 'I've thought about this and I'm not being a jerk or anything but what I want to do is get equal artist royalties or one song per record.' He said, 'Not a chance on the song on the record. It's just me and Paul, that's it. Me and Paul talked about this before we started this and I'm tired of it.' Then he said, 'I don't really see management going for it.'" Having essentially quit the band, Harrison headed home.

When he arrived in England, Harrison met up with guitarist Tim Renwick. Sutherland Brothers and Quiver was winding down and Renwick had plans for a solo album. They rehearsed and did some recording. Renwick planned to do the bulk of the recording in Barbados and offered Harrison $1,000 to participate. In the meantime, Harrison had heard of auditions with Mick Jones, and he went around to play with him. Jones was impressed enough to offer Harrison a position in Foreigner.

Meanwhile back in the States, Poco was asked to participate in the historic M.U.S.E. (No Nukes) concert series at Madison Square Garden. They were invited after running into their former lighting director Tim Sexton while on tour in New Jersey. Young called up Harrison and asked him to come back to play the date. Harrison recalls, "Rusty rang me out of the blue and said, 'We're doing the No Nukes thing at Madison Square Garden in New York, and it's going to be a live album. It's really a drag we haven't got you here, we miss you real bad.' I said, 'Well, I told you my situation.' Rusty said, 'Well, like I said, writing is out, Charlie. Tell you what, would you come back and do the Madison Square Garden? Paul and I have talked to management but we'll figure something out.' I got paid, I can't remember, but I got paid a pretty damned good price for it."

With Harrison back in the band, Poco played the No Nukes show on September 23. The band was second billed to Crosby, Stills and Nash. They were recorded live as part of the project, and a live version of *Heart Of The Night* was placed on the Christmas release of the album NO NUKES. "That thing went platinum!" Cotton exclaims. "That's the most money I'd ever made in 20 minutes." Phil Kenzie joined them on stage to perform his sax solo. Young muses, "I'm real proud that we were involved with that project. Tim Sexton, who's the guy who got Tim [Schmit] into movies, was the musical director of No Nukes and he's our old lighting director and he invited us to be involved in that project." Poco played a modest 30-minute set before a rowdy, anxious crowd waiting for the "reunion" of CSN. Bullard smiles, "Yeah, that was a lot of fun. I remember we were there the first night and saw Tom Petty and Bruce Springsteen play, and then my wife was with me and we went backstage. I ran into Bruce and talked to him a little bit. It was his birthday that day. That was a real thrill."

After the show, Harrison and Young met and Young told him, "Well, this is what's happened. We'll give you equal artist royalties,' which turned out to be 4 and a half cents, but I never made a damned penny of it. I didn't really delve into it, you know? I should have signed a contract saying, 'Void of all other debt.' In other words, when I start getting it. But I didn't because I was stupid."

Not knowing any better at the time, Harrison accepted Young's offer. He told Renwick and Jones that he was staying with Poco.

The rest of the band received a similar deal. Regardless of the intended generosity, the rest of the band never saw any additional money from record sales. The reason was that unknown to their band mates, Young and Cotton were in tremendous debt from their previous incarnation as Poco. The royalties earned by the band never exceeded the amount that Poco was indebted to the record label. Chapman, Harrison, and Bullard made their living on their share of the money earned on tour.

The group took another prestige gig on October 20 when they opened for Graham Nash at a performance to benefit the Cousteau Foundation. The concert was held at the Ventura Seaside Arena in Ventura, California. The highlight of the show turned out to be an unadvertised reunion of Crosby, Stills and Nash. Poco played a crowd-pleasing set. Bullard recalled, "I do remember playing the songs, and literally two feet to my right was Jacque Cousteau dancing and bopping to the music. It was a real thrill to have him groove right next to me throughout the whole set." All the bands used Poco's equipment setup, leading to some difficulties when Bullard surrendered the keyboards. "I don't know where it started or why, but everything was tuned down a half step. All the instruments were tuned down a half step, meaning piano as well. So it took a while to settle in and actually be in tune. I remember Craig Doerge brought like one of his own pieces of gear [laughs] so he had to play the piano like a half step down from his stuff - like on the same song!"

Although a fall-winter tour of colleges was contemplated, Poco instead took a well-deserved break. The year 1979 had proved to be outstanding for the band. The success of LEGEND was a pleasant surprise for Young and Cotton. The increased visibility, overcoming of tremendous odds, made the pair feel vindicated. Cotton told Richard Randle of KTTV years later, "We were against the wall, we had no management, no record company to take it to, we put our nose to the grindstone and there it was! We were proud of it and very surprised too! I mean...in the middle of the disco era." It was, in retrospect, a bit of a fluke. The record-buying public was not headed in Poco's direction.

The whirlwind success of LEGEND had been an exciting and energizing time for Young and Cotton. "*Rolling Stone* finally reviewed us," Cotton laughs. "They really didn't like the band for some reason. But they did a feature on us that came out when we were in New York. Ah, finally! But they never mentioned us again." Both musicians had been justifiably proud of the effort and were looking forward to continuing the trend. As Poco began pre-production work for their follow-up album, they asked their new label MCA for an increase in their recording budget. Instead of a positive response befitting a gold record earning band, MCA executives demanded the band perform a humiliating task in order to get the money.

12
Under the Gun

Before offering up any additional funds, executives at MCA insisted that Poco audition some of their new material before the label would give them the money. For a band with the professional background of Poco, the group naturally resented the insult but was left with virtually no alternative. "We put together a tight set and the suits came down to listen," Chapman recalls. "After the audition, they said 'Great!' and gave us the money, but it was humiliating."

As 1980 dawned, the music scene was undergoing a big change as punk rock and new wave acts were gaining more attention and many of the old guard were falling by the wayside. Additionally, the sale of ABC to MCA had crushed the band. Suddenly all the executives that they had such a great rapport with were gone in a massive corporate housecleaning. Their replacements had little sympathy or understanding of Poco.

Consequently, when Poco's management made the request for additional funds for their recording budget, MCA executives were less than thrilled with the prospect. Some poor business decisions by MCA Records had hurt their bottom line. From their standpoint, Poco already appeared on shaky financial ground from previous debts and the cash payment to Grantham to buy him out. When they considered the additional bills racked up in 1978 to record LEGEND, MCA was looking at an already sizeable investment in the group that the sales of LEGEND did not overcome.

Poco also changed management in mid-stream as they went with Crosslight Management, dumping Hartmann and Goodman. Chapman feels, "It was basically a Rusty and Paul thing. They probably felt like they weren't getting the support. 'cuz they had America, who were doing pretty well. Graham Nash. It was strange. Peter Golden had a reputation for having a lot of clout in the music business."

Having finally received the additional funds in early 1980, Poco was finally ready to record their first MCA album. They had some discussion with Richard Sanford Orshoff again, but conflicts that arose during the recording of LEGEND plus differences in their approach to the recording sessions prevented the deal from coming together. Orshoff recalls, "We approached the next record as if I was going to work on it. We met and talked about it but it didn't gel. There were some incidents in the studio with studio personnel [during LEGEND], engineering questions. They didn't love the idea of only recording just seven or eight hours a day, five days a week. These were guys that had been Poco for a long time already, and here's this guy who comes out of nowhere and says, 'Here's how we're gonna do it.' But now they've got a hit. Now they have a big hit, and now they want to do it their way. And of course, I have my own ideas of why that record was successful and wanted to make sure that we continued that same approach. But there was nothing specific that led to us not working together. It was a combination of things."

Needing a new producer, Poco auditioned a number of potential candidates including John Carter, Barry Beckett, and Chuck Plotkin. Eventually, Poco hired Heart producer Mike Flicker and entered Village Recorders in West Hollywood in April. Young initially was Flicker's biggest supporter. "Mike had done records with Heart," explained Harrison. "Rusty really liked the way those records sounded." Chapman felt that Flicker had a clear vision of what Poco needed to do with their next album. "Mike's big pitch was 'You've made a lot of great records over the years. Now you have to inject a little 'Come See' into it. You've got to put something on the record that will make people want to come see you. Something exciting.' He wanted it to be more of a rocking thing, which was fine because that was very much what Rusty and Paul wanted at that point."

Rusty Young had been listening to what was happening in music and felt that the emergence of Bruce Springsteen and Tom Petty signaled a return to a more basic rock and roll sound from the disco and punk leanings of the more recent past. His choice of Mike Flicker as producer reflected his desire to have Poco tap into that audience. Cotton agreed, "Mike was the 'Guitar Guy' because of Heart. Not everybody can get serious about guitars, but he'd bring in his old Marshall cabinet in and say, 'Plug into this, Paulie!' I loved that."

The recording sessions began in March 1980 at Village Recorders and included Kim Bullard as a full time member after having used studio musicians for keyboard parts on LEGEND. The idea was to strengthen their studio sound using more upfront guitars. "There's a lot of R 'N' B influence and a real rock feel to this album," Cotton said at the time. Young agreed. "A major difference between this and previous Poco albums is that the guitars are really featured and brought up to the right level." Young decided to hedge his bets in working with a new producer by insisting that engineer Joe Chicarelli be brought in to work on the album. Chicarelli had largely been responsible for the technical sound of LEGEND, and Young thought that was an important element to keep. Unfortunately, the partnership between Flicker and Chicarelli proved to be uneasy, making the end product a rather schizophrenic mix of the two's styles. Bullard explains, "It wasn't a great marriage. They both had their kind of styles and ways of doing things - Mike and Joe. As it is with some situations, both of their talents got diluted in the process. If Joe had just made the record, it would have been a distinct stamp, it would have been one thing. If Mike would have clearly made it, it would have been another thing. But you combine the two together, and neither of them really got to do what they wanted to do."

At the time of the album's release, Young had positive things to say about Flicker. "We trusted his perception more than our own to get the right balance which we might have overlooked. We needed his point of view, his outside influence." But the fact was that Flicker wasn't happy with the effort. He told MCA that he felt that the band only had half an album and had encouraged them to record more. But Young and Cotton disagreed and submitted the album as recorded. Flicker's lack of support did not go over well with Young and Cotton. Denny Jones also reveals, "He had a very padded expense account. He spent a lot of time embellishing. I thought he wasted an awful lot of money."

The material was arranged towards a much less polished sound. "Rusty had a feeling on UNDER THE GUN," explains Bullard. "He didn't want to over rehearse anything because he thought songs happen at a certain time when they're learned until the band finally kicks in and really plays it. He wanted to capture that in the studio rather than a rehearsal hall, and then go and try to recapture it. So there wasn't an extensive amount of rehearsals for that. Although,

we ended up really analyzing it a lot once we got into the studio."
Chapman contrasted the mood of the sessions for UNDER THE GUN
with LEGEND, "We recorded at Village Recorders in Studio D. I
think we did about two weeks of tracking. It went much more
quickly actually than LEGEND. LEGEND was pretty spread out because there was no pressure to do an album. Once we'd had the hit
with LEGEND, there was a little bit of pressure to get the thing
done. That part of it was different. We were trying to get more of
a live thing so that part of it was different. Apart from that it's hard
to say except that it was more compact or whatever. On LEGEND
we could take a week off, come back whenever. Pretty laid back. If
you were in the studio and things weren't working, we'd go see a
movie [laughs] with the clock running at $100 bucks an hour! On
UNDER THE GUN, it was a little more intense." Veteran session men
Phil Kenzie and Steve Forman were brought in during May to overdub their talents on four of the album's tracks.

UNDER THE GUN was released in July 1980. It was a fairly
solid follow-up to LEGEND but its release nearly 18 months after
their hit album failed to take advantage of any momentum. The title song was the opener, and it was a catchy Cotton tune based
around a memorable, yet simple guitar riff. Cotton reveals, "The
song came about because of disharmony in a relationship. It's a
one-on-one level kind of song. Those are the kinds of tunes I like to
write: one-on-one songs but that everyone can relate to." Young's
While We're Still Young followed, and it had excellent guitars and
lead vocals by Cotton. Again Cotton makes use of a nice guitar fill
that is the song's hook. *The Everlasting Kind* was a Young ballad
that was similar in feel to *Crazy Love*. Harrison and Bullard contributed high, breathy harmonies. Cotton drew on some strong rhythms
for his *Down To The Wire*. The side ended with Young's excellent
Footsteps Of a Fool (Shaky Ground) featuring Phil Kenzie on alto
sax.

Rusty Young's rhythmic *Reputation* opened side two. Cotton's
fine *Midnight Rain* got things back on track. *A Fool's Paradise* was
an average Young song that he wrote about a former band mate.
Cotton peaked again with *Friends In The Distance*. Some fine guitar
work rescued Young's *Made Of Stone*. Young's reaction to MCA's
disinterest in Poco was personal and cutting. *"Made of Stone* just
came to me," admits Young. "It was written in a half hour and it
was releasing an anger that had built up inside." Overall the album
seemed solid, although it did lack a real standout tune.

MCA released *Under The Gun/ Reputation* as a single along
with the album. It hit the charts but stalled before reaching the

coveted Top 40. Its #48 showing was a real disappointment to the group, who felt that it was the album's superior track.

Poco even joined the video age with a clip directed by Mike Nesmith to promote the single. The band went to Pacific Arts studios in Monterey for a two-day shoot at the end of July. The video was designed around a boy-girl theme. After seeing the results at MCA, the band decided that it was a pretty weak effort. Bullard says, "We went up to Monterey where Michael Nesmith was. They had little vignettes, a storyline that they wanted to do. People driving a car, coming to this little club...it was for *Under the Gun*. It was actually for the single on the second record. And it turned out really lame. They had some goofy kind of special effects during the guitar solo. [Laughs.] Paul Cotton's girlfriend or wife at the time, Frieda, was the love interest sitting at the bar. It was really kind of embarrassing. I remember Rusty thinking it was a bad career move, just a bad scene. It just got buried." Chapman's recollection was similar. "It was a conceptual piece set in the West. We didn't like how it turned out so we made sure it wasn't widely seen, if at all."

Young did most of the press surrounding the release of UNDER THE GUN. "We kept the strengths of LEGEND," Young maintains. "The qualities that appealed to people and put it into songs like *The Everlasting Kind* and *Midnight Rain*. The rest of the album has a strong rock feel, especially the single. [It's] the most powerful thing we've done to date." His upbeat assessment of the album eventually decayed as the album failed to match its predecessor's chart showing and MCA seemed unwilling to push it in the marketplace.

Poco planned to headline a national tour after the album's release and rise to #50 on the album charts. A year of touring in 1979 had exhausted the group, and they made plans to restrict their roadwork to only a couple of months in 1980. The tour began in August with Poco booked as headliners. Right away, Poco experienced problems when keyboardist Kim Bullard injured himself roller-skating right before starting the tour. "I broke a bone in my hand," explains Bullard. "Well, they used to have this club at the corner of La Cienega and Santa Monica. It was a bowling alley and pool hall, and it was bought out. Cher used to go there a lot. It was a big bar and roller rink, and the two just don't mix. I got tangled up in a big old wreck. These people were really drunk and roller-skating. And I broke this particular bone that takes about a year to heal. It was not fun." Despite the injury, Bullard took precautions to allow him to remain available to the band. "I had it set in an octave. I brought a keyboard in and had them put the cast on with my hand in an octave spread." This arrangement allowed him to continue to play with his hand in the cast.

Despite Bullard's injury, Poco honored their commitments on August 6 in Riverside and on August 8 and 9 at the Universal Amphitheatre. Poco's show in Riverside had opening act LeRoux capturing the crowd, but Poco came out and took the crowd right back. Local reviewer Hal Parron noted, "Few bands come out for a second encore in a small venue, particularly when it's not sold out. But what Wednesday's audience lacked in size, it made up in enthusiasm. Appearing for a second encore, Young muttered close enough to the microphone to be heard: 'We've got to come back here.'"

Billboard reviewed the show at Universal, and reviewer Ed Harrison wrote, "With its new found rock energy and consistency engaging melodies, Poco should be making strong records and live appearances well into its second decade." Both shows at the Universal Amphitheatre were sell-outs.

But despite the big crowds, Poco postponed the rest of the tour until mid-September. Despite press releases to the contrary, Bullard contends that his injury was not the reason for the cancellations. When the group finally got back on the road, they found the crowds were sparse. They played colleges and small venues in the Midwest and East Coast through the middle of October with John Hall as opening act.

The long tour of colleges was a throwback to the early Poco days. Chapman explains the rationale behind the move. "The reason was that the concert business had been turned up on its head, as had the whole record business. There had been a real boom in the late '70's and then all of a sudden in the early '80's there was a bust. You had this huge success with Fleetwood Mac, FRAMPTON COMES ALIVE, Bee Gees, the disco thing. It was really unprecedented. So instead of this boom, all of a sudden - I don't know if it was the recession or what - I don't know what happened. People from labels were being let go, all of a sudden overnight the concert business plummeted. So I think the rationale behind the college tour was that it was a safe bet. It had somewhat of a built-in audience."

In spite of promise of a safe bet, the critical response to Poco for most of the college tour was less than stellar. At DePauw University, critics complained, "What good can cheering for the living dead do?" When Poco played Lair Ballroom, the reviewer observed, "It almost seemed like the group was tired of what they were doing. Paul Cotton was playing riffs with what appeared to be a minimum of enthusiasm, as if he had played everything 117 times before and couldn't be bothered with any excitement for such a small crowd."

Poco's live set was an interesting blend of older material with debuts of new material from UNDER THE GUN such as *Made of Stone* and the title track. Fans at Universal Amphitheatre heard a sterling set whose highlights were the familiar hits from LEGEND. When the tour resumed in September, the group had revamped the set, adding new tunes *It's a Game* and *Reputation* along with *Indian Summer, Magnolia,* and *Too Many Nights Too Long.* The band also introduced an acoustic set back into their concerts with a hot blue-grass medley of *Blue Water/Fools Gold/Rocky Mountain Breakdown.*

After many of the college shows, Bullard, Chapman, and Harrison would join with John Hall and scour local towns for clubs that had live music. They formed an informal group and played rock standards, as well as original material by Bullard and Harrison. Bullard says, "That was a fun tour because afterwards we had this band called Loco instead of Poco. We would go to whatever club had live music and with John, me, Steve, and Charlie and we would do sets. John had an amazing vocabulary of songs, and we would just have a ball. We'd play Beatle songs, play whatever. A lot of Sam Cooke, whatever he wanted. Actually, we would do a couple of warm-up sets, I would sing a couple, and Charlie would sing some. We had a lot of fun on that tour."

This version of Poco, perhaps more than any other, liked to socialize both on and off the road. Denny Jones recalls, "Poco liked to party and it usually focused around my room. It was a pretty close band at times." Bullard felt that Young chose to remain distant. "He and Paul were not getting along very well. So Rusty would just sit in his room." Jones explains, "Rusty was...I don't want to say aloof. But he had problems with dialogue. Rusty wasn't really tolerant of Charlie's antics. The parties would get out of hand. The entire band would be there except Rusty. He didn't go for all the rest of it so I can see where Kim might think that." The road was a wild place for this edition of the band. Bullard recalls, "We were into this thing at the time with our crew. Our crew was all English, and it would end up with champagne buckets on our heads, food fight, complete warfare. Real insanity."

While Poco was on the road, MCA released another single in October, editing *Midnight Rain/ Fool's Paradise.* This outstanding Cotton song got only to #74 on the charts. Surprisingly, Poco chose not to perform it while on tour.

In November, the UNDER THE GUN tour turned towards the West Coast with dates in North and South Dakota, Colorado, and California. John Wilkens of the Santa Barbara *News-Press* wrote a positive review. "Poco's major challenge in concert these days is to skillfully toe the line between the old and the new. The group did just that with ease and exuberance yesterday at the County Bowl, dividing the 16-song set evenly between early material, which showcases considerable instrumental talents, and the most recent songs, which have finally made a five-member band a popular one."

Two months later MCA tried the *Crazy Love* clone, *The Everlasting Kind*, as an edited single, but it didn't chart at all. Sadly, the momentum was gone. Poco had had its day in the sun.

UNDER THE GUN deserved a better fate. Rusty Young has consistently been rather hard on it, saying that Poco was not happy with it from the beginning. They did expect the single *Under The Gun* to be another hit, however. Young felt that UNDER THE GUN lacked the "earthy Poco elements." It was clear that Young and Cotton weren't sure what direction to take the group in. They initially chose to work with Mike Flicker because they wanted a big guitar sound. But after its release they complained it lacked the acoustic music Poco was best known for. "That record was a real disappointment, I must say," Young recalls. "Because we thought that it was a real good record and should have done well as a follow-up to LEGEND, as big as LEGEND was." Still it is, in some ways, a superior album to LEGEND. Paul Cotton's contributions are uniformly excellent. Indeed, the real failing of UNDER THE GUN was the lack of quality Rusty Young material, which may be the reason he remains so critical of it.

The album didn't get much attention from the critics. What few reviews were published were not encouraging. The *Aquarian* noted, "UNDER THE GUN, Poco's 15th LP, sounds like outtakes of last year's gold LP, LEGEND." The *Independent* observed, "It's emotional, sensitive, but also serious."

Another crucial aspect of UNDER THE GUN's failure was that MCA's management did not appreciate Poco. Rusty Young recalled, "It was the first record we did for MCA, and there were a lot of political problems going on. *Under the Gun* [the single] came out and was the #1 AOR cut for a number of weeks and got massive airplay, and they didn't sell any records. I don't want to get into all the details but [MCA] had a lot of business problems that really just murdered us." Bullard describes the feeling within the band, "I think when it didn't sell, they [Young and Cotton blamed the record company. I remember *Y.M.C.A.* was out by the Village People, and everybody was saying 'Why MCA?' Like why are we on MCA? You know, rather than working with what they had, it became a battle."

Bullard also explains part of Poco's problems with MCA stemmed from an accounting problem that cost the band a considerable amount of money in royalties after MCA acquired ABC and LEGEND was a big seller. "Here's what happened. LEGEND blew out a ton of units and ABC was absorbed by MCA. At that time, they had a distribution deal with GRP which guaranteed returns. Now when it went over to MCA, they didn't guarantee returns. So they didn't have a real good notion of where their product was going. All of a sudden, those units were lost." After MCA took over, they found warehouses filled with product, mostly Poco's album. Rather than deal with the inventory problem, MCA sold the inventory to a distributor for a cut-rate price and failed to pay royalties on the product. The market was quickly flooded with cutout bin copies of the LEGEND album, which cut into sales of the full priced product. Richard Orshoff doesn't doubt that the incident took place. "I don't know about the cut-outs being dumped, but I do know that the album was certified gold, which is 500,000 copies, and the next royalty statement I got was for 303,000 copies or so. So I do know that there were a couple hundred thousand copies unaccounted for."

MCA's lack of responsibility in clearing up the mess led to some bitter feelings between the group and the label. Poco had experienced this kind of lack of support before, and it grated on them. Both Young and Cotton decided that if MCA weren't going to give them any support, then Poco would go on their way and fulfill their contract without attempting commercial product. That plan worked too well.

The last two albums Poco delivered to them to fulfill their contract best exemplified the growing disillusionment with MCA. Both were pet projects that Cotton and Young dreamed up even while Schmit and Grantham were members of the band. When informing the music press about the upcoming projects, Young was openly critical of MCA, feeling they did little to promote Poco. "We kind of knew it wasn't going to be a commercial record," Young told William Ruhlmann. That was too easy a cop-out, according to Bullard. "Those were throw away albums. They just wanted to get out of the contract, which seemed to be self-defeating. It was an OK label. You know, make a good record. It never does any good to make bad records. I don't think it benefits anybody to make records that aren't 100 percent effort. Like, what are you saving yourself for?"

Poco booked time at Soundcastle Studio in Silverlake with Mike Flicker in March 1981 and recorded a batch of tunes that Young and Cotton had been sitting on for years. After the disappointing chart showing of UNDER THE GUN, where electric guitars were dominant, Poco focused on more acoustic tracks and sought a balance of their sound. Rocking up-tempo songs were generally avoided. More of the material was oriented to telling the story and ballads, and mid-tempo tunes kept the lyrics up front. Young and Cotton rarely saw eye-to-eye with Flicker on their approach, and when he found his suggestions were being ignored, he stopped showing up at sessions. Young and Cotton went on as before, essentially producing the record themselves, with the aid of favored engineer Joe Chicarelli and John Mills. Poco wrapped up the sessions in mid-May.

The project was released in July 1981. BLUE AND GRAY was a concept album based on the Civil War. Young and Cotton wrote songs that they felt dealt with the feelings on both sides of the conflict. "Well, it's about the Civil War," Young recalled, "you know, which is pretty left field, I grant you. But at the time we were on MCA Records and MCA, we felt, weren't really into Poco. They weren't selling records for us, and it was a great time to try something. We didn't figure it was a great commercial venture, but it was something really artistic. We felt it was our chance to try something really artistic and forget about selling records, since they weren't selling records for us no matter what we did." BLUE AND GRAY hit the racks to an indifferent public, getting as high as #76 on the album charts.

The album opened with Young's *Glorybound*. It was a fine scene setter with Young's acoustic and Cotton's understated electric guitars blending nicely. His *Blue and Gray* had some fine moments also. Young told Robert Klein on his syndicated radio show, "*Blue and Gray*, that particular tune we've had for three or four years. We'd play it but because it was about the Civil War it wasn't the kind of song you could put on an album that's an eclectic album of ten tunes. It was a little too special." Cotton made his debut with *Streets of Paradise*. Young's *Writing On The Wall* followed. He told *BAM*, "The whole thing came to me in two seconds, and I finished out the message that was in those [opening] lines. Every once in a while, you get a song that's really inspired." Cotton's *Down on the River Again* closes out the first side.

Side two opened with Cotton's strongest cut, *Please Wait for Me*. Cotton told Jim Ladd, "Yeah, that's just one-on-one romance thing with Atlanta burning in the background." Young hits the mark with *Widowmaker*, a song influenced by the murder of John Lennon. "*Widowmaker* became one of my favorite solos of all time. I used Mike Flicker's old Marshall rig on that. Sounded great" Session singers Venetta Field, Clydie King and Denise DeCaro placed some ominous background vocals on the track. Young's *Here Comes That Girl Again* was an excellent Poco love song. Cotton falls short on *Sometimes (We Are All We Got)*, and the album ends with a thrilling gospel number, *Land of Glory*, written by Young. Vocalists Venetta Fields, Clydie King, and Denise DeCaro added their talents to the track.

BLUE AND GRAY did have its moments, but the concept obviously forced some lackluster material onto the album. It was also much more laid back, featuring more acoustic instruments. Although there was some quality cuts on BLUE AND GRAY, Poco needed a much better follow-up to the disappointing UNDER THE GUN. Unfortunately, this album wasn't it. It was almost impossible to promote with no strong candidate for a single. Still, Rusty Young liked the album and felt that BLUE AND GRAY "shows what we do in a more natural way, more acoustic and not the real rock and roll stuff. I think it suits our band better and we're more comfortable with it." Paul Cotton also cites BLUE AND GRAY as his favorite Poco album.

In September, MCA tried a single, *Widowmaker/ Down On the River Again*. Although it was a catchy number, it failed to dent the Hot 100. Poco made an appearance on the syndicated music program *Solid Gold* on September 19 to promote the single. Cotton and Young were decked out in cowboy hats and boots, and Young showed off a rather scruffy beard.

Considering the distressed touring economy, Crosslight booked them as opening act for the Little River Band. The tour began in Denver on September 7 and ended six weeks later in Miami. The Seattle show drew a positive review from *Times* reviewer Patrick MacDonald. "A few years ago [Poco] was on its last legs, surviving on past glories and falling out of favor because of its old-fashioned, hippie-style country-rock. But Poco got a transfusion, with new members and a more contemporary style and came back to life. Poco had sound problems, including recurring feedback, and didn't get as much time as it should have – the crowd wanted a second encore but didn't get it. But Poco showed that a band can come back to life if it has talent and desire."

It was a grueling tour schedule as Poco crossed the country by bus, often leaving right after the show and driving through the night to get to the next tour stop. While their tour bus was state-of-the-art, it still wasn't the same as sleeping in a hotel bed. Poco played a tight 45-minute set every night that showcased LEGEND and UNDER THE GUN, and routinely ignored their latest release with the exception of *Widowmaker*. The tour was not an inspiring experience and Poco fans were disappointed by the shorter set. It did keep Poco in the public eye for the late summer and early fall although they didn't get much radio airplay. The tour was enjoyable from the band's standpoint. Bullard recalls, "We covered a lot of ground. We had a lot of fun with those guys. There were two factions in the Little River Band - one was the fun guys, the other was the sticks in the mud. They had two different buses even to split up the guys.

We had a fun time with the fun guys. Go to Malibu Grand Prix and race against them and stuff. You know, just stuff you do on the road."

The tour showed that both bands complimented each other. Harrison points out, "It was one of the better [pairings] for me. Because at that point they were pretty big and we were doing pretty damn good. If you think about it, if you're a concert goer, at that point it wasn't too much of one thing. It was great music, really like it, and there's not too many bands to this day that play that sort of music." Both Little River Band and Poco performed with notable precision. However, by taking the tour, Poco limited their national exposure. Little River Band had already played the New York and Boston areas before Poco joined the tour. For the first time since they had been actively touring, Poco did not book any dates in their traditional stronghold of the Northeast.

The BLUE AND GRAY tour began a surprising three months after the release of the album. The reason was that Poco used the time immediately after BLUE AND GRAY's release to craft their final MCA album. The album had been recorded at the Soundcastle in just less than two weeks in late July 1981. Harrison offers a possibility as to why Poco completed the album so quickly. "I think it was probably a bit of all around pressure from several different organizations in the music world that were saying, "You're spending too much money!! [Laughs.] Get it done!" At first the band considered calling it ONE A DAY because they recorded and mixed a song per day until the album was completed. Instead they took its title from the working title of UNDER THE GUN. They called it COWBOYS AND ENGLISHMEN. A sneak preview of the album appeared in January 1982 in the form of a single. An edited version of *Sea Of Heartbreak/Feudin'* was released and sank without a trace.

MCA followed the single by releasing COWBOYS AND ENGLISHMEN in February 1982. To any true Poco fan it was obviously an "end-of-the-contract" album. All the material came from outside the group except for Young's *Ashes/Feudin'* and Cotton's *There Goes My Heart*. Top-notch material and performances were sorely lacking. Pieces like the Everly Brothers' *The Price of Love* and Gordon Lightfoot's *Ribbon of Darkness* worked fairly well, but Poco failed to improve on the originals. Cotton reached into J.J. Cale's catalogue again to cover *Cajun Moon*. Still, the band insisted they had fun doing the album. Too bad so few enjoyed listening to it as evidenced in the album's #131 chart showing. When asked if the two projects might not prove a setback to Poco's recent career climb, Young jokingly told *BAM*, "It doesn't matter what type of music it is, or how rock and roll you are...we stopped caring about labels a long time ago...after this album, maybe a polka album. Poco goes Polka!"

Despite saving their own material for their first album on a new record label, Young and Cotton were not willing to use material from either Bullard or Harrison. Bullard explains, "No. They didn't want to open up that door. I think honestly it was a lot more to keep Charlie under wraps than anything to do with me as far as I remember. Charlie was very volatile. He was quitting all the time and rejoining. There was always this drama around him. Drink substancing out a lot. He thought he had songs. Whether mine were as good or better, whether his were, that's very subjective, but I know that it would have been an impossible scenario to have a band and have my songs on the record and not Charlie's. That would have been impossible so I think in order to keep the floodgates from bursting open, they just had this unspoken policy." Harrison was even more explicit. "Never. No way remotely close. Zero. Nada. No, at that point that was like, 'I'm done. I'm baked. Time to get out.' And I still stuck around. It was a mistake."

Denny Jones offers his assessment of Harrison's behavior. "He was the wild-card, take it from me. At times almost uncontrollable. There were instances I remember on the road where he and Paul almost got into a fistfight. We had to put him under clamps and almost sent him home. When he did drugs, he got totally out of control. A very gifted musician but he was a fighter...feisty, mouthy, wild man." Harrison's volatile nature kept the band and crew on edge throughout his tenure.

MCA's commitment to the success of the album was decidedly less than previous efforts. It didn't take a genius to realize what was going on. MCA did a minimal job of promotion, choosing not to include a lyric sheet, opting instead for a folded insert with song and musician credits and a few photos of the band at Silverlake. The critical outlook on the album was practically non-existent. Despite the music press's ignoring their latest release, Poco was nominated for a Grammy in the Country Instrumental category for *Feudin'*, a track from the COWBOYS AND ENGLISHMEN album. The group was amazed on learning of the nomination. Chapman noted, "I never even thought of *Feudin'* as a separate song. It was a part of *Ashes* to us." Still, the band, with the exception of Cotton, attended the Grammy show resplendent in their tuxes. They cruised the backstage parties and enjoyed the live music during the broadcast. But the Academy gave the Grammy to Roy Clark instead, and Poco went home empty-handed.

Poco's tenure with MCA ended amid great frustration and apathy. For Rusty Young and Paul Cotton, the future was bright, if for no other reason that they were no longer obligated to a label that didn't care about them. The challenge was to find a label that did.

13
Shoot For the Moon

Despite the chart and sales performances of their last two albums, Poco had no difficulty securing a new recording contract with Atlantic Records in late 1981 in large part due to the connections between the label and their management company. Although figures were never made public, the Atlantic contract was a lucrative one. Chapman recalls, "I think the reason we went with Atlantic was Peter Golden and Bill Siddons had a relationship with Atlantic because of Crosby, Stills and Nash. Atlantic paid us an enormous amount of money which spent every dime on paying the back debt. [Laughs.] So we were sort of out of the fire and into the frying pan." That may be true, especially since Bullard recalls the excitement of a new contract was palpable. "They would always say, 'Just wait until we get out of here and into a new contract. We'll be rolling in the dough.' But we never saw it."

Doug Morris of Atlantic came down to see Poco in rehearsals and heard several tunes that convinced him that Poco was an asset to the label. Morris was especially taken by a new tune of Paul Cotton's, *Break of Hearts*. Poco signed the contract and began working on a new album in February 1982. Finally dropping the charade that Mike Flicker was still associated with the group, Young and Cotton undertook production of the album with engineer John Mills serving as co-producer. The band laid down tracks at Soundcastle Studio, including a couple of songs that were left off the album. In March, sessions moved to Jennijudy Studio in North Hollywood where Steve Forman and Phil Kenzie joined in. Four more tunes were cut, including another song set aside once the album was released. An overdub session took place at Capitol Records to add orchestration to three tracks. Still not quite satisfied, Poco booked time at Sunset Sound and recorded an instrumental track with Steve Forman adding percussion.

Young recalled the feeling of joining a new label, "The whole feeling was very up and enthusiastic. Everyone was excited about a brand-new situation. We were proud of the first album we gave them, but I'm not sure that it was the kind or record that Atlantic thought we were going to deliver." Chapman's attitude was slightly different. "I think we were still feeling pretty good. But in some ways maybe a bit of dissension was setting in. Everyone was kind of excited about being on Atlantic Records. That was the big thing that everyone was talking about. Rusty and Paul had been sort of holding material back for this record. So there were a lot of expectations, and in some ways the expectations didn't really pan out. We didn't really get there." The sessions progressed through March before moving to both Capitol Studios and Jennijudy Studios for overdubs with percussionist Steve Forman and saxophonist Phil Kenzie. By May, the album was mixed and ready for release.

Poco played some scattered concerts during the summer of 1982. They played a three-date stand at the High Sierra in Lake Tahoe with Marshall Tucker Band. In late June, Poco undertook what they termed the Bayou Blitz Tour. They played club dates throughout Mississippi, Louisiana, and Texas. They also opened a few shows for the Beach Boys. They opened a 4th of July show at the Irvine Meadows Amphitheatre for Christopher Cross. Poco also performed a show aboard the *U.S.S. Presidential* docked in New Orleans. The tour also allowed Poco to visit Alaska for the first time, playing the Sheraton Hotel in Anchorage. Bullard recalls, "Yeah, we made it to Alaska. That was great. We played in some hall. It was actually in a hotel. They didn't have a lot of big halls. That was really great! We went salmon fishing and had a blast."

R. Brian Bennett of the Anchorage *Times* was not impressed with Poco's first time in Alaska. "The band looked bored playing its popular hits but this concert-starved audience ate it up. It took the encore numbers of *Hoedown* and *Slow Poke* to bring the band and the crowd to mutual enthusiasm. Keyboardist Kim Bullard was the only Poco member who appeared to enjoy the entire evening. He looked as if he were in another realm, playing his piano to his favorite Poco album instead of performing on stage."

With two albums released in 1981 by MCA, Atlantic held off on the release of the album Poco had turned into them back in April. Finally, in September Atlantic released the new album. GHOST

TOWN was the title, and Atlantic released an edited version of the title track as a single. *Ghost Town/High Sierra* managed to enter the charts for a couple of weeks in October, stalling at #108. The single featured an entirely different guitar solo in addition to a reduced time. The album itself proved to be a major disappointment to both Atlantic and Poco. It barely managed to get on the album charts at #195. It was by far the worst showing ever by a Poco album. *Ghost Town* was Young's social comment statement on urban America. "We had noticed as we traveled around the country that a lot of the inner cities looked abandoned and boarded up. When I was growing up in Colorado, my great-grandfather had a huge ranch with a ghost town on the property - and those inner cities reminded me of that."

The LP opened with a full orchestrated version the title song. It was a production piece similar to *Rose Of Cimarron*. Nick DeCaro did the string arrangement. Cotton supplied a typical tune, *How Will You Feel Tonight*. Cotton revealed that he wrote the song about a fellow Poco member, but wouldn't reveal whom. Young followed with the acoustic ballad *Shoot for the Moon* filled with traditional Poco harmonies. "I usually had one song on each Poco album like this one," Young told Barry Alfonso. "I like writing in a romantic vein." *The Midnight Rodeo (In The Lead Tonight)* was a rather uninspiring Cotton tune. Cotton told Barry Alfonso, "Back in 1980 or so I was really hooked on watching rodeo on TV. The announcers would run off these buzzwords and I'd start writing them down. That's where *Midnight Rodeo* came from; although I'm not sure they actually do have rodeos at midnight." Young's *Cry No More* ended side one.

The flip side opened with Cotton's outstanding *Break Of Hearts*, a song he admitted was about his impending divorce. Phil Kenzie returned to add a tasty sax solo and strings were added, as well. This song above the others had convinced Doug Morris to sign Poco. Young's *Love So Cruel* was pretty average with simple lyrics and several hooks that sounded like reruns of older Young songs. Young's vocals were not very strong on this track. *Special Care* was also a fairly forgettable Cotton song about life on the road. The version sounds stilted and there is a noticeable lack of melody. Cotton told Barry Alphonso, "We were doing these very long tours by bus at the time. We probably averaged out to 10,000 miles when we'd tour with the Little River Band from Seattle all the way to Miami. And I'd think, 'I've got to get a song out of this.'" Young did better with *When Hearts Collide* despite more weak vocals. Only at the end does he sing with any passion or energy. In fact, it sounds like a rehearsal take. The sedate instrumental *High Sierra* ended the album on a disappointing note. Cotton wrote the song although the label incorrectly credited it to Young. It was the first mellow Poco instrumental to see release.

Three songs were attempted during the sessions that didn't make the cut. *Fast Company, 12:05*, and *Runnin' To New Orleans* didn't meet the band's expectations. Although studio time was devoted to them, it isn't clear if completed tracks exist or whether the attempts were broken off before vocals and overdubs were added to them.

In December, Atlantic released *Shoot For The Moon/ Midnight Rodeo* as a single, and it stimulated enough interest to climb to #50 on the charts. In years past, that would have been cause for celebration, but not in the wake of two disappointing albums. Chapman complains, "It made Top 40 but it was so bogus. The charts were based on airplay, not on sales. I think it's still that way. So it looked good on paper, but it didn't sell a bit. And by that point, we weren't playing the big rooms anymore." Poco appeared on the syndicated TV show *Solid Gold* to perform the single, but that was the only noticeable promotion that the band received. The lack of ads in the trades or heavy advertising by Atlantic Records was puzzling given their sizeable investment in the group.

As the band began its latest tour, MCA released a greatest hits package entitled BACKTRACKS in December consisting primarily of tracks from LEGEND, but it got only to #209 on the album charts.

The tour that Poco undertook after the release of GHOST TOWN took them back to clubs and small halls. Their drawing power had diminished dramatically. Jones explains, "At that time, they were back to playing smaller places. It was kind of sad. We didn't have the bus. We went out in the dead of winter back east driving rental cars. We were very lucky driving around in winter. It was dangerous." Undaunted, Poco actively promoted their new album on tour, adding *Ghost Town, How Will I Feel Tonight, Special Care*, and *Shoot For the Moon* to their set. They began gigging in late November in southern California and Colorado and toured steadily until April 1983.

The intimate setting of clubs allowed the group to reconnect with their core audience. Their appearance at the Old Waldorf in San Francisco found the band in high spirits and Young doing jokes during the song introductions. When bassist Charlie Harrison broke a string, Young teased, "I don't think Tim [Schmit] ever broke a string in all the years he played with us!" The late show closed with a sizzling version of *Legend*, and the band encored with the Buffalo Springfield tune *On the Way Home*.

Poco moved on to shows at the Palomino and the Golden Bear. The tour was off to a great start. Noel Davis of the *Orange County Register* picked up on it at the Golden Bear. "You can tell when a band is really hot by the way the musicians keep flashing each other secret, knowing smiles. Paul Cotton and Rusty Young smiled a lot during the band's early set Saturday night." But as the tour progressed, it became clear that all was not well. A winter tour through Canada and the East took its toll. With Poco not playing premiere venues, the GHOST TOWN tour was not up to the usual standards. "God, it was like *Spinal Tap*," bemoans Bullard. "It was just horrible. We were playing to half-filled American Legion halls in towns where no groups would play." Aside from the less than idyllic venues, the tour routing was also draining. Harrison complains, "Yeah, you'd have tour routing like San Diego, Chicago, San Francisco, Tennessee, Texas, New York, Washington State...it was ridiculous. At that point the fire was gone. The fuel is spent."

Despite some of the out-of-the-way shows, Poco did manage to return to the Big Apple. Poco's two-night stand at the Lone Star Café was the band's first New York City performance in two years. The five-piece band made for a crowded stage setup, but the shows were strong and Poco's New York audience gave them a standing ovation on both days. Poco had arrived in the Northeast in the dead of winter. Their show at the Brandywine Club on February 11 had to be canceled when a blizzard struck the Delaware Valley. "It was pretty dangerous driving in that," Jones sadly recalls. "We finally got buried by 27 inches of snow in Philly and lost two shows. And all the profits from that entire run were gone. We sat in the hotel and drank up all the booze in the bar. Hell, we were isolated. Trapped. We ended up having to dig our rental cars out of snow drifts to get out of there." In the aftermath of the Philly cancellations, Young fell seriously ill and a raft of dates was canceled.

Once Young recovered, Poco resumed touring with a series of shows in Canada, Montana, and Wyoming. The concerts included a couple of college dates with the Marshall Tucker Band in late March and early April. On April 2, they performed at the University of Montana. Reviewer Sam Richards decried the absence of older material in both band's sets. "Neither band did enough obscure material – especially Poco. Fifteen years and 15 albums later, they play more hard rock and much less country – what a pity. Also, of the 12 songs Poco performed, nine were from either their latest album GHOST TOWN or from 1978's LEGEND. Only one song, *Rose of Cimarron* was older than LEGEND and it featured an excellent slide guitar solo by Rusty Young."

Poco rolled into Seattle on April 5, 1983, to play a club called Parker's. It was the tour's final date and the band was exhausted. After opening the set with *Under the Gun*, Poco played *Sea of Heartbreak* to a surprised crowd. They continued with a standard set. After closing with *Legend*, Poco returned to encore with *Rose of Cimarron*. However, during the introduction the lights inexplicably went out. Young profanely rebuked the crew, who instantly slapped them on, but the tension was obvious. To his credit, Young shook the incident off and led the band through another three songs before bringing the show to a close.

After the tour, Atlantic released another edited single *Break Of Hearts/ Love So Cruel* in April 1983, but it didn't chart at all. Atlantic wasn't pleased with the showing of their latest acquisition and neither was Poco. Young has admitted that GHOST TOWN was a pretty weak effort. "I think a lot of it had to do with the sound of the production," Young recalls. "I think Paul and I didn't do a very good job on that." But he also pointed out, "Firefall had just broken up and I think they wanted us to take Firefall's slot on their label. Firefall was always kind of a light, airy kind of act, lots of vocals, aimed at commerciality and when GHOST TOWN wasn't that, I think we lost them." It was clear that Atlantic's promotional efforts were not notable. Virtually no advertising was placed in the trades, and the first choice for a single showed the company's lack of imagination.

The end of the GHOST TOWN tour proved to be a crossroads for the band. Chapman explains, "I think at that point there started to be a lot of dissension. It was tough. Financially, things were really tight. I think Kim Bullard had sort of had enough at that point. He was starting to do a lot of other things. Actually, Kim, Charlie, and I had a side project that we tried to get a record deal on. So there were all these other things going on, and all of us were starting to do other things." Still unable to garner any earnings from the latest Poco album, the rest of the band began looking elsewhere for income. Bullard, Chapman, and Harrison joined up with Spencer Davis after the GHOST TOWN tour and did a small American tour as his backup band to supplement their income.

The side project put together by Bullard, Harrison, and Chapman was a band called the Mumbo Jets. It included all three players from Poco along with lead guitarist Steve Farris, who later hooked up with Mr. Mister. They worked up some original material, but the project never got off the ground.

Long time tour manager Denny Jones also called it quits. The decline of Poco's fortunes led Jones to take up some of the numerous offers he was being given. He initially took a job with

Nazareth. By 1984, Jones was managing Michael Jackson's Victory tour and later worked for Kenny Loggins and Little Feat. He recently retired from the road after four decades.

During a break from touring, Poco got involved in a film project. They recorded a Rusty Young song to be included in the FAST TIMES AT RIDGEMONT HIGH film soundtrack. *Leave It Up To You* was an upbeat, '50's style romp that had Poco sounding its most carefree since the early days. While it could be considered a style at odds with the usual Poco sound, it was also their most commercial sounding release in years. Unfortunately, it was not released as a single by Asylum, who licensed the track from Atlantic. Poco brought in John Mills as engineer and co-producer on the track.

Shortly after the session for *Leave It Up To You*, Kim Bullard left Poco to rejoin Crosby, Stills and Nash on tour. The frustration of living in a band that didn't make full use of his talents had grown too much for Bullard. "I was ecstatic when they called," explains Bullard. "I was really looking for a reason to get out to there." While his time in Poco causes him to wistfully consider the possibilities that were ignored, Bullard managed to leave the band on good terms. "I didn't wish them ill, but a Poco record to them was whatever songs they happened to write during that time, not the best record that Poco as a band could make. See, Poco as a band could have made fabulous records. We could have involved some other writing. We could have had an expansive view of what the band was and really turn it into what it had the potential to be. But they didn't want that. They had a bigger share, and they didn't want to hear about anybody else writing or co-writing. And ultimately it was to their detriment."

After a break, Poco prepared for their next album with the intention of cutting an "80's style" album. Young explains, "We wanted to see how '1980's' a record we could make. We made a conscious effort not to put steel and not to have any country overtones." "I call that 'Toto meets Poco,'" explains Cotton. The approach was supposed to shake things up for both Poco and Poco fans, but it wound up doing so in some unexpected ways. Rusty Young recalls, "Richard Landis [Juice Newton's producer] started off the record by firing Charlie [Harrison] and Steve [Chapman] and bringing in session players. And then he didn't get along with Paul and I very well, so he dropped out about two weeks into the project after cutting the basic tracks. It was a time of real turmoil for us." "Landis was a problem," Cotton claims. "He kept pushing a tune he wrote. [Laughs.] Turned out to be a pretty good one though, and Juice Newton covered it."

Young's recollection brings up some very serious questions. How did a hired producer have any sway over group membership? It is apparent that Young and Cotton had lost control of their own destiny at a crucial juncture. The pair obviously felt that the current lineup was unable to create an "80's sound" so they were initially willing to let session musicians take over. Chapman tones down the controversy simply stating, "Richard just felt he wanted to bring in his guys and make the record. And that was his decision. And at that point the whole thing had come apart so much that we said, 'Hey, that's fine.' You know what I mean? And it was still called Poco, but that version of the band essentially broke up at that point. And that was the end of it." In fact, Chapman returned to play percussion on several tracks after Landis had left the project.

Landis began the sessions at Conway Studio in Los Angeles on August 13, 1983. He assembled a band consisting of Neil Stubenhaus on bass, Vince Coliauta on drums, George Doering on guitar, Randy Kerber on keyboards, and Landis himself. For a week the sessions continued with Landis cutting the basic tracks and instrumentals for 12 songs. Landis completed his studio work on August 30. Shortly after, Landis was relieved of his production duties.

Cotton and Young once again took over production of the album. They invited Joe Chicarelli to engineer the project and serve as co-producer. Chicarelli had helped Poco during the recording of several of their albums. Despite any misgivings about Landis' tact for removing their rhythm section, both Young and Cotton used most of his backing tracks, no doubt more due to budgetary reason than anything else. Poco also brought in keyboardist Richard Gibbs, known for his work with Oingo Boingo, to play on some of the songs. Gibbs performed keyboard overdubs on nine tunes at Can Am Studios in Tarzana in October 1983. In November, Young and Cotton entered Can Am Studios and put down their contributions on the nearly completed tracks.

Unsure that Gibbs' work would be acceptable to Poco fans, Young and Cotton invited former member Kim Bullard to participate on the record. Bullard recalls, "Yeah, I did a lot of work on that album. That was a pretty cool record actually. I think I played on a lot of that. We did a lot of work on that. We were up at George Doering's studio. Coming in as a session guy. I thought it was really nice of them to call and it was good to work. It was a professional scene and everybody got along great." Bullard entered Doering's studio on January 3-4, 1984, and put keyboard overdubs on all 10 songs that were selected for the album. Later in the month, guitarist George Doering overdubbed his guitar work on nearly every track as well.

Cotton also had an idea to help Poco fans adjust to the unfamiliar style that Poco was recording. "To me, the Poco sound is all about the voices. That was the reason for having all the guys on there. We wanted to bring the band into the '80's, but still have those great harmonies and melodies be a part of it." "All the guys" were former Poco members George Grantham, Tim Schmit, and Richie Furay. Young explains how the reunion came to take place, "I went to some club or something and Tim [Schmit] was there. I said, 'We're in the studio, why don't you come on by and sing a harmony part. I have this song I'd love to hear you sing harmony on.' I think it was *Save a Corner of Your Heart*. 'Boy it would be great to hear you and me.' because I'd never sung with Tim. And Richie was in town doing a church thing, it just so happened, and I've kept in contact with everybody over the years. The guys were in town and we were having a good time making this record." George Grantham concurs, "Well, you know Rusty got a hold of me. He wanted everyone to be on that record. It was a lot of fun and it was real quick. Ithink I spent a day and a night there and then flew back to Nashville."

Richie Furay had been out of the music business for several years and had established a ministry in Boulder. The invitation to participate was a pleasant surprise. "It was a fun time of reconnecting with the guys; joining them as a guest artist was a good moment for me," he acknowledged. "When I left the band there was tension, and these moments along the way helped to bring us to where we are today – good friends who enjoy and respect each other as people and musicians."

Atlantic issued a single prior to the album's release. *Days Gone By/ Daylight* went to #80 on the charts after its April 1984 release.

Atlantic released INAMORATA in May 1984. In all respects it achieved exactly what Cotton and Young had intended by displaying a more modern Poco sound. *Days Gone By* began the album, and it was a distinctive Cotton song with harmonies by Furay. The country blues of *This Old Flame* was a nod to Poco's roots but didn't really fit the feel of the rest of the album despite some excellent harmonies. Written by Reed Neilson, Young told Barry Alfonso, "Reed's a friend of mine. We loved this song - it should've been a hit single for us." Young's *Daylight* featured the high harmonies of George Grantham. "We cut that track with some great musicians, Neil Stubenhaus and Vince Colaiuta. We experimented on that one, with just me playing guitar with the two of them. They came up with an amazing rhythm track, so we left it real sparse." Cotton's stylish *Odd Man Out* rocked in a more modern vein with metallic guitars and an accented rhythm. "I was really into Robert Plant's early solo work," recalled Cotton. "I kind of approached this song in tribute to what he was doing. That's Richard Gibbs playing a lot of the keyboard things on there." The first side ends with the outstanding *How Many Moons*. This Cotton song features acoustic lead guitar and brilliant Tim Schmit harmonies. "Tim Schmit blended nicely with me on that one," Cotton told Barry Alfonso. "That's us at the ending. He's great with vocal parts like that."

Young opened the second side with the solid *When You Love Someone*. Young's later assessment of the performance was less that positive. "I'm not sure that we got the best version of that song that we possibly could, but I think it's real pretty and goes through some neat changes." Cotton's *Brenda X* continues the '80's feel with metallic guitars and a descending keyboard riff and echoed vocals. The working title of the track was *Inamorata*. *Standing in the Fire* featured an unidentified black vocal quartet on backing vocals. Cotton recalls, "That song is kind of my blue-collar experiment. I originally wanted to do it the way Gregg Allman might have, but Rusty was into Michael Jackson's THRILLER at the time and had me sing it a whole other way." Young's *Save a Corner of Your Heart* features excellent production. The background vocals are smooth and reminiscent of 10cc's *You're Not in Love*. It was Young's strongest melody in some time. Young thought so too. "I think it's one of the four or five best songs that I've ever written. At the time, I felt like things were slipping away for Poco, as far as how people looked at us. We'd been around for 12 years at that point, and I felt as though we had lost their attention. What I was saying in the song was 'There's all this other stuff going on, but don't forget about us.' I hope someday that somebody will recut that one." Tim Schmit added some airy backing vocals that smoothed out the cut. The album ends with Cotton's evocative *The Storm* boasting some additional Furay harmonies.

Poco did cut backing tracks for two other songs that were left off the album. *Shakin' the Night Away* and *Anyone but You* were cut during Landis' tenure on the album in August 1983. Vocals were added to *Shakin' the Night Away* in November, but it too was relegated to the outtake reel.

INAMORATA was superior in every way to Poco's first Atlantic release. *Relix* called it "their most inventive...in a number of years." Without question, INAMORATA was well produced and well balanced. The *Aquarian Weekly* was not so generous. "Richie Furay and Tim Schmit return to aid a hand in the latest in a long series of Poco albums. It's nice to have them back in the fold, but they fail to do much to strengthen the record. Hopefully there will be better things in the future to prove that Poco's best work isn't all behind them." The Toronto *Globe and Mail* stated, "This record is undoubtedly a relic, but it's a generally attractive and curious effort. The band was always best at country picking, though, and the stabs at hip over-production here are wasted, as the material too often slides into AOR tedium."

However, there was virtually no promotion behind it, and for the first time in years no lyric sheet or individual musician credits were included in the package. Young was discouraged with Atlantic's lack of effort. "I really don't understand how record companies work at all. They paid a lot of money for us. We're expensive. But they're not working the record. I'd say that 10 to 15 percent of the stores in the places we're playing don't have the record. If they're not putting the records out there, how do they expect to make money?" Sadly, INAMORATA spent only seven weeks on the charts, getting only to #167. It did do better than its predecessor, however. Young had perceived the situation correctly: Poco had lost the attention of even their most fervent fans. One can hardly help noticing that Atlantic's minimalist packaging seemed designed to foster the notion that Furay, Schmit, and Grantham had rejoined the band for the album. In fact, most rock reference books to date still state unequivocally that the trio had re-formed Poco. What also seems clear from studio documentation is that very little of INAMORATA was performed by Poco, including Young and Cotton.

Atlantic issued another single *This Old Flame/The Storm*, but it proved a poor choice since it didn't accurately reflect the album. Like many other Poco singles, it didn't chart.

Young and Cotton did not go back on tour right away to promote INAMORATA. Their band had made other arrangements for the spring. Bullard, Chapman, and Harrison joined Spencer Davis on a U.S. club tour that ran from February through May 1984. Chapman and Harrison returned to Poco in preparation for another tour after completing the 20-date tour. As it turned out, the tour proved profitable since Harrison made friends with keyboardist Rick Seratte during the tour and invited him to replace Bullard on the upcoming Poco tour.

Chapman, Harrison, and new keyboardist Rick Seratte rehearsed with Young and Cotton for another tour. The mood of Poco's senior members seemed down. The reluctance of Young to go back on tour was obvious to his band mates. "The band got back together but Kim didn't want to do it," explains Chapman. "I think he'd gone back out with Crosby, Stills and Nash at that point so he was gone. Charlie started the tour and then dropped out. There was this guy Rick Seratte on keyboards. Rusty, Paul, and myself,

Rick. Charlie dropped out after a date in Denver. He got pretty squirrelly [laughs] so that was that. Then a guy named Jeff Steele came and played bass."

Harrison recalls how Seratte joined the band. "I had known him a short while. He needed a gig, and he came down and ended up doing it. At that point we had to share rooms, which threw me even more because we were in debt. They told me, 'You can room with Rick. He's the new guy. You know him.' I didn't know him. And Rick can get a bit nervous now and again. At least at that point he was. Anyway it just wasn't meant to be - us sharing rooms. It just pissed me off. I thought, 'I've got to get out of here. I can't stand this.' It wasn't Rick's or anybody's fault. It just happened that way, you know. Rick was just the new boy so all the questions were being fired on me."

Charlie Harrison had been a source of trouble throughout his tenure with the band. Demanding that he be allowed to sing lead vocals and write songs, Harrison proved to be an irritant to Young and Cotton, neither of whom were willing to allow that big a role in Poco to Harrison. According to several members, Charlie had quit and rejoined the band several times. During rehearsals for the INAMORATA tour, it was clear that the downturn in Poco's fortunes and Bullard's departure had lit a fire under Harrison yet again. Another factor was weighing in on his dissatisfaction with the band. "I should have quit two years before. I never should have done GHOST TOWN, let alone another tour."

Although Harrison's attitude was collapsing, Poco managed to play their first couple of gigs with him in the lineup. A collector's tape exists of a warm-up show in Vail, Colorado. Harrison plays bass during the show. They opened with *Sea of Heartbreak* followed by *Ghost Town*. The band switched to acoustics and played the obligatory *Bad Weather* and *Crazy Love*. The band charged into *Heart of the Night*. Seratte's keyboard solos were shaky. Poco pulled out a surprise with a charged version of *Down to the Wire*. Seratte's extended solo was blistering and bordered on maniacal. *Shoot For the Moon* slowed things down before Poco played its latest single *Days Gone By*. After Young introduced the band, he led them through a series of country tunes, *Rose of Cimarron*, *Hoedown*, and *Slow Poke*. The last song features another spirited keyboard solo by Seratte as he clearly gained confidence as the show progressed. Poco finished the set with a riotous version of *Legend* and *Good Feeling to Know*.

The next night, Poco headlined a show at the Rainbow Music Hall in Denver. Charlie Harrison hit the bottle hard and barely made it through the set. During one of the encores, Harrison collided with his microphone and knocked the stand to the stage. With

Harrison's subsequent refusal to play an additional encore, the band had had enough. Harrison admits, "The next morning I got on the bus and they all got off. Every bloody one of them got off. [Laughs.] So I got off the bus and into the van, and they got out of the van and back on the bus! And Denny [Jones tour manager] came along and said, 'I think after last night, that's it, Charlie.' 'What happened last night?,' 'You really don't remember?' I went 'No' and he smiled at me like I was kidding, and they hopped on the bus and left. I flew out and that was it."

Poco returned to Los Angeles, and Cotton and Young quickly began desperately scouting out a replacement. Rick Seratte suggested that they check out a local bass player he knew from the club circuit. Jeff Steele recalls, "The first person I had contact with was Rick Seratte. He called me out of the blue to see if I would be available or interested to go on the road. I knew Rick from playing local LA gigs. I'm sure all the band members were racking their brains and calling everyone they knew to find a quick replacement for Charlie."

The band arranged to come see Steele play as a sort of live audition. "They came down to see me play with a rock cover band at a small club called Poncho and Wongs in Redondo Beach," recalls Steele. "It was Rusty, Paul, Rick, and Steve Chapman. After a set and some drinks Paul said, 'How would you like to hit the road with us?' I remember being so damn excited! I partied my ass off that night with the guys! The next day they gave me a cassette tape to listen to...I learned all the songs...and rehearsed the following day. I think the day after we hit the road! This all happened in about three days from the time they asked me to join the band."

Back out on the tour less than a week later, Poco hit Milwaukee and Chicago's Park West with their new bass player. After his first gig, Steele celebrated late into the night. The next morning he showed up five minutes late to the bus and found that his new band had left without him! Steele confirms, "The band left without me to teach me a lesson and left instructions at the front desk for me to get my ass to Chicago! I had to take a cab!!! I was never late after that. The next gig was at Chicago's Park West...and it was great because being from Chicago, all my friends and family were there!"

Now with their new bassist in tow, Poco played a couple of shows opening for the Beach Boys in the New York-New Jersey area in late August 1984. The shows were in large venues at Jones Beach and the Garden State Arts Center in Holmdel, New Jersey. They also split a bill with Exile at Club Casino in Hampton Beach, New Hampshire. On August 30, a late summer thunderstorm struck the Saratoga Springs area. As thunder and lightning loomed, Poco and the Beach Boys braved the elements at the Saratoga Performing Arts Center Amphitheatre. However, before Poco could open the show, power dimmed and caused a 20-minute delay. The *Saratogian's* Jim Reilly gave Poco a brief nod in his review stating, "Poco opened the show for the Beach Boys with [a] 50-minute set that had spirit and a nice sound but never really caught fire, although the instrumental finale came close."

Poco also did a couple of shows opening for the Little River Band on the tour.   In early September, Poco played two nights at the Lone Star Cafe in New York City. In the New York press, Rusty Young fended off rumors of the return to Poco of Tim Schmit and Richie Furay. "A lot of people are real curious about Richie and Tim coming back," Young told the New York *Daily News*. "But it doesn't relate to ticket sales - not enough that it becomes a number one priority for all of us." Poco returned to the Paradise in Boston before heading south to play dates in Atlanta and Florida.

While out on tour, Poco played a historical set, including only *Days Gone By* from the new album. This was in stark contrast to their previous tour which included five songs from their GHOST TOWN album. Apparently, Poco wasn't into promoting INAMORATA any more than Atlantic was. Among the older Poco songs included in their set was *Good Feelin To Know*, and the band encored with the Buffalo Springfield song *On The Way Home*.   It isn't hard to imagine that Young and Cotton were disappointed with the whole INAMORATA experience.   The firing of Harrison was just the beginning.   When Poco returned to the concert trail, the pair found themselves on stage with two virtual strangers in Seratte and Steele. Cotton took Steele under his wing and generally included him in any post-show socializing. According to Steele, Rusty Young remained distant, and never warmed to the new recruits. Poco's shows that summer showed a band marking time. They added only one new tune off INAMORATA, showing that they were not presenting the image of a band moving forward.

As he often had in the past when Poco's chart performance fell below expectations, Rusty Young blamed their record company. He was frustrated that INAMORATA was hardly visible in stores as they toured. It was obvious to him that Atlantic was not supporting the album. He told New York DJ Pete Fornatale that the experience forced him and Cotton to rethink where they wanted to take Poco. Obviously, a modern-sounding Poco wasn't what their fans wanted.

In August, Atlantic tried again by releasing *Save A Corner Of Your Heart*, but it didn't chart either. INAMORATA was a disappointment, and Atlantic chose not to exercise the option on their contract and dropped Poco from the label's roster. That turn of events ended any hope of another live album, which Rusty Young had mentioned quite a bit in recent interviews. It had been a hard lesson. The tour to support the album had been a short one by Poco standards. When the group returned to Los Angeles, Seratte and Steele were let go. If nothing else, the tour had given both Cotton and Young ample time to mull over their options. The attempt to make Poco into a more modern rock band had fallen on deaf ears. To return to the LEGEND styled band seemed to be losing ground. The pair wanted Poco to keep moving forward. One direction kept calling out to Paul Cotton and he felt the time was right for a bold move.

14
One of These Days

Crosslight Management wasted little time after receiving the notice that Atlantic Records had dropped Poco from their roster. Within a few weeks of the end of the INAMORATA tour, the firm announced that it was seeking to place Poco on a Nashville-based label more suited to the band's country appeal. It was the first sign of a new direction for the band. As for both Cotton and Young, they had some new old ideas for Poco. "We thought that with the coming of country rock," Young recalled, "and country music then getting more hip and progressive, that it would be a good move for us."

"I kind of had an inkling that it was the last straw," explains Cotton. "We had to get next to the country guys. I thought that it would enable us to do our own thing. Nashville, it turns out, was looking for the new Alabama, and they thought that that might be us. Besides, I'd met George Strait in LA with his manager Erv Woolsey, who happened to work for our label ABC at the time. Erv and I became friends after meeting out there. He actually wanted to manage us, but Rusty thought that was wrong."

Cotton headed out for Nashville and began working with musicians such as Faith Hill's husband Dan. But nothing firm arose for him. Five months later, as Rusty prepared to follow his partner out to Tennessee, Young asked Chapman to come along, but instead he chose to remain in Los Angeles. More and more, music was becoming a sideline for Chapman. He began exploring the business end of the industry and eventually began a management company, handling his old band mate Al Stewart. Understanding perfectly, Young left for Nashville determined to return Poco to its country roots.

Once Cotton and Young were settled in Nashville, they looked up former drummer George Grantham, who was playing behind Ricky Skaggs, and convinced him to rejoin Poco. Now a veteran of the Nashville scene, Grantham was fairly secure in his role with Skaggs, but the pull of Poco proved too strong. Grantham told Robin Flans of *Modern Drummer*, "It feels good to be back with Poco. It's going to take some time to get readjusted to it...I haven't forgotten it though. When we're doing a song I did years ago with them, it feels like it was just yesterday." Grantham had a limited recording role with Skaggs, but was a member of his touring band. The lure of a revived Poco in Nashville convinced Grantham that he could do better financially with Poco. The realities of Nashville made Grantham realize that the disputes of the past over shared publishing revenue were nothing to argue about this time around.

Within a few month of their arrival, Young, Cotton, and Grantham auditioned several bass players at the Picker's Pickup in Nashville. Among the candidates was a curly haired bassist from Minnesota named Jack Sundrud. After listening to a long line of prospective bass players, the trio settled on Sundrud. Surprisingly, Sundrud didn't hear the good news directly. He recalls, "A few days later John Dittrich, later the drummer for Restless Heart and Buffalo Club and a Gail Davies band mate, told me that he heard 'a blond, curly headed bassist was the one who got the job.' I had a perm at the time."

Sundrud recalled in 1986, "These guys [Poco] moved there about a year and a half ago to pursue country-rock. I'd got word through the grapevine that there were auditions, and I got myself an audition and the rest is recent history."

Poco began intensive rehearsals before debuting their new lineup for the road. It was quite a departure for their new bassist. "We rehearsed a lot," explains Sundrud. "I was used to doing one rehearsal and going on the road with people. Poco was accustomed to being a unit so rehearsal was more a part of the way they did things. Songs were not just copped from the record, arrangements had grown over time." Aside from learning the older Poco songs for the live set, the band also worked up some new material.

Cotton and Young were extremely supportive of their new member and knew that Nashville would be a new experience for them. They immediately looked to Sundrud for some help. "I was surprised," Sundrud recalled. "They listened to a few of my tunes later the first day." Although much of his material was more country in nature, Sundrud brought some rock-type songs to rehearsals, and the band decided to include a few in their set. "Jack was a great guy, man," Grantham claims. "He was more recently the lead singer in Great Plains. Great singer-writer. Super easy guy to work with. He fit in really well with the group. He's a great singer, too. So, it sounded great. It was a good group with Jack." Cotton would later tell Richard Randall of KTTV in Colorado that Sundrud had a "great voice...real stable...good solid bass player...easy to get along with. He was always encouraging us. He was a fan, as well as a musician."

The move to Nashville by Poco caused a flurry of activity. Paul Cotton recalls, "We had a handshake deal at RCA over lunch. Joe Galante, who's still there. That never matured. We did a Christmas song for Epic, a Sons of the Pioneers tune that I picked. It was supposed to be on an album with Merle [Haggard] and Willie [Nelson], all the Epic artists. That never happened. And then MCA approached us and high-pressure L.A. managers turned them off."

In February 1985, the music trades were circulating rumors that Poco was about to sign with MCA Records-Nashville. Considering the distaste with which Poco felt towards MCA after its purchase of ABC Records, it was hard to imagine them going back to work for the label. But Young confirmed that MCA invited Poco to come to Nashville. The Nashville Division of MCA was totally free of the problems the band had experienced in Los Angeles. Unfortunately, Poco's managers weren't able to nail down a contract. Grantham confirms, "We supposedly had a record deal and everything. And that all fell apart when they got to Nashville. We had a meeting and Jimmy Bowen met with us, and I guess he didn't like our attitude or something. Something didn't click there, but next thing we knew, we didn't have the record deal. So I had left a job based on that and it just fell apart. It was really sad. It's different in Nashville. They handle it differently." Sundrud agrees, "It was one of those music business things, I guess. When I first joined the group, we met with then president of MCA Jimmy Bowen to discuss the upcoming record. Not long after that, there were disagreements between the label and the management as I recall, and the deal fell though before it really started."

After years of reflection, Rusty Young explained, "When I came to Nashville in 1985, the record mogul was Jimmy Bowen. We sat down with him and we had just come off a record where Paul and I had hit singles. Jimmy Bowen started telling us what we couldn't have on a record – certain guitar sounds, certain drum sound, two lead vocalists. Five years later in Nashville, they were making the records they said we couldn't make."

Despite the disappointment of losing what was supposed to be a guaranteed record deal, Poco continued to rehearse and develop new material. The addition of Sundrud energized them. They were recording demos, using their own funds. Sundrud recalls, "We recorded quite a few times. All of them in Nashville at several different studios. We were experimenting mostly. Trying things to see how they fit. I think Poco was trying to find out if there was a place where their sound intersected with what was going on in country music at that time." Cotton concurs, "We started recording on a 12-track in Rusty's living room just trying the recording thing on our own. But no deals were happening." Although none of these demos have ever seen the light of day, Sundrud confirms that at least two of his compositions, *It's Been Years* and *Right Before Your Eyes*, were recorded by Poco during this time. A total of four demos were recorded by Poco during 1985 with Grantham on drums and Sundrud on bass.

The new Poco debuted on the road in April 1985 at the Country Club Saloon in Edmonton, Alberta, Canada, playing a series of shows at a recently opened country music club. Another show in Ft. Lauderdale, Florida on May 7 showed that despite the stated change of direction, Poco played a 90-minute set that revealed they had changed very little in their live approach. The set list was virtually the same as their sets in the post-LEGEND years with the exception of adding in a few of Sundrud's tunes.

Crosslight Management was still courting Music Row, and on June 5 they got Poco a prestigious booking to headline the annual Nashville Music Association show at the Tennessee Performing Arts Center in Nashville. The purpose of the show was to interest record companies in signing the featured acts. Since label A&R men had not attended NMA shows in large numbers in the past, *Billboard* reported that organizers sent limos around town to pick them up and take them to the show. While Poco was politely received, no contract offer was forthcoming as a result of the performance. Young and Cotton later revealed that the problem for Poco in Nashville was the country music establishment's desire to have Cotton sing everything and their refusal to allow Young to play his own steel guitar. Their frustration led to a decision to stay close to home and work on material rather than book extensive live dates.

The summer shows gave fans some new tunes to enjoy although Poco still played a majority of older songs. Rusty Young's *One Of Those Days* and Jack Sundrud's *Chasin' Love* were pleasant songs, neither of which were hardcore country. "*Chasin' Love* and *Rhythm of Love* are stories of the overpowering emotions of youth," Sundrud explains. "That time when testosterone spoke louder than reason. The latter was co-written with my sweetheart Sue Braswell." One of the summer's highlights took place when the band returned to California to play the Palomino Club in North Hollywood. The set was progressing smoothly when problems started. Immediately after breaking a string on his electric guitar, Young switched over to his lap steel mounted on a stand, which began slowly sliding to the floor as the stand it was on began to loosen. Rather than stop the song, Young continued to play from a squatting position. To top the night off, Jimmy Messina was in the audience and joined Poco for a couple of songs including a rousing version of *You Better Think Twice*. It was the first time that Messina had sat in with his former band since he had left back in 1970.

Poco was dealt another blow when Crosslight Management decided to close its doors during the fall of 1985. Poco replaced their Hollywood managers with Bob Titley, manager of Brooks and Dunn and Kathy Mattea. Cotton laughs, "He used to say [drawls], 'All I want to do is make enough money to buy a burger stand back in Colorado. And of course he ended up managing Brooks and Dunn." The band signed with Entertainment Artists for booking. Despite the new Nashville connections, Poco coasted, playing weekend gigs and continually failing to come up with a recording contract. After Crosslight's tactics had cost Poco a contract with MCA-Nashville, neither Young nor Cotton appeared anxious to hook up with traditional rock and roll management. Their decision to hook up with a Nashville manager indicated a willingness on their part to play the game.

Poco managed to stay sharp by playing occasional shows while honing material for another attempt at getting signed by a label in Nashville. Rusty Young was not particularly pleased with the way things were going for Poco. "We did some dates after that while we were here in Nashville. Paul and I would go out. The agent would call and say, 'Listen, I've got an offer for two weeks if you want to go out. You'll make X amount of dollars. Do you want to do it?' The truth of the matter is that Paul got himself into a situation where he needed to have a cash flow. It's called divorce. As I look back on it, I wish I hadn't, but we did go out and do shows, so that it would help him get himself set up. I owed it to Paul."

The lack of a recording contract and a reduction in live work took Poco out of the public eye. Although there was never an announcement of a breakup, most major music media assumed that Poco had split up after being released from their Atlantic contract in 1984. No new album in the offing seemed to confirm that the band had expired to the national music scene.

This low profile soon cost Poco the services of Grantham, who returned to the more lucrative session scene in Nashville. While Young and Cotton could rely on songwriting royalties from past Poco albums to get them through lean times, Grantham had no such safety net. "I had to get something where I knew I was getting in-come...having money coming in, you know?" explains Grantham. "It was all up in the air then. That's when I had the offer to work with Steve Warnier."

Without Grantham, Young and Cotton turned to their old LEGEND companion Steve Chapman to play drums during their occasional live outings. Young called Chapman and he agreed to join up for some limited touring. After some brief rehearsals, Poco toured again with Chapman on drums. Poco returned to the Lone Star Café on December 4 and participated in a flood relief telethon in West Virginia on December 7. John Denver, Tom Chapin, Richie Havens, and Kathy Mattea also performed. On January 18, 1986, Poco played two sold out shows at the Westport Playhouse in St. Louis. *Post-Dispatch* reviewer David Surkamp wrote, "Although the group retains its cowboy boots and steel guitar, little country music remains in Poco's rock sounds. In its place, the group has constructed a streamlined approach to its music that is modern, accessible and more commercially rock-oriented." Surkamp's review seemed to strike at the heart of Poco's problem in Nashville. Despite Young and Cotton's stated intention, Poco wasn't prepared to do any country music that Nashville would find acceptable.

Chapman recalls his return to Poco. "We only toured in summer time. By that point I had gone back with Al Stewart and I was playing with him. But I would spend weeks at a time at Rusty's cabin in Nashville and stay with Jack. Oh, I loved that. I mean, that was one of my favorite tours actually. It was a different thing. We played outdoor summer fests, clubs, some other things. It was real good...just a four piece. It was a lot of fun and very easy 'cuz I think the band was very good. Jack was a great vocalist and wrote some great songs. It was a lot of fun."

After a break, the summer tour took Poco to Georgia, Charlotte, North Carolina, Orlando, and Chicago. In July, Poco joined Johnny Rivers to headline the Spirit Festival at the Liberty Memorial in Kansas City. They returned to the West Coast in August to play the Coach House in San Juan Capistrano before returning east. The routing was difficult, but with plenty of days off in between shows, the band didn't suffer as it had during the 70's. The live work was invigorating, but it didn't help Poco gain a foothold in Nashville. Rusty Young was struggling with the inability of Poco to make an impression in Music City. He again began to rethink what Poco should be doing.

In July 1986, Poco revealed in an interview with Pete Fornatale that after their club tour, they intended on recording an "alumni" album featuring all the previous members of Poco including

Richie Furay. This was a revelation since Furay had retired from the music business to become a full time pastor in Boulder, Colorado. Young assured everyone that Furay would be a part of the project and had even written a couple of songs for it. While an alumni album might have been seen as a threat to their new bassplayer, Sundrud was supportive. "I thought it was a great idea," he enthused. "I always knew that I had nothing to do with the success or the history of Poco. I enjoyed working with them and would have liked to have seen some more success come from my time with them, but I'm a realist. Reuniting the original band was something a lot of folks, including myself, would love to see." Unfortunately, the project was set aside. Perhaps the logistics were too difficult to pull off, or more likely, the failure to have a record company's financial backing for the sessions doomed the project.

One show from the 1986 touring season was captured by a fan on tape when Poco returned to Philadelphia for the first time in several years to play the Chestnut Cabaret. Although their set was heavily drenched in reverb from the house sound system, Poco played an interesting set that had several new numbers in it. Sundrud's *Rhythm of Love* sounded like a potential single, offering a catchy chorus. Poco performed two new songs, *Trouble With Love*, written by Pam Rose, and Mary Ann Kennedy of the duo Kennedy/Rose and *Too Old To Die Young*, written by Kevin Welch. While they were pleasant enough, they didn't sound like big hits as performed by Poco. *Too Old to Die Young* later became a country hit for Moe Bandy. For the second straight year, Paul Cotton had failed to perform a new composition in concert, making one wonder if the move to Nashville had been wise from a creative standpoint. Poco returned an acoustic medley to the set of *Keep On Tryin'*, *Pickin' Up the Pieces*,and *A Child's Claim To Fame*. Unfortunately in Philadelphia, the acoustic medley sounded ragged and under rehearsed. The remainder of the set was performed in usual fashion.

In September Poco returned to the Coach House and the Kono Hawaii in Santa Ana before opening shows for Nicolette Larson in Chicago, the University of Akron, Ohio, and Boston. Chapman and Sundrud played in Larson's backup band during those shows. Sundrud explains, "In fact, it was from seeing me in Poco that Nicolette asked me to do some dates with her. She also recorded a version of *Rhythm of Love*." Poco played two sets at the Westport Playhouse in St. Louis on October 4. The *Post-Dispatch* raved, "While Poco certainly capitalizes on the strength of its harmonies, what stood out more than any element Saturday was the group's overall instrumental talent. Young, in particular, delivered masterful performances on pedal steel, 12-string, mandolin, banjo and dobro. The

band got several standing ovations from an obviously biased crowd."
Sundrud's *Rhythm of Love* proved the highlight of the set. Cotton
revived *Ride the Country*, and reviewer Louise King lauded the selection of *On the Way Home* as the encore.

Still hoping for a recording contract, Poco recorded at least
eight tunes during several sessions in 1986. One demo session included Young and Cotton at Rusty's cabin recording songs with a
drum machine. Later, Young invited Steve Chapman out to Nashville where the group went into the recording studio to lay down
some new material. Two tunes were by outside writers, and the
rest by Cotton, Young and Sundrud. Confirmed tunes include two
that would later show up on Paul Cotton solo projects, *High Water*
and *Across a Painted Sky*. In mid-October, Poco submitted a three-
song demo to CBS-Nashville. Rusty Young told inquisitive fans before a gig at the Lone Star Café in New York City that he was hope-
ful that a deal would be in the offing. But CBS wasn't interested and
passed on offering a recording contract.

While there was disappointment at another rejection, life in
Poco was much different than during the early 80's. Chapman explains, "I just remember that the music was great. I had taken a
break from it , and there wasn't the pressure like in the latter days
like GHOST TOWN or INAMORATA. There was amazing pressure to
make it work then. There was tension in the group. Money was
tight. But going back and doing this in '86, there was none of the
pressure. Let's just make music and have a good time."

That lack of pressure made touring enjoyable, but there was
also a lack of motivation to push the band in the marketplace. Poco
continued to play sporadically into 1987, but failed to interest anyone in signing them to a recording contract. Based solely on the six
new songs that Poco played live during their "Nashville Years," it is
obvious that there was little there to lure a label into signing them.
While the material is listenable, especially the three written by
Sundrud, there were no songs of exceptional quality.

Poco was not a full-time job by this point. Chapman's memories of only touring during the summer are substantiated by Sundrud's other work while a member of Poco. "After the initial burst
of activity when I first started with Poco, there was quite a lot of
downtime actually. I worked some with Nicolette Larson, Dickey
Betts, the O'Kanes, and a few others. I also waited tables and
played live and studio gigs around Nashville."

The 1987 summer tour took Poco to many of the same venues,
small and intimate. During the summer of 1987, Poco played an obscure club, Oscar's, in Santa Barbara. Local resident Jimmy Messina
showed up with guitars in hand and sat in during both sets. *The*

Santa Barbara News-Press observed, "When the band launched into Neil Young's infectious Springfield tune, *On the Way Home*, it mattered not that it was a ragtag version, this was nostalgia on a steamy skewer. At the late show [Messina] joined the band for *Act Naturally*, the Loggins and Messina tune *Listen to a Country Song* and the Poco gem *You Better Think Twice*."

The 1987 live set reverted to more of a best-of collection of songs. Perennials like *Magnolia, Rose of Cimarron, Bad Weather*, and *Indian Summer* were performed, along with nearly one-half of the LEGEND album. Cotton resurrected *Ride the Country*, and a shaky acoustic medley of *Keep on Tryin', A Child's Claim to Fame*, and *Pickin' Up the Pieces* was featured. As they had done for several years, Poco closed the show with the Buffalo Springfield classic *On the Way Home*. Sundrud's contribution to the set was a rocking *Crime of the Century*. Sundrud offers, "*Crime of the Century* was a blues-rock oriented song of failed love co-written with John Neal when he and I were in Dickie Betts band."

As 1987 waned, interest in the group waned with it. Sundrud noted, "I wouldn't say the mood was great. Poco wasn't working much. We recorded some more stuff but nothing became of it. There was talk of the reunion." There was little doubt that both Young and Cotton were both marking time. Their inability to change the Nashville mind set about Poco caused them to stagnate creatively. With no recording deal forthcoming and no new album in nearly three years, the pair was in essence taking the money and running. And there wasn't much of that to be had.

Young and Cotton reached a rather obvious conclusion late in 1987 and decided to put Poco to rest. Chapman faded into the background and entered artist management. He recalls, "I don't think they told me that they'd quit. They just stopped calling." Sundrud agrees, "I don't recall there being a decision to fold Poco. It was obvious that things were not going all that well. We saw each other less frequently, but Poco has always been a dynamic entity. I didn't feel that Poco was over - with or without me. There was inactivity and we all moved into other things." One of those other things for Sundrud was Michael (*Bluer Than Blue*) Johnson's backing band. From that connection, Sundrud met producer Brent Mahler, who encouraged Sundrud's songwriting. Eventually, Mahler convinced Sundrud to start his own band.

The stifling atmosphere of Nashville eventually forced Paul Cotton to move on. He relocated to Sarasota, Florida, in 1987 and began exploring new musical themes. He took some time off and began sailing. The sea captured his imagination, and Cotton began writing songs that reflected his new environment. He recorded three demos on his own while in Florida. In the fall of 1987, he visited Young at his cabin in Nashville and recorded at least four more demos, including *One Long Last Look*.

For all intents, Poco was through. The end came so quietly that there were no post-mortems in the media. In fact, Poco's profile had been so low that most mainstream media had assumed the band had folded back in 1984 in the wake of INAMORATA. The Nashville experience had been a frustrating one for the band. Although Cotton and Young had high hopes upon arrival, it was quickly clear that it was not going to be an easy road. "Nashville is insecure," observed Cotton. "They don't want to change. When we moved to Nashville, they wanted to make us the next Alabama." Poco was not about to become a clone of another Nashville group, even a successful one.

15
Legacy

Paul Cotton's creative resurgence after his move to Florida continued. The change in location proved to be an inspiration to Cotton, who quickly began writing new songs. In April 1988, he recorded four demos in Nashville. Included were songs such as *Sarasota on the Bay*, written by Nashville friend Earle Bud Lee, and *You're Still a Friend of Mine*, written about former partner Kal David. Cotton also did a cover version of Van Morrison's *Into the Mystic*. The demos showed Cotton aiming at a less country and more adult contemporary style. Many of them featured multilayered guitar lines and some keyboards.

Shortly after, Cotton wound up with a solo recording deal. "That deal came about through a friend of my ex-wife's. She'd call me out here and decided to spend some time in Florida and ask me if I had any tunes, bring them out or get 'em demoed somehow. They flew me out there for three or four months, and I stayed with a friend out there who had played bass in Poco filling in for Charlie."

Former Poco bassist Jeff Steele confirms, "In fact he lived with me for a while, and I produced an entire demo of songs, which got him his record deal for CHANGING HORSES. I think it sounds better than the actual record! We co-wrote *From Across a Crowded Room*. I also played bass on a couple of songs on CHANGING HORSES. I put a band together around Paul and we played some small clubs in the south bay area. Good times! It's unfortunate that Paul didn't have good management during that time period. I think his solo career might have taken off."

The demos produced by Steele eventually led to a contract with Sisapa Records. Cotton entered the studio with veteran producer Paul Brown in 1989. "I went into the studio in Sherman Oaks with the A-team in L.A. I tapped Toto for Steve Lukather, Michael Landau, Garth Hudson from the Band played on *Heart of the Night*, Portia Griffin sang, Christopher Cross on two songs, Gary Mallabar from Steve Miller." The album opened with a tight, melodic remake of Chris Rea's *I Can Hear Your Heart Beat*. Cotton's strong rhythmic tune *I Walk the River* follows. Another outside tune *Tiger on the Lawn* features some tasty lead guitar work. *Here in Paradise* is a look at some of Cotton's new approach to his songwriting. The side ends with *One Long Last Look*, a Poco demo. The second side starts with a re-make of *Heart of the Night*, with Cotton taking a more modern take on the classic Poco tune. *After All These Years* and *Jamaican Rain* are solid tunes that Cotton sings with tremendous feel. Another Poco demo *High Water* follows. The album ends with *Across a Crowded Room*, written by Jeff Steele, Poco's bassist from the 1984 tour.

The CHANGING HORSES project was a positive experience for Cotton. He really didn't mind not being part of the LEGACY project. "I was doing my first solo album at that time," Cotton explains. "I was doing exactly what I wanted to do at exactly that time. I had a huge budget and the best session players in Los Angeles. I had a row to hoe, I had to do it, and I'm glad I did it." That big budget came primarily from a trust-fund source. "The guy with the money was trust-funded. His dad was one of the richest men in the world. [Laughs.] This kid got a million dollars a year just for doing whatever he wanted to do. So he threw this money at the project, Sisapa picked it up, and they made money on it."

Sisapa Records was a small label formed by artist J.D. Blackfoot and Bob Liebert. They had a small group of artists signed to the label, including Marshall Tucker Band and Crazy Horse. "They wanted my album for their first release. There I was, I had this song *One Last Look* climbing up the charts, getting great reviews...the owner decided he didn't want to be in the record business anymore. He was getting into CD production or something. The whole thing folded completely. Nothing was left. They don't own my songs. They didn't care 'cuz he had enough money. Boy, that was a sign of the times to come."

The collapse of Sisapa Records crippled any attempt for Cotton to tour to promote the album. "There was no help there. I did headline Earth Day in Columbus, Ohio, with Lou Gramm. I had the best band in Columbus. Then I went down to Florida and opened for Marshall Tucker and that was it. That's all I did."

Rusty Young began his post-Poco career by joining Vince Gill's touring band with friends Reed Nielson and Richard Neville. He also did some scattered session work, but primarily it was Young's intention to sit back and take things easy for the first time in his adult life. The Vince Gill tour provided Young with the opportunity to play a tour without worrying about carrying the load. When Gill's path crossed the hit country duo of Foster and Lloyd, Young and the pair found many common interests and eventually agreed to team up when they returned to Nashville to try to write together.

However, as 1988 began to wane, Young contacted several of his ex-Poco mates, including Jimmy Messina and Richie Furay to do a project together. It stemmed from the "alumni" album concept first mentioned in 1986. Although the initial idea was to reunite ALL former members of Poco, Young's efforts eventually evolved into a full-blown reunion of the original five members of Poco. The ball began rolling when Young and Messina decided to work together on a project. Rusty Young explains, "I talked to Jimmy I said, 'Why don't we do something - the time is right.'" Shortly thereafter, like the next week or something, I saw Richie, and I told him. He said, 'Boy, I really would like to do something too. Why don't we do something - the three of us.' Then I got back to Jimmy and he said, "I've got a great idea - let's make it the original band - let's call Tim - we'll get George. Let's go in and make that record we didn't make 20 years ago."

Young supported Messina's concept, but was hesitant about having to ignore his partner of so many years, Paul Cotton. But Young wanted to work with Messina so he bowed to Messina's wishes. As for Cotton, he was philosophical. "A lot of fans looked for me in that project, and I was approached about doing it, but it never worked out," Cotton said. Young told Lydia Carole DeFretos of *Harmonies*, "We decided it was going to be the original group. At one point, the concept was run by Tim - we ran it by him. We talked about doing the original five, we talked about doing everybody - all seven, including Paul Cotton and Tim Schmit with the five originals. To be honest, Tim wasn't really interested. But it didn't matter because that really wasn't the concept we wanted anyway." "I spoke with Timmy," explains Messina, "and Timmy had a reluctance to becoming a part of it. I'll paraphrase what I remember that he had spent a lot of time in the band, there was a lot of water under the bridge, and it was just not something he wanted to revisit."

Young set about to contact Randy Meisner. He called Alan Kovac, Meisner's former manager, to get Meisner's phone number.

"One of my first calls was to Allen Kovac, who's our manager," Young says. "I was under the impression that he managed Randy. He did manage Randy Meisner for some period of time. As it turns out, Alan wasn't managing him but he said, 'This sounds like a great project. I'd really like to get involved.' He called Randy and talked to Randy about doing it. He came to us and said, 'If I manage you guys, here's what I think I can do for you.' He organized putting the five of us together." Kovac's Left Bank Management group was currently riding a very hot wave in the person of Richard Marx. Kovac's presentation was impressive enough that the group agreed to sign with Left Bank.

Richie Furay recalls, "I think everyone was in place when I was approached. I know the idea was kicked around to bring Timothy and Paul on board but that quickly was brushed aside – stating 'Let's bring out the original band.' I don't think Timothy was too keen on the idea, but it would have made for a 'take it to the next step' opportunity."

With the business side taken care of, Randy Meisner, George Grantham, Jimmy Messina, Rusty Young and Richie Furay got together in southern California to consider the possibility of doing an album together and touring. The five men converged on Messina's recording studio in Santa Barbara in January 1989 to test out how things sounded. They jammed on a few Poco riffs as well as Furay's classic *Kind Woman* and decided that there was a sound still there among them. Over the course of three days, the five men talked about what the project would and should entail. They made it clear to Furay that they didn't want the reunion to become a platform for his religious beliefs. Furay agreed, provided that the band did not ask him to compromise his beliefs with the material that they would perform. All of them seemed comfortable with the ground rules and told Kovac to see if there was any label interest in a Poco reunion album.

Kovac went right to work and found a willing record company in RCA Records. Messina told *Billboard*, "RCA Records President Bob Buziak was the key to the deal. Bob was actually the one who saw the vision and was willing to finance the project so that we could actually get done what we needed to do. He believed enough to gamble on taking a group that hadn't been together in 20 years, and he put his money where his mouth was. He was really instrumental in making this happen." Poco made its demands and they were expensive. Since the band was scattered throughout the country, it was bound to be expensive bringing them together to record and tour. Still, RCA offered them a good deal and Poco accepted it. A contract for one album and a supporting tour was signed with RCA.

The label also fronted the money for two videos to help promote the band.

Messina remembers, "Things started to get pulled together. Left Bank said, 'It's a great group, we'll get the original members together, we can get thousands and thousands of dollars for concerts.' To be honest with you, I think Kovac was very, very excited about the band and genuinely liked the band." This enthusiasm originally fueled the reunion as each member viewed the reunion with an optimistic eye.

Messina was stunned by what happened next. He relates, "They told me, 'Jimmy, you're not going to produce it.' I said, 'Uh, OK. What do you want me to do?' 'We just want you to play and sing.' 'That actually sounds kind of nice. You mean I don't have to wear two hats?'" Kovac suggested that the band use David Cole. Young told *Harmonies*, "Allen [Kovac] said, 'Here's the producer for this project - this guy makes hit records. He knows how to deal with five personalities like you guys.' It's a unique project in that you've got guys who have done it their way for the most part. We needed someone that could stand back and say, 'Okay, that's what you think.' And he said, 'David Cole's that guy.' He was right." Messina and Young met with Cole and found that they would be able to work together without any problem. But Messina was still not convinced that was the right thing to do.

The reformed Poco entered the studio in March to record with David Cole producing. Each of the members submitted several songs for consideration. Outside material was submitted as well, including a song by Richard Marx. Cole and representatives of RCA listened to the demos and decided what material the group should record. As Messina told *Relix* writer Mick Skidmore, "They chose the material that they thought would make the best and most rounded-out album. We were subsequently notified as to which songs would be recorded and we took them and went into a rehearsal period and made it work for us." After a decade's reflection, Messina went even further in his assessment. "*Call It Love* was not a song that we would have written," contends Messina. "We were told that was the hit single. There were other songs that were given to us that were supposed to sound like Poco, but it was someone else's vision of what Poco would sound like. That was unbelievable that they wouldn't trust us with our music. After a while I got the feeling like someone was trying to possibly create an image that would be Poco in this day and age as opposed to letting us be who we were. And that may be because they didn't hear any songs that they thought were Poco and were radio-like."

It wasn't until after LEGACY's release that news was slowly leaked that problems had been encountered during the recording sessions. George Grantham had "personal problems" and was unable to do any drumming. As he explains, "I had just gone through some personal things that took me away from being able to be involved in that at first...rehearsing and....when it came time to record, there was stuff going on with me where I just couldn't commit to it. So when I could go to LA, I finally did and I was at the studio every day, but they had already rehearsed with another drummer and he was the one doing the album, playing the drums on it. Boy, I wish that could have been different. I really would have liked to have been part of that. Vocally I was, but not as far as playing drums." Messina confirms that Grantham had some medical problems that kept him from participating in the recording sessions. "We had to find someone else," confirms Messina, "because here we were in the studio again and I'm thinking, 'Gee, this is familiar.'" Instead, Gary Mallabar and Jeff Pocaro took over during the sessions. Some band members were also upset when producer David Cole decided to go with more outside material instead of the band's original songs. Meisner had been unable to offer any original material. He had to rely on outside songs.

Another conflict arose when the band got together at Messina's Ojai Ranch to begin rehearsals. Richie Furay objected to several of the songs they considered recording. He felt the subject matter wasn't suited for him to sing and still maintain his credibility among his congregation. The band had barely made it through a couple of tunes before Furay called a halt to the rehearsal and told his band mates that he didn't think the reunion was going to work for him. It initiated long discussions that eventually lead into the night. The result was that the entire group was willing to try to find a way to make it work.

One song in particular bothered Furay, *Call It Love*. The song was written by Ronnie Guilbeau, Richard Lonow, and Billy Crain. The original lyrics contained the stanza, "I make you wet, you make me sweat." There was no way that Furay was going to sing that line. In fact, it wasn't a song that Poco would have sung at any stage of their career. Some concessions were made and Messina re-wrote the lyrics, but Furay still refused to participate on some tracks. Especially disappointing from Messina's perspective was Furay's refusal to sing on his tune *Look Within*. Messina had begun the tune years earlier when he heard Furay during the early stages of his preaching career. When he learned the pair would be working on the reunion project together, Messina finished off the song especially for Furay to sing on. However, Furay's perspective was that it was nothing but new-age philosophy that was not Christian, and he refused to sing on it.

Despite a great deal of media attention, Messina was quick to correct some misconceptions, however. He told Jim Monahan of WNEW, "Richie wasn't responsible for any music not being released." He was unable to participate fully due to his church commitment, as well. As a result, the original Poco really didn't record together. The album was mostly the work of Messina, Meisner, and Young.

RCA released a debut single off the album in August of 1989. *Call It Love/ Lovin' You Every Minute* gained immediate radio play and hurried up the charts. Rusty Young's lead vocals over a memorable rhythm guitar riff led to Poco's second biggest hit when it crested at #18 on the charts.

RCA hired director Michael Bay to put together music videos for the band's first two scheduled singles. Furay was concerned and called Bay directly to warn him that he would not appear in any video that conflicted with his values. Bay assured him that there wouldn't be a problem. Indeed, when filming took place Bay filmed the band lip-synching to *Call It Love* and *Nothin' To Hide*. When the videos were screened, Furay was disappointed to find scenes of men hosing down women in the desert had been interspersed with shots of the band. Although he demanded that Alan Kovak lead the effort for making changes, Kovak refused, saying he'd seen it and didn't find anything wrong with it. Instead Furay contacted RCA directly, and they made it sound like they were willing to edit the video. RCA promised to screen the edited video for Furay at the RCA convention in Nashville where Poco was scheduled to perform.

Poco arrived in Nashville on the eve of the RCA convention ready for their first public appearance together. Rehearsals went well and Furay finally asked to see the newly re-cut video. RCA executives called a meeting of the band and informed Furay that the video would not be edited and that it had already been released. Furay was enraged and despite a threatening thunderstorm, left Nashville without performing with the band. Frustrated, Poco went ahead with the performance and anxiously awaited the album's release.

LEGACY appeared late in August. It opened with the outstanding Poco tribute written by Richie Furay and Scott Sellen entitled *When It All Began*. Furay and Sellen had provided the lyrics to a melody written by Anthony Krizan and Stephen Pasch. The single *Call It Love* followed. Randy Meisner made his debut on a song written by Van Stephenson and Jeff Silbar called *The Nature Of Love*. Grantham was upbeat about including outside material throughout his career with Poco, but the choice *of The Nature of Love* left him puzzled. "That one," sighed Grantham, "I really didn't think that song fit." Furay also complained about the risqué lyrics of this tune and prevailed upon Van Stephenson to alter some of them. Young contributed *What Do People Know* which featured some fine acoustic picking from Young and Messina. Young had intended Furay to sing the song, but he wound up taking the lead vocals when Furay's participation dwindled during the sessions. Two selections by Messina rounded out the first side, *Lovin' You Every Minute* and *Follow Your Dreams*. The former was a ZZ Top styled rocker, and the latter was an acoustic piece with bright Poco harmonies. Both Messina tunes dated back to the early 80's. *Lovin' You Every Minute* had been included on Messina's Warner Brothers solo debut, and *Follow Your Dreams* had been used in the soundtrack of the 1983 film *Independence Day*.

The second side opened with *Rough Edges*, a song written by Young along with Nashville writers Radney Foster and Bill Lloyd. Meisner did lead vocals on it and the following song. *Nothin' To Hide* was written and produced by Richard Marx and sounded similar to Meisner's big Eagle hit *Take It To The Limit*. Young struck again with *Who Else*, a nice mid-tempo song with fine harmonies. A bonus track not included on the vinyl release was Messina's contemplative *Look Within*. Remarkably, Messina began the song back when he was originally with Poco. He dusted the tune off and completed it specifically for the reunion project. The album ends with the stirring Furay song about the homeless, *If It Wasn't For You*. Furay was putting his vocals on this final tune, and it proved to be a struggle. He recalls, "The chorus is extremely high, so high that when I sing the song today, I play it in a different key. But on that day, I was struggling to tackle one of those hard-to-reach parts. I'll bet I sang that same line for ninety minutes, and I was getting frustrated to the point where I'm sure other people noticed it. When at last they told me I had gotten it right, I wanted to take a break – but it wasn't in the cards. There were twenty people waiting inside the control room to wish me a happy birthday, and it turns out that one of the reasons they'd kept me singing for so long was to sneak everyone in without my noticing."

LEGACY received good reviews, and the initial single pushed sales of the album into the gold range. Messina told *Rolling Stone* that there would never be another Poco album unless the original five members recorded it. Fans of Paul Cotton and Tim Schmit pointed out that they had been members much longer than Messina, Meisner, and Furay combined. Messina later amended his comments, suggesting that Poco record occasionally using various groupings.

LEGACY was released during a summer filled with classic rock band reunions. The album's performance on the charts made it stand out as one of the few to get much attention. This is likely in large part to Cole's contemporary production and the song selection calculated to appeal to a more modern audience. LEGACY had drawn considerable fire from hard-core Poco fans for its lack of Poco qualities. But gold Poco albums are quite rare and it was hard to argue with that.

No immediate tour plans for Poco were announced. During a spate of radio promotions, Poco pointed out that the flurry of reunion bands out on the road made touring a very financially risky proposition until after the new year. If the album continued to do well, Poco would consider touring at that time.

RCA made a push for European sales by sending Meisner, Messina, and Young to the Continent for promotional visits and a few acoustic radio concerts. "We did travel all over," Meisner remarks. "We went to Europe for a month to promote this whole album. Out of a month we played twenty four days and we would get up at five in the morning, go to every radio station in Europe and plug this album. It didn't do a darn bit of good."

Sales of LEGACY stateside soon warranted some sort of public appearances to assist in promoting it. Poco made a network TV appearance on *The Arsenio Hall Show* on October 4. They performed *Call It Love* and did an acoustic medley of *Take It To The Limit, Crazy Love* and *Your Mama Don't Dance*. A month later they appeared on *The Tonight Show* and performed a shaky version of *Call It Love*. After some tense negotiations, Furay made both appearances and agreed to participate in the six-week tour stipulated in his contract.

The year 1990 dawned and plans were made to go out on a short tour to accommodate Furay's tight schedule. A two-week tour of opening gigs for patron Richard Marx was booked by Left Bank. They hired keyboardist David Vandercore to play the tours to help fill out the arrangements. While Poco rehearsed for their first tour in several years, RCA released an edited version of the Richard Marx song *Nothin' To Hide/If It Wasn't For You* as a single in November. It started slowly, eventually peaking at a disappointing #39. Another video was produced using a very similar style to the clip used to promote *Call It Love*.

Disputes over lyrical content continued to plague the band. Furay continually found it difficult to sing some of the songs in Poco's prospective set. Amazingly, Furay objected to the bridge of Messina's *Your Mama Don't Dance*. "I'm dumbfounded," confides Messina. "Richie wanted to re-write the bridge so that the lyrics work for him. So now Richie and I are back in conflict again. Here's a song that's been a hit for 20 years with no government censorship or religious opposition to it. I don't understand it. But being the problem solver that I am, I say, 'Ok, you re-write it but we've got jobs to do in the meantime, what do we do about that?' Furay was able to convince both Messina and Meisner to let him revise the lyrics to a couple of their tunes before touring.

Poco's tour supporting Richard Marx began in late January 1990. They scheduled a couple of warm up club dates, one of which they canceled to make a second appearance on *The Tonight Show* to perform *Nothin' To Hide*. The tour finally got underway in Pittsburgh on January 24. Their nine-song set lasted just over 40 minutes and showcased Furay, who had taken a back seat on LEGACY. The set included old favorites such as *Rose Of Cimarron, Good Feelin' To Know*, and *You Better Think Twice*. Poco also highlighted tunes from LEGACY such as *Call It Love, Nothin' To Hide*, and *When It All Began*. Although their set showed the usual opening night jitters, they were obviously having fun. The crowd was less than responsive except for *Call It Love* and *Nothin' To Hide*, the latter song because of its affiliation with the headliner, Marx.

RCA pulled another single out to coincide with the tour in February. *Nature Of Love* featured an open-ended interview as a bonus on the CD single. While it did garner some airplay, *Nature Of Love* failed to hit the pop charts.   The tour was an interesting experience for the veteran rockers. Being an opening act to a teen idol was a sobering experience. The audience of mostly pre-teen girls didn't react particularly well to Poco's material, especially the songs done from Poco's early days. New York *Post* writer Gene Santoro praised the band's NYC appearance while pointing out some rather poor treatment at the hands of Richard Marx crew prior to their appearance at Radio City Music Hall. He wrote, "As they demonstrated to the delighted crowd, they haven't lost the easy-going sense of fun and the formidably enduring voices of their youth. Just pickin' and singin' in the small part of Radio City's gigantic stage not covered by [Richard] Marx's elaborate rig, they played oldie faves and recent hits with fervent, amiable professionalism, and got a standing ovation - a rare feat for an opening act."

The tour stayed east of the Mississippi, and Poco ended the two weeks of shows on what appeared to be a positive note. Poco ended the tour performing a headline gig at the Diamond Club in Toronto. Playing a full 90-minute set for the first time, Poco played plenty of solo tunes from their days after Poco. Richie Furay even performed a Christian tune entitled *Rise Up* during his portion of the show.   But there was tension beneath the surface. Meisner explains, "Richie Furay is a minister in Boulder, Colorado. So when we went out we had to change our lyrics like on the song *Hearts on Fire* we had to change the line "I had myself a tall one waiting in the bar I didn't want to leave here until I had her in the car" it got to Richie. I had to respect Richie but one night we were playing in Toronto and the crowd was really good and I sang the original lyric and Richie got kind of upset about that."

In April, Poco made another live appearance at Farm Aid IV at the Hoosier Dome in Indianapolis, Indiana. All five members participated and their acoustic medley was aired on TV. It would be the last time the original members of Poco performed together. One reason was that at Farm Aid, Messina finally agreed to sing the revised lyrics Furay had written for *Your Mama Don't Dance*. But despite Messina's intent, twenty years of habit intervened. "I had agreed to change the lyric," Messina confesses. "I'm singing the song like I've done for twenty years, and I go on autopilot and sing the wrong lyrics. And Richie comes absolutely unglued. I don't know what to say. It certainly wasn't something I did on purpose. But I think that someone who's put out the effort to make the change and who's comfortable with it, which Richie was, it was really a bad thing for me to do." Messina's attitude reflects a decade of hindsight. At the time, Messina challenged Furay's criticism and stormed off the band bus in anger. It would be quite some time before the pair would reconcile.

The summer concert season loomed ahead, and Left Bank managed to book a long headlining tour for Poco. They booked dates all across the country, unlike the opening tour where they only played east of the Mississippi. The tour began in July, but this time Poco went out without Richie Furay. The trouble encountered during the Richard Marx tour was a significant reason for Furay's departure. It proved too difficult for him to reconcile his religious beliefs with the rock and roll life. The refusal by RCA to edit the videos to suit him and his band mates failure to sing the revised lyrics he had provided were too much. In addition, several members of his church in Colorado had quit in protest of his participation in the Poco project and Furay felt he had to give up music again.

Young maintains, "When it came to the summer tour, even though he'd committed to it, he said, 'I'll do half of it, how's that?'" But the rest of the group declined and told him he might as well return to his ministry. Young defended the decision in an interview with William Ruhlmann in *Relix*. Young said, "We probably never would have done that except for the fact that Randy, Jimmy and I had been out working, promoting the record for eight months ahead of that." There was quite a bit of bitterness in the wake of Furay's reneging on his tour commitment. In interviews for an upcoming re-issue CD from Epic/Sony, Messina, Young, and Meisner held little back in pointing the finger at Furay for Meisner's original departure. Young confided to one fan, "I'm glad that Richie's not along. He keeps seeing the devil in everything. It just wasn't fun anymore." During their summer shows, Young and Messina greeted the inevitable shouts of "Where's Richie" with sarcastic remarks. As the tour wound on, however, the remarks were toned down.

Messina was a bit more charitable after several years of reflection. "I don't blame anybody. We are who we are, and we had gotten diverse. Richie had a congregation, and he had responsibilities and obligations to them. I think his heart was into making the reunion happen, but it just became difficult for him to juggle his prior life and his present life. And that was probably the reality for all of us."

With Furay gone, Poco scrambled to rework their projected set list. The set had been expanded for the summer tour, allowing both Messina and Meisner to play several older songs from their days with Loggins and Messina and the Eagles, respectively. Poco augmented its lineup by recruiting former Poco member Jack Sundrud to replace Furay on rhythm guitar and David Vanecore on keyboards.

Sundrud explains how he rejoined Poco. "After [the Richard Marx] tour, Richie Furay decided not to continue on with the tour. Anyway, that's when Rusty called me. He asked me to do the rest of the tour with them. I was delighted. It was fairly short notice. We rehearsed in LA for about two weeks." Sundrud was so excited about participating that he postponed a recording project with a new band that he had put together for six months.

Poco opened the summer LEGACY tour on June 24, 1990, at the Del Mar Fair in California. Shows followed at the River Fest in Madison, Summerfest in Milwaukee, and Taste of Minnesota in St. Paul. By July 7, Poco arrived at Winter Park, Colorado, for the American Music Festival. Surprisingly, Richie Furay joined Poco at the show and the set was adjusted to open with *When It All Began*. The Denver *Post* noted, "But when the band launched into the song on stage, Furay's microphone cut out, and the potential triumphant entrance turned into one of embarrassment and frustration." Rain thinned the crowd but over 2,000 showed up to brave the elements. Furay later explained that he decided to participate as a favor to the promoter, who had advertised Furay's participation. A week later, another Poco alumnus showed up at their July 13 show at the Ventura Concert Theatre in California. Guitarist Paul Cotton joined the band during their encore of *Legend*.

Although Poco headlined these early shows, by mid-July they were sharing the bill with headliners like Chicago and Dave Mason on shows in the Midwest. Crowds were sparse, but the people who did show up were boisterous Poco fans pleased to see them touring again. Sundrud was pleased to see Poco on a major tour and to be a part of it. "It was great to see Poco on top again."

RCA released another single, *What Do People Know/ When It All Began* during the tour. It didn't chart and featured a clumsy edit that marred the song. The performance of the song live was superior to the recorded version as Messina really opened up on acoustic lead. The band was tight and very energetic. Their show at the Circle Star Theater in San Carlos was played before a small house, but Poco played a lively 90-minute set. Among the non-Poco songs performed were Meisner's *One More Song* from his solo career and the acoustic medley of his Eagles hit *Take It To The Limit* and Messina's *Your Mama Don't Dance*. The bulk of LEGACY was performed except for Furay's songs. Poco also debuted a new Messina song entitled *Sinners and Saints*. Young was adamant that if Poco were to record a second reunion album, he'd make sure that song was on it.

Life as a young boy was filled with unrest
Time was my teacher, revealing its test
I managed to slip through my destiny late
And into the arms, of my ultimate fate

A chance of a lifetime was thrown at my feet
The offer was simple, but the price wasn't cheap
A band full of poets rebellious and free
Showed me a new life, a new life for me

Now I ride with sinners and I sing with saints
and I do what I can to avoid what I cain't
I'll pass of the judgment, now make the call
I'm a playin' my hand, the way the cards fall

So I packed up my suitcase and I set out to see
What life on the road could offer me
From city to city we traveled by day
Night fall would find me on a new stage we'd play

The crowds would go crazy demanding more time
The music would soar and the poets would rhyme

When the encore was over we fled from the scene
To the hideout we'd scurry in a long limousine
So many places in such a short time
The faces are friendly, but one is divine

Her eyes are enchanted the muse has touched deep
There through her body the music it speaks
Conversing with vision, no need for a word
There in her glance a question is heard

Oh, the sweet joy of knowing the man and his song,
Will rest in the heart as the poets, as the poets,
as the poets roll on
                              Sinners and Saints (Jim Messina)

"That was written in Europe with Rusty and Randy," explains Messina. "Being on the road with those guys flashed me back to being with Poco and Buffalo Springfield, and the feeling of what it felt like when I first stepped into the limelight and had the fringe ripped off my jacket to feeling the conflicts that were going on in my heart with Richie. The feeling that I got while writing this song was here I am back in the same place again with Richie and Rusty and Randy and George. And I'm having this hollow feeling inside me again. What is this? Is this the chemistry of our personalities, our behaviors? We have such opportunities. The world wants to know who we are and what we think. We have this opportunity, and we can't keep it together long enough to make that happen with one another."

The tour also took in The Ritz in New York City on August 8 with Dave Mason. Dan Aquilante of the New York *Post's* review remarked, "Poco, who played the Ritz Wednesday, is a sad shadow of its former self. But even through the show dragged for the most part; at times the band regained some of its past glory. The evening's best piece was a new, unrecorded Messina tune *Sinner and Saints* other than that and a couple of Loggins and Messina songs (most notably *Nobody But You*), the night was filled with heartless harmonies and faulty phrasing by a group whose band mates have only the past in common and play together with punch-the-clock passion." The early dates were less than spectacular in terms of turnout, but their East Coast shows did quite well and the audience reaction there was strong. Poco's show at Waterloo Village in Stanhope, New Jersey, was a triumph. The raucous crowd cheered madly at everything, and the band extended their set to an hour and a half. It was one of the few shows that the band strayed from a very rigid set list.

In August, Poco joined the 1990 Marlboro Music Tour, playing a month of dates with .38 Special and Angel Train. Many of these booked dates took place on military bases such as Quantico Marine Base, Pope Air Force Base in Fayetteville, North Carolina, Camp Lejeune in Jacksonville, Florida, Fort Huachuca in Tucson, Arizona, and Pearl Harbor in Hawaii. Their date at Pope Air Force Base had to be canceled when units were shipped to Saudi Arabia for the Desert Shield/Desert Storm maneuvers. Many others allowed off-base personnel to attend when it was clear that there weren't enough base personnel left after deployments to Saudi Arabia to make up a sufficient audience.

After a month's rest, Poco flew to Japan to play a five-date tour. Nearly 2,000 showed up at their opening performance at Nakano Sun Plaza Hall on October 15. Shows followed in Tokyo on October 19, the Bottom Line in Nagoya on October 21, and wound up the tour the next day at the Osaka Takatsuki Shimin Kaikan. Japanese Poco fans were supportive and reviews of the performances were positive. Randy Meisner was especially singled out for applause based in large part because of his recent solo tours in Japan. Jack Sundrud found the whole experience to be positive. "The audiences were very polite, yet appreciative. We were treated royally by both the fans and the promoters."

Poco remained positive about the summer tour despite the mixed reactions and the reviewers harping on the absence of Richie Furay. "It was great to work with that whole bunch," explains Sundrud. "I was treated very well by all concerned. It was the first big rock tour of which I had been a part. I loved seeing Poco back on top. It was very rewarding in that sense." What the summer tour did show was that the reunion wasn't as much a celebration of Poco as it was an attempt to jump-start the solo careers of Messina, Meisner, and Young. Very little Poco music was played and with good reason. Messina and Meisner were responsible for almost no Poco songs of note.

Renewed interest in Poco did lead to the release of a two-CD set from Epic/Legacy in November 1990. For the first time, Epic put together a quality Poco product. Scouring the country for master tapes, Epic compiled an excellent collection of recordings from Poco's tenure on the label. Bill Irwin worked hard to provide a quality product and proved to be quite a detective when it came to hunting down master tapes. The sonic quality of much of the material was vastly improved, with many of the songs being remixed. Individual members of Poco were consulted regarding availability of rare tracks, and the band history was included in the CD booklet. A double CD did not leave much room for everyone's Poco favorites, but Epic/Legacy managed a pleasing blend of the familiar and the unreleased that covered the band's years with Epic.

FORGOTTEN TRAIL included nine unreleased tracks, including several from the CRAZY EYES sessions. Among the unreleased tracks made available for the first time were *Last Call (Cold Enchilada #3)*, a Rusty Young instrumental whose title parodied the Flying Burrito Brothers' *Hot Burrito #1 and #2* cuts; *Lullaby in September*, a touching Jimmy Messina song that was intended as a gift to the Furay's in anticipation of the birth of their first child; an acoustic version of *You Better Think Twice*; and a trio of tunes, *Nothin's Still the Same, Believe Me*, and *Get in the Wind* from the CRAZY EYES sessions.

Critics had high praise for FORGOTTEN TRAIL, citing Sony's restraint in issuing only two CD's and the nice balance of well-known tracks and unreleased material.

The end of the LEGACY tour left a sour taste in the mouths of Poco members. Messina philosophized, "The time when Poco had the will and the desire to be a group was when we were younger and had the same goals in mind, which was to be successful with our music, and we were pretty much on equal terms. We all had different goals, and we now lived in different places. We had families and lifestyles that were so unrelated to one another that it made it difficult to sit down and refocus the energy on the same situation. It was one of those situations where if everybody had been there for the same reasons, it could have been a very enjoyable experience." The whole experience had been a struggle. Young admits, "People don't change; you still have the same kind of personalities, the same kind of conflicts."

In addition, Left Banke Management had gotten Poco involved in a morass of legal trouble. "Allen Kovac had made some commitments to some people that we would play that we didn't get to once the group busted up," professed Messina. "We went and performed to honor some commitments that he made on our behalf."

The group had also managed to get personally obligated for a large amount of merchandise that didn't sell during the tour. The band took a substantial financial hit, and they ended up having to commit to a few shows in 1991 to placate some promoters. The ultimate impact of the merchandise situation and missed shows was that none of the members of Poco have made any money from the LEGACY project.

Messina explains that Poco's LEGACY tour had a bitter legacy of its own, "By the time the thing was over, I think we could barely finish our last tour. Not making enough to keep it on the road. We signed agreements that we all felt said something different than they did and ended up having to basically reimburse advances back to people, and ended up not making a dime and probably going into the hole for some of them. Some of them couldn't take the hit; some of us were able to – which was bad. It was not a good thing."

Meisner concurs, "Let me tell you what really happened. This was going down around the time of the Persian Gulf War and our management had arranged all these things on military bases. We had all this merchandising to sell and when we got to all these army bases we were playing to empty crowds because all the troops were in the Persian Gulf. After that we played a few more things but I ended up paying all this money for merchandising rather than making money on it."

After the LEGACY tour, George Grantham departed, joining a new version of the Flying Burrito Brothers with John Beland and Gib Guibeau. Grantham's role in the recording of LEGACY was virtually nil, but he had proved to be a solid drummer during both tours. The new version of the Burritos worked for a short time on some demos, recording a total of six songs in 1991. However, when a record deal was signed and the recording began, the Burritos chose to add studio veteran Ronnie Tutt on drums and Grantham moved on. By 1992, he was out of the music business entirely.

In the wake of the LEGACY tour, there was some speculation in the press about a second Poco reunion album. In spite of a gold album, RCA did not make money on the Poco reunion. The high overhead cost of getting the quintet back together and promotion efforts kept the profit margin slim. RCA indicated the label had no interest in a second Poco album. In February 1991, Left Banke announced the formation of Impact Records, a joint venture label with powerhouse music conglomerate MCA. The announcement listed Poco as one of Impact Records clients.

Randy Meisner's attentions were diverted when a Nashville DJ began playing an old cut *Learning the Game* off the 1985 Black Tie album. It caught on, entering the *Billboard* Country charts on December 15, 1990. Black Tie was in demand for media appearances. But despite the sudden attention, Black Tie failed to catch on with the country audience. By the early part of the year, Meisner was again available.

After some hurried rehearsals, Young, Messina, and Meisner went out on the road to play a few shows to make up for the promised appearances during the summer of 1990. They kept overhead low by touring as an acoustic act without a drummer. During one of the 1991 acoustic shows, Rusty Young confirmed to fans from the stage in Allentown, Pennsylvania, that the trio was working on a second Poco reunion album. Messina explains, "Randy and I and Rusty, after we got through all the crap, had come to my studio and brought some songs together to see what we had. Actually we were really enjoying each other's company."

Messina arranged for the trio to go into his studio with producer Michael Clute to record some demos. Although the general idea behind them was to interest a label in another Poco record, Messina was more interested in seeing if working with Young and Meisner was worth investing his time instead of continuing to work on his solo projects. "The reason I chose to do that was to see if we could work together, to see if there was some magic there. Because both of these people were two people that I enjoyed being reunited with and to this day truly appreciate and respect for the contributions they've made in my life. But what I realized was that Randy is a great singer. He writes, but not that much. Rusty is a really great writer. As a singer he's more of a singer-songwriter and at the time, my voice had developed to the point where I just liked singing with people with a fuller range and quicker to grab parts. The experience I had with Randy and Rusty was one that would be a lot more difficult as an artist to work with. And honestly, I felt that I just wanted to work as a solo artist."

After fulfilling the last of their obligations Stateside, Poco returned to Japan for a short series of shows. Meisner, Messina, and Young took Gary Mallabar along to play percussion. They opened on July 26 at the Bunkamura Orchard Hall. They followed with shows at Lake Yamanaka and ended their Japan tour with a performance in Osaka. Opening the shows was ex-Eagle Bernie Leadon and Seldom Seen. At most shows Poco invited Leadon to join them on their encore of the old Eagle tune *Midnight Flyer*. Leadon's spirited banjo playing brought a touch of old Poco to the shows. In Japan, Meisner again drew constant calls from the audience due in part to his solo tours there. Meisner delighted fans by debuting a new tune *Long Time Blue* written with songwriter-friend Bruce Gaitch.

The 1991 acoustic tour, modest as it was, appeared to have put a quiet end to the career of Poco. The trio of Meisner, Messina, and Young parted to begin work on other projects, and Poco was laid to rest for what appeared to be the final time.

16
When the Coast is Clear

The remainder of 1991 was quiet as the former members of Poco were all busy on various projects outside the band. Paul Cotton's CHANGING HORSES had done very little in the marketplace, especially after Sisapa Records closed its doors shortly after the album's release. Still, it had provided Cotton with a creative outlet aside from Poco. With the band on hold, Cotton began work on a second solo album. He laid down a number of demo tracks during 1991, but wasn't able to interest another label.

For the first time in his professional career, Rusty Young began work on a project outside of Poco. Young along with Patrick Simmons, John Cowan, and Bill Lloyd formed a group named Four Wheel Drive. When originally putting the project together, Bill Lloyd had even considered ex-Byrd Gene Clark but was unable to contact him. Tragically, Clark died shortly after Lloyd's failed attempt. Randy Meisner was also approached as the bass player, however he dropped out of the project when he learned of the time commitment involved. The Four Wheel Drive project was intended as a one-time album of country-rock stars in the tradition of the Travelin' Wilburys. Four Wheel Drive spent nearly a year and a half writing and recording songs for RCA-Nashville under the sponsorship of the head of A&R for RCA, Josh Leo.

Unfortunately, Josh Leo and the rest of his staff were fired mid-way through the project, and the group lost its label support. Surprisingly, RCA allowed the band to complete the album. However, after hearing it, RCA determined that the material was too

pop for country and too country for pop, a throwback to the difficulties Poco had experienced with radio at the start of their career.
RCA filed the Four Wheel Drive tapes away and released the group
from the label. Young bitterly recounts, "At RCA, the guy that made
the decision not to release the record is the same guy who told
Vince Gill that he didn't have a career and dropped Vince from the
label. The same guy is not releasing our record and that frustration
just really is a tough one to swallow, when you know you've done
really good work, and there are people who would really like it, and
it doesn't get out because of some guy you have very little respect
for." The album featured four songs written by Young, three of
which he did the lead vocals on. Among the tunes was a version of
Old Hat, co-written with Jack Sundrud, that used piano and strings
that closed the album.

In addition to the Four Wheel Drive project, Rusty received a
call from promoter John Erdle in January 1992. Erdle asked if Poco
would be interested in participating in the Taste of Colorado Festival in Denver in September. Young told Erdle that the reunion band
was no longer performing. Erdle asked if Young and Cotton would
be willing to get back together as Poco. After contacting Cotton
and learning that he was interested, Young confirmed that they
would play the Taste of Colorado Festival. Young made it clear to
Erdle that this was a new lineup of Poco, not the reunion band.
That was acceptable to Erdle.

Paul Cotton recalls Larry Larson as the true force behind the
reformation. "Larry Larson, our first manager, called us up out of
the blue," Cotton contends. "You guys need to get back out on the
road. And he fixed up some things for us to play." Young and Cotton put together a new lineup after some brief auditions. Drummer
Tim Smith and bassist Richard Neville provided backup vocals as
well as the rhythm section. Neville was a former associate of
Young's prior to his involvement with Buffalo Springfield, and Smith
had played drums briefly with Four Wheel Drive.

Larry Larson began representing Poco and soon lined up additional dates for the band to play besides the September date in
Colorado. Young and Cotton gave Larson clear instructions to plan a
limited number of engagements. If they were fun and the audience
responded, they would continue. If not, Poco would once again
fold. It was a very similar situation as the Nashville years when
Poco played a limited number of dates, allowing Young and Cotton
to pursue other interests. The limited number of gigs also allowed
the group to focus on a basic live set that would not require a substantial amount of rehearsal time. The quartet met in Nashville and
put together a 12-15 song set that highlighted Poco's recent career,

focusing on the songs that were likely to be the most familiar to the casual Poco fan. Cotton smiles, "It was just a way to keep his secretary busy, I think. She turned out to be really good for us. Her husband Michael Thompson ended up playing keyboards for the Eagles!"

Beginning in the summer, Cotton and Young toured the country again on a small scale as Poco. The emphasis was low-key and low overhead. The band went out without roadies or lots of equipment. To keep costs down, they rented their backline at each concert site rather than travel with amps and drum kit. The band themselves served as their own roadies and set up and tore down their own gear. Young cut down his traveling arsenal to steel guitar, acoustic guitar, and electric guitar. No banjo, mandolin, dobro, or other instruments. The tour routing was understandably scattered as Poco tried to establish themselves again on the concert circuit. Their first gigs were in June in Wisconsin and Florida. Right way, the critical response was positive. Poco played two dates late in August in southern California. They also played a free show in Indianapolis, Indiana. Poco opened for America at Kansas City's Spirit Festival on September 3, 1992. Robert Eisele of the Kansas City *Star* noted, "To attempt an acoustic set in the wide-open expanses of the Liberty Memorial mall takes intestinal fortitude but opening act Poco pulled it off. The 15-minute all acoustic middle segment spotlighting the nimble fingers of guitarist vocalist Rusty Young was the highlight of the 50-minute set."

The initial response from promoters and fans alike had been so positive that Young and Cotton gave Larson the green light to book further shows for the group. Poco appeared at the Taste of Colorado Festival in Colorado Springs, and Richie Furay appeared with them both days. Local TV reporter Richard Randall with KTTV interviewed them during breaks between sets. Furay was obviously enjoying the opportunity to play a couple of old tunes in front of an audience again. Later in the month, Poco joined an all-star lineup at Charlie Daniel's 15th annual Volunteer Jam at the Starwood Amphitheatre in Nashville. Shows in October included the Livin' on the Levee festival in West Memphis, Tennessee. On December 11, Poco played two shows at the Konocti Harbor Resort at Clear Lake, California. Their set was a nice blend of classic Poco, along with all of Rusty Young's lead vocals from LEGACY. Young debuted a new song *Old Hat*, which was to be included on his album with Pat Simmons, Cowan, and Lloyd. Again, Paul Cotton did not play a new tune, but gave an interesting basic rendition of *Bad Weather* without the distinctive lead lines. This version, claimed Young, is how Poco first heard the song when Cotton played it for them in Richie Furay's living room in Laurel Canyon. Poco followed the performance with a couple of sets at the Catalyst in Santa Cruz on December 12.

This new version of Poco could be inconsistent at times but clearly kept the spirit of Poco alive. "I thought that band really rocked," Cotton says assuredly. "But we never recorded anything so I'm not really sure how we sounded." Reviewers harshly criticized the band's rhythm section in the early going. One reason was Richard Neville's over-achieving on bass. Cotton playfully recalls, "Richard tends to over-play. He'd say, 'Well, I was born the same day as Jaco [Pastorius]." 'So?!?' 'And I can play just like him.' But not with Poco! I remember one time when his mother showed up at a show, he goes into Jaco right in the middle of a song!" But by year's end, the band had solidified their sound and delivered entertaining sets consistently.

While Young and Cotton had modestly revived Poco, both kept their solo options open. Despite their debacle at RCA Records, Young and the Four Wheel Drive band weren't willing to give up, and they continued to shop themselves around Nashville. In 1993, they successfully signed with Warner Brothers Records. Jim Ed Norman, head of Warner Brothers Nashville Division, chose not to purchase the masters of the RCA album. His opinion was that the group needed to focus more on a sound friendly to country radio. Norman also felt that the group should have one lead singer to generate a familiar sound. Although that was not true to the original concept of the group, the band decided to give it a try.

John Cowan was selected as the lead voice of Four Wheel Drive and the songwriters in the band began composing new material. Within six months, the group had successfully completed their first recording sessions and submitted them to Warner Brothers. Norman was supportive but was not entirely happy with what he heard. Instead, he sent them back to the studio to come up with some more songs that were radio friendly. It was a frustrating experience for the veterans of the record company wars, but they were committed to their new group. Each of the writers continued to come up with material and the band recorded demos of these new tunes.

Knowing that his new project was still in the formative stages, Rusty Young kept Poco alive. He and Cotton went out on the road again in 1993. During the spring Larson booked Poco on a package tour with Edgar Winter, Steppenwolf, and Dave Mason called "Grand Slam Jam." Cotton remains perplexed at the decision, "Yeah, that thing with Steppenwolf, Edgar Winter...that thing went all over the country. That was really weird to start back up on something like that." Depending on the venues, different combinations would appear on the bill. On May 18, Poco joined Dave Mason at the Luther Burbank Center in Santa Rosa, California. They played a spirited set and then asked Young's Four Wheel Drive band mate Patrick Simmons to join them for the encore. After shows at the Circle Star Theatre in San Carlos and the Universal Amphitheatre, Poco joined America for a brief swing through Oregon and Washington. Poco stayed busy throughout June and July, concentrating on venues in the Midwest and in Colorado. In July, Poco headlined in St. Louis. David Surkamp of the *Post-Dispatch* reviewed their show. "Interestingly enough Poco's program did not rely on a 'greatest hits' format alone, although chestnuts such as *Crazy Love* and *Call It Love* filled the blanks nicely. An acoustic interlude actually produced some of my favorite moments of the show." Later in the year, Poco went back to the clubs, playing many of their staple venues like Jannus Landing in St. Petersburg and Konocti Harbor Resort in Clear Lake, California. The 1993 set was only an hour long, leaving no room for any new material, only the old favorites. "It was too hard to find time to rehearse," explains Cotton. "We were all over the country, and it just wasn't economical to get us together for rehearsals. It's still that way."

Poco's drawing power was still strong enough to draw on the nostalgia circuit, however it still frustrated Young that Poco no longer attracted a contemporary audience. "We're not an act that is going to appear in our underwear and use four-letter words like a lot of acts do. It really saddens me to see what it's come down to." More and more, Young appeared to be distancing himself from his rock and roll history and focusing on his new band.

Rusty Young and Four Wheel Drive also managed to do some live dates during August 1993 opening for the Doobie Brothers. The dates allowed the new band to get some live work in, and it also allowed Pat Simmons to tour with his old band. Pat Simmons and John Cowan did double-duty by performing with both Four Wheel Drive and the Doobies. Four Wheel Drive was often unbilled so fans rarely knew what to make of them. Their short sets generally consisted of a mish-mash of well-known tunes from the member's former bands with a couple of Four Wheel Drive tunes tossed in.

As a result of this visibility, Four Wheel Drive quickly found that there were a number of bands out there with the same name and the threat of lawsuits loomed. Rather than fight it, the band dropped the name Four Wheel Drive. After some brief discussion, Young, Lloyd, Cowan, and Simmons chose to go with a suggestion of Simmons', the Sky Kings. Warner Brothers allowed the musicians plenty of time to rehearse and get their material in order. They spent much of 1994 working on tunes, songwriting, and searching for an acceptable musical direction. While the time spent was vital to the Sky Kings' development, Young felt the pressure to keep his partner working.

With the lack of movement on their solo careers, Young and Cotton turned their attention back to Poco. In 1994, Young and Cotton returned to the road with Neville and Smith again playing back up. In March 1994, Poco returned to Alaska to play the Cabin Fever Festival in Anchorage. While there, Young put Poco into proper context for Anchorage Daily News reporter Brenda Woody. "Poco is one part of my life. But I have three careers going at the same time." Poco's 1994 shows were sparse as Young's attentions were diverted to his other recording project. More and more time was being spent with Bill Lloyd and John Cowan in Nashville trying to find the right blend of contemporary country sounds and their respective musical backgrounds. Still, Poco continued to play solid, professional sets for small, devoted crowds. Young and Cotton added a couple of Richie Furay tunes back into their set during the 1994 shows. *A Child's Claim to Fame* and *Kind Woman* were pleasant surprises, and occasionally they also brought back *Good Feeling to Know* as well.

Meanwhile, Cotton began working on a new set of demo recordings and shopping for a label in 1994. "That whole project started with that song *The Coast is Clear*," explains Cotton. "Richard Neville actually wrote the lyrics. He stayed with me for three days in LA and he had that thing finished. But he didn't have any music for it. [Laughs.] So once again I find out what I do best and put that together with a Neil Young sort of urge." The sessions began with Thom Landt and Mike Botte assisting Cotton in Botte's White Elephant Studio in San Diego. They recorded a number of tunes with Botte on bass and emulators. Botte had just acquired recording equipment that had 24-track capabilities. Cotton recalls, "We had to learn the recording studio. It was Adat at the time...24-track. He had three of them lined up. So we did a crash course on the fly." The trio spent quite a bit of time learning to use the equipment, but eventually managed to do preliminary recording on about a half dozen tunes. Sessions then continued in Landt's Avenida Reposo Studio in Escondito. Cotton commuted to California to record, ultimately making over 20 trips. They were able to complete six or seven tracks for the proposed album.

Cotton eventually convened sessions in Austin, Texas, with former Loggins and Messina drummer Merle Bregante, guitarist John Inman, and bassists Charles Larkey and Kyle Brock at Crib Works Studio. The Austin sessions resulted in the songs *Lanikai*, *High Water*, and *Santiva* being completed. These sessions became commonly known as the WHEN THE COAST IS CLEAR project. Six songs were recorded including *Just Out of Reach, It Never Goes Away, The Sunset Kidd,* and a cover of Van Morrison's *Into the Mystic.*   While rumors swirled that Cotton was about to sign a solo deal with either Marguaritaville Records or Rhino Records, a deal was never completed, and the songs remained unreleased. Many of the demos eventually found their way out to the collectors' market. Still, a solo career continued to elude Cotton, but it was all he had to look forward to.

However, 1995 was another light year as Poco continued to limit its live performances. Warner Brothers was anxious now to see the results of the Sky Kings rehearsals and were pressuring Young to concentrate on recording a new album. Poco also chose to pare down some of the road shows by doing acoustic duo shows and leaving Neville and Smith behind. The set list of these acoustic shows had Poco doing some different tunes for a change. Cotton dusted off *Cajun Moon* from the COWBOYS AND ENGLISHMEN album and *Too Many Nights Too Long* from ROSE OF CIMARRON. Young debuted a new tune *One Tear at a Time* from his unreleased Four Wheel Drive project. Many of these acoustic duo shows began a trend that would blossom a decade later at the Wildwood Springs Lodge in Missouri. The intimate venues and relaxed attitudes of Cotton and Young allowed for a livingroom feel to their shows.

The Sky Kings continued to rehearse and finally got permission to go into the studio to begin recording their album for Warner Brothers. They immediately ran into problems when Patrick Simmons decided not to knuckle under to pressure from Warners to concentrate on the Sky Kings project. Michael McDonald had consented to joining a Doobie Brothers reunion tour during the summer of 1995. When Warners balked at Simmons' participation, he chose to leave his new group for the more lucrative reunion market on May 26, 1995. Young didn't feel the decision was a bad one for the band. "I personally never liked the idea of four people, because I think it spells real trouble down the line," he predicted. "No one gets to sing as much as they want and no one gets to write as much as they want." The Sky Kings continued to work, taking some time off for a few Poco dates during the summer. By May 1995, the Sky Kings had completed their album, mixed it in August, and began a short tour opening for Hank Williams, Jr.   The Sky Kings live band included drummer Fran Breen, formerly with Nanci Griffith and the Waterboys, and Peter Hyrka on fiddle, keyboards, and guitar.

With the Sky Kings signed to a major label and poised to kick off their new career, Young decided that once again Poco had reached the end of the road. Cotton had high hopes for the recordings he was making and agreed the time was right to focus on his solo career. The pair approached their final gig in relative obscurity. Larry Larson booked Poco to play the Deadwood Days Festival in Deadwood, South Dakota, on September 16, 1995. Tim Smith was committed to another project at the time so Young and Cotton called on former Loggins and Messina drummer Merle Bregante to fill in for the show. Bregante had been working with Cotton on his solo project so the match-up seemed perfect. Prior to the show, Young informed the local media that the performance would be Poco's last one. "This will be the last Poco show," Young told the Rapid City *Journal*. "It seems ironically fitting that the band dies in a town named Deadwood." Over 6,000 fans attended the show with most of them not knowing they were seeing Poco's swan song. Despite some problems with the sound system and a few missed cues by Bregante, Poco's 10-song set was warmly received, and Young and Cotton left the stage to a standing ovation.

Despite the announcement of Poco's finale, Young accepted a couple more bookings in the New York/New Jersey area in January 1996 for a brief farewell tour of the Northeast. As Young told fans that Poco were hanging it up, a relaxed duo did informal acoustic sets at their final gigs at the Turning Point in New York and Club Bene in South Amboy, New Jersey. Cotton debuted a new song *The Coast is Clear* from his pending solo project, and Young played *One Tear at a Time* and another new one, *I Must Be Doing Something Right*. With advanced word, fans in the Northeast recorded and videoed the shows for posterity.

Warner Brothers finally released the first Sky Kings single *Picture Perfect* in March 1996. The band had also filmed a promotional video, and Warners supported them on a radio promotional tour. But despite the fact that the single managed to get on the charts at #52, Warner Brothers decided not to commercially release the album, choosing instead to wait for a stronger single. Warners canceled a scheduled June release date. Young was crushed, but realized that the country market was different and decided to wait it out.

Richie Furay announced that he was going to record an album of worship tunes and asked Rusty Young to participate. The session took place on May 24, 1996, in Nashville where Furay did some recording in part to accommodate Young's participation. The album IN MY FATHER'S HOUSE, featuring an upbeat array of worship songs, was released in the spring of 1997.

With the Sky Kings now on hold, Rusty Young decided to make use of the time for some additional Poco shows. Larry Larson got into action and more shows were booked for the summer, including an appearance on June 1 in St. Louis' Riverport Amphitheatre with America and the Little River Band. The *Post-Dispatch* noted, "A 40-minute set allowed them just seven songs and they took four to get warmed up to the point where vocal harmonies blended just right and the music punched. Until then, to paraphrase Gertrude Stein, they had the syrup, but it wouldn't pour." The reviewer caught a nuance that plagued several Poco shows during the early 90's. With both Young and Cotton participating in other activities, there was virtually no time for extensive rehearsals for these road shows. Consequently, there were shows that showed the lack of rehearsals.

While Poco toured, Warner Brothers released the Sky Kings' second single That Just About Says It All on July 26, and it quickly disappeared. With no video or advertising, the single didn't have a chance. Warner was not happy with the performance and set aside the release of the CD indefinitely. With no certainty about the Sky Kings' future, Young, Lloyd, and Cowan agreed to keep their options open.

Young kept Poco alive while Warner Brothers mulled over the Sky Kings' future. Larry Larson booked a handful of dates in 1996, including an appearance at EuroDisney in France late in the year. It was a rare Poco show on the Continent and they performed before a full crowd.

The Sky Kings had one last chance when Warner Brothers asked the band to go back into the studio and cut three tracks for another single in December 1996. Warners picked a remake of Elvin Bishop's *Fooled Around and Fell In Love*. The single was released in April 1997 and was widely ignored by country radio. Based on the disappointing reaction by country radio to the Sky Kings, Warners elected to shelve the album and released the band from their contract. Bitterly disappointed, the Sky Kings played a farewell show at the Bluebird Café in Nashville on June 14, 1997. Thankfully, Rhino Handmade released the Sky Kings album along with a number of demos in 2000.

Poco reappeared on the concert trail in 1997 with a scattered itinerary of dates. Nothing new was offered in the set lists, although they played *On the Way Home* and *A Child's Claim to Fame* in honor of the induction of Buffalo Springfield and Poco founder Richie Furay into the Rock and Roll Hall of Fame during May. There were some discussions about trying to give Poco another shot, but Rusty Young was disheartened and seriously contemplating getting out of the business in light of the Sky Kings failure. His frustration with the music business seemed to be overwhelming. Poco continued to spend more time on the road in 1998, but with very little in the way of new music to offer. Aside from the occasional Poco

date, Rusty Young took nearly a year off, doing no writing, performing, or session work.

Sure that Poco's time had long past for another shot at the big
time, Young and Cotton decided to set their sights a bit lower.
There was talk of recording a demo to be shopped around to small,
independent labels.   But it never happened.   Cotton explains,
"Rusty really shut that avenue down. I kind of wondered why he
stopped it. He really wanted to maintain that Poco identity and
they [Richard and Tim] weren't singers." Tim Smith decided that
his time with Poco had come to an end. Other opportunities continued to call him away from the Poco scene. Smith's announced last
show with the band came in June 1999.

With another dozen or so shows left on Poco's schedule,
Young turned to a neighbor as a replacement. George Lawrence explains, "Rusty was my neighbor in Nashville in the late 90's. We
lived in the same neighborhood. My new wife at the time, Nancy,
had known Rusty for years and introduced me to him. Of course I
knew who he was, and I think he was aware of who I had been working with around Nashville and Muscle Shoals." Lawrence had played
with the pre-Mr. Mister band called Pages. In 1980 while with that
group, Jim Messina's backing band Oasis approached him to play
with them in Santa Barbara. "I stayed in Jim's guest house for a
couple of months," recalls Lawrence. "There was talk of me working the next Messina tour and album. Though I ended up playing and
recording with Oasis for a couple of years along with other projects,
I rehearsed with Messina for a couple of weeks but it didn't work
out. I was already a studio veteran by that time, used to doing a
couple of run-throughs and then recording the song, and was just
not into rehearsing songs for weeks on end, which is Jim's method.
It works for him but not for me." In the early 1990's Lawrence
moved to Nashville and met Rusty Young. By 1997, Lawrence was
the staff drummer for Muscle Shoals Studio.

In preparation for the shows, Young brought his guitar over to
Lawrence's house and played him the set list. Lawrence charted
the songs out and wrote them down. A brief rehearsal followed and
Lawrence was ready to go. As it turned out, Poco played only a few
shows before Young and Cotton decided to cancel their remaining
summer dates and take a break.

With Poco on a break, Paul Cotton returned to the studio to
begin work on his belated second solo album. The tracks recorded
in 1994 were ignored in favor of new material. The project began
almost by accident. John Thaler, President of Futuredge Records
approached Cotton in the spring of 1999. Thaler explains, "I contacted Paul through his publishing company, Black Bayou Music, for

the purposes of obtaining a license to use the song *How Many Moons*. During the conversations Paul indicated a desire to record another solo project. After several months of discussions, an agreement was reached." Cotton recalls, "The correspondence kept going and no one was beating down my door except him. I'm sitting there with a half a dozen new tunes, itching to record them. I was working with another guy, Ron Mazelli, who ended up writing lyrics to three of them. So we cut a deal and started recording."

John Thaler and Thom Landt co-produced the album with Cotton. Sessions began in November 1999 at Anthem Recording in Phoenix with basic tracks being laid down. "We tried for an organic feel," explains Cotton. "We did that down in Phoenix, recording bass and drums on tape. That's Richard Neville on bass. Decided to put him to work. [Laughs.] He was really good for that. Except that he was my roommate during that time, so I got no rest and I lost my voice. Then we got back to L.A. and I lost half my hearing. I never thought we'd get through it." Recording continued into the early part of the year at Diamond Mine in Northridge, California. Rusty Young added some vocals and instrumentation at a studio in Nashville in March, and a final mix was immediately completed. Released in April on Futuredge, FIREBIRD was a mature work that was consistent with Cotton's previous Poco output with few surprises. Along with eight new tunes, Cotton re-recorded *Ride the Country* and an acoustic version of *Bad Weather*.

The album got off to a strong start with *Woman With a Broken Heart*, co-written with Ron Mazelli. It was a strong mid-tempo song with tasteful guitar riffs and a measured vocal performance. *There's a River* is a smoky ballad with a punchy chorus. *Firebird* features a hypnotic bass line by Neville and intertwining lead guitars by Cotton and Thom Landt on slide. *Not Out of Mind* is a ballad co-written with Ron Mazilli. Cotton chose to re-cut *Bad Weather* with minimal instrumentation, primarily acoustic guitar with some Rusty Young steel runs and harmonies. *Across a Painted Sky* was a Rusty Young tune that was demoed for Poco during their Nashville years. Cotton plays some tasty guitar over a driving beat. Young and Bill Lloyd offer backing vocals. *Do What You Do* is a mellow acoustic-based song with a languid feel. It was written by Cotton and Ron Mazilli. *Don't Stop the Carnival* has a sprightly Caribbean feel and a bossa nova beat. *All the Way to You* is an instrumental with Caribbean flair and a very danceable beat. Cotton transforms his Poco classic *Ride the Country* as an acoustic tune with steel and banjo accents by Rusty Young and mandolin by Bill Lloyd. *Let the Wind Blow* closes out the album.

In comparison to the slick production of Cotton's previous solo work, FIREBIRD felt like a return to a more classic style. Thaler confirms, "We felt that it was important to be more traditional and true to the sound that made Paul famous." Cotton explains his approach, "I think the new album is really an extension of Buffalo Springfield and my love for that band, and kind of where ROSE of CIMARRON left off with Poco and hopefully flowed through with the inspiration." Cotton put together the Paul Cotton Band composed of his son Chris on drums, Thom Landt on guitar, Steve Jones on bass, Joe Morris on percussion, and Tony Mandraccia on guitar and performed a few shows to promote the release of FIREBIRD. He didn't make a big push, however, and was content with a modest promotional effort.

One could question why with such a solid solo product in the marketplace, Cotton didn't chose to make a full court press in promoting the album. His previous solo effort had stumbled when his label folded. John Thaler and Futuredge appeared to be ready to marshall their resources including the internet to push Cotton's FIREBIRD. Instead, Cotton turned back to Poco. The reason was that the pull of the horse was strong and it appeared to be gaining strength as it entered the next turn.

17
A Horse That's Running

As a new century dawned before them, Young and Cotton began serious discussions about Poco's future. They decided to end their managerial relationship with Larry Larson and signed with Nashville manager Rick Alter, who also handled the reformed Firefall and Pure Prairie League. It didn't take long for Alter to determine that label interest in Poco was virtually nil without some additional members with a connection to the band's storied past.

Negotiations with several record labels took place in early 2000 with Sony Records indicating an early interest. Rusty Young shared, "Sony has said that they would like to do it and we're negotiating. Sony wants to have a big hand in what material is on the record and what is done. And some of the other opportunities are with no one other than us doing the record but with a smaller company. It's just in the baby stages of it all and we need for Sony to say, 'Here's a check, get started' – and so we're waiting for that." As things turned out, the deal with Sony never came together, however the negotiations had some consequences.

In June, Rick Alter made the announcement that Richard Neville and Tim Smith had been asked to leave Poco. In their place, Jack Sundrud and original drummer George Grantham had returned. Richard Neville confirmed that he and Tim Smith had been forced out of Poco. Neville revealed on the internet, "Tim Smith and I were forced to leave the band due to record company politics and management pressure. In order for Poco to continue the powers that be felt it necessary to have more original members as in George to replace Tim, and Jack Sundrud to replace me."

In looking back on the 90's version of Poco, Paul Cotton admits, "We had become our own best cover band. [Laughs.] Not as good as the original but still pretty good. We needed some singers." Rather than revisit the LEGACY regrouping, Young and Cotton decided to bring original drummer George Grantham back into the fold. Young and Grantham had crossed paths at a Tom Hampton showcase in Nashville and rekindled their friendship. With both of them living in Nashville, they began socializing, usually a weekly gathering for dinner. The pair began talking about working together again. The appeal of the return of the original drummer to Poco was not lost on Young. Jack Sundrud, also living in Nashville, was asked to come back on bass. This lineup dating back to 1985 had more visibility in the Nashville area.

The lineup change came rather abruptly with a touring season already underway. The quartet hurriedly scheduled some brief rehearsals in Nashville in order to make a June 15 show to open for Firefall and Pure Prairie League. It almost didn't happen. The trio from Nashville spent the night before in the Dallas Airport after a flight delay. They arrived in Reno tired but anxious to debut the new lineup. Poco performed a short five-song set on an outdoor stage. During their short set, first a train and then a motorcycle interrupted Young's attempt at singing *Crazy Love*. A few weeks break in the tour allowed the group to undergo some intense rehearsals to get Grantham and Sundrud up to speed on a full set of songs. In July, Poco returned to the road, and their initial shows went back to a basic one-hour set of Poco standards. Since rehearsal time was limited, it took a couple of months before they worked some other songs into the set that showcased their increased vocal capabilities. *Keep on Tryin'* was eventually returned to the live set, and Jack Sundrud was given a solo spot in the set to perform his song *It Must Be Love*, a #1 country hit for Ty Herndon.

Alter outlined plans for a more active Poco during the remainder of 2000 and into 2001. In July, Poco played the Music on Main festival in Frisco, Colorado. Richie Furay sat in during the show and enjoyed reconnecting with George Grantham. Jock Bartley of Firefall began sitting in during Poco sets whenever the two bands shared the bill. Poco toured across the country focusing on smaller venues. As their tour dates increased, Poco felt reenergized. Young recounts, "Where we're at, it's great fun. We get to go see our friends, people that have been important to us over the years. And the band sounds great. I think it's the best it's sounded really ever, so we're having a high old time." Alter often booked them with his other clients, Firefall and the reformed Pure Prairie League. Poco ended the year with a prestigious New Year's

Eve show at the Universal Amphitheatre in Los Angeles with Christopher Cross and America.

Another positive aspect to the increased visibility of Poco was the internet. The ability to pass information along to other fans throughout the country began to pay off with better attendance at shows. Before long, a virtual community of Poco fans, known affectionately as Poconuts, had developed and established them on the 'Net. In response, Poco entered the computer age in 2002 with a website that provided up-to-date tour information, occasional posts by band members, and a thriving online community board to discuss Poco and other topics. Aside from allowing Poconuts to establish new friendships, the website provided that Poco shows could be announced well in advance, allowing fans from across the country to make plans to attend. The attendance of Poco's shows began to increase, and the crowds were now clearly filled with Poconuts.

With six months of road work behind them, Poco took the late winter to focus on their first record in decades. In late January and February 2001, Poco entered the studio to lay down backing tracks. Despite the additions of Grantham and Sundrud, a recording deal with either a major label or an independent had not materialized. Instead, the band financed the recording sessions using its own funds. Young, Cotton and Sundrud had tunes to offer, and they whittled the batch down to a manageable size. "Paul and I haven't recorded together for years and it's been a lot of fun for us," Young told a reporter in Jacksonville, "We've grown as players, writers, and singers. It sounds like Poco and I think we're better at what we do. It's really some neat songs." Basic tracks were completed by the end of February on 11 songs.

Poco hired Michael Clute to produce the album with Rusty Young. Clute worked for Poco in the late 80's as their soundman on tour and engineered demo sessions. He had also been involved with the post-LEGACY demo sessions. Now a successful producer in his own right, Clute was a perfect choice to help Poco back into the recording world. Despite the initial momentum on the backing tracks, the sessions dragged on between live dates and Clute's other commitments with Restless Heart and Blackhawk. Early in the process, word spread that BAREBACK was the working title of the album. The band managed to finalize the recordings late in 2001 after completing their tour commitments, and mixing of the tracks took place in February 2002. By the time the album was completed, the decision to set aside the proposed title track was made, and the album was renamed RUNNING HORSE.

The band continued to perform live between the scattered recording sessions. Late in 2001, Poco played a group of shows in the Pacific Northwest that became known in "fandom" as PocoFest. Paul Cotton performed a solo show on August 30, playing several songs from CHANGING HORSES and FIREBIRD, along with a couple of Poco classics. Poco then played shows in St. Maries, Idaho; Centennial Amphitheatre in Moses Lake, Washington, and finished up with a show in Riverview Park, Spokane, Washington. Richie Furay also attended and performed as the opening act for the Poco shows. Poco fans from across the country flew or drove to the shows. An estimated 14 states and three countries were represented. Then in October, Rusty Young and Paul Cotton performed a couple of acoustic shows at an intimate setting at the Wildwood Lodge in Steelville, Missouri. The response was so great that Poco has been booked to perform at Wildwood every year since to sellout crowds.

With the album in the can, Poco set out for another year on the road. An interesting aspect of the touring year of 2002 was that Poco members were busy on other projects throughout the year that called for them away on occasion. In January, Jack Sundrud had a previous engagement and Richard Neville was asked to return for one show on bass. George Grantham was sitting in with Pure Prairie League in July so Young called on Tim Smith to replace him for a show in Deadwood, South Dakota. The show was to honor firefighers who had saved the town from a raging forest fire during a severe drought. As luck would have it, a summer downpour ended Poco's set after only three songs. Then late in the year, Paul Cotton had a solo show to play so Poco called on Jock Bartley of Firefall to play lead guitar.

Poco released RUNNING HORSE via their Internet site in November 2002 just in time for the Christmas season. The album was a tasty compilation of material written over the past couple of years. It was a soft-sounding album with some nice material from each of the band's writers. The album begins with *One Tear at a Time*, which the band had been playing live for a number of years. The blending of voices and Young's breathy lead vocal is a nice reminder of Poco's heyday. Cotton's tasty *Every Time I Hear That Train* showcases an acoustic-sounding mid-tempo workout. His vocals show wear, the backing vocals are sterling. Young adds some banjo for flavor. Young's *If Your Heart Needs a Hand* is a bluesy workout with keyboards subtly wailing in the background. Craig Fuller of Pure Prairie League adds some vocal harmonies and acoustic guitar. Jack Sundrud finally gets a song on a Poco record with *Never Loved...Never Hurt Like This*. It is a soft, acoustic ballad with mandolin by Young and tasteful riffing by Cotton. *Forever* is a Rusty Young ballad written about his son Will and his long-time girlfriend. The driving riff is reminiscent of *Call It Love*. Great Poco harmonies bolster the recording. It is Young's strongest tune on the record. Sundrud's *Never Get Enough* is one of the few upbeat tunes on the album, but it isn't one of Sundrud's strongest compositions. Young does play some scorching lap steel on the track. *If You Can't Stand to Lose* is a slow Young ballad that never seems to go anywhere. Cotton returns for *I Can Only Imagine*, a typical mid-tempo that sounds a bit like some of his mid-80's work. It doesn't feature a particularly strong chorus, but as usual does feature some tasty Cotton guitar work. Sundrud's highlight is *Shake It*, an exciting rhythm piece that brought some new sounds to the Poco canon. Grantham's percussion work is spectacular and Young's slide work is hot. Rusty Young adds another acoustic love song with *That's What Love is All About*. He adds some nice pedal steel guitar to the track that features those soaring Poco harmonies. The album closes with Cotton's nod to the legacy of Poco with *Running Horse*. High flying vocals, curling steel lines, a strong Cotton lead vocal, all the right ingredients for a perfect Poco tune.

RUNNING HORSE was Poco's first record in over a decade. Released on the Drifter's Church label, the album was initially available only online. Young noted, "We did this CD ourselves. We didn't have a record company. You never could have done that 10 years ago." The album was later released commercially in America and Europe. A subsidiary of Sony distributed the CD domestically.

The critical outlook for RUNNING HORSE proved supportive. If there was any complaint from hard-core Poco fans, it was that the album didn't really have any high-energy rocking tracks. When confronted with the assessment, Young made the case, "We don't set out to do a rockin' album or a mellow album. We just write what we write and play it best we can." Shaun Dale of *Cosmik Debris* noted, "Maybe it's the return of original drummer George Grantham, who left in 1977, or the introduction of the new guy, Jack Sundrud, but the band, which includes founding member Rusty Young and Paul Cotton, a member for over 30 years, sounds great, with new songs that are equal to any of their classic hits and a level of energy that puts the young'uns that have come up behind them during their 13 year recording hiatus to shame." Duke Egbert of the *Daily Vault* opines, "Surprise, surprise folks. This is why we actually listen to the CDs. RUNNING HORSE is pretty damned good. Far from being another nostalgia retread, RUNNING HORSE proves that Poco hasn't lost a step. Fans of country-rock music should really check it out. *Roots Music Report* gave it a five-star rating and said, "Poco is back and will be running up the charts with the release of Running Horse. It's all on this CD. A mixture of Roots Rock written by the members of the band. Great Production! Poco's talent shines with great harmonies and a variety of killer vocal performances." Scott Plank of *Ear Candy Music* wrote, "Unlike a lot of '70s bands that return to make lackluster albums, Poco shows that they still have what it takes to entertain. If you long for records like the Eagles **used** to make, pick up RUNNING HORSE. You won't be disappointed."

The year 2003 was spent on the road promoting the new album. Poco began touring in April and played scattered dates through mid-December. The road work was energizing. Young explains, "We're not youngsters anymore who ware fighting over who gets the next single and all lthose things. We're all old friends now. We're having a ball." Poco added the title track *If Your Heart Needs a Hand* and *Never Get Enough* from their new album to the set list. The spring concert showed a more confident band who were adapting to their new material quite well. Jack Sundrud was being given a larger role in the set list and using it to good advantage. After a quiet month of May, the group played a series of four shows in Colorado in June and then in July played several in California with Richie Furay and Chris Hillman and Herb Pedersen opening for them. Dubbed PocoFest II, the California dates again attracted fans from all over the country.

The series began on July 18 at the Orange County Fair. Due to the restrictions imposed by the fair, Poco played two short sets. The following night at the Canyon Club in Agora Hills, Poco stretched out with a 18-song set. It was a memorable night with Furay and Hillman collaborating on tunes and joining Poco during their sets. In San Diego at Humphrey's, Furay played an entire set with Poco to start their portion of the show. The three shows continued to highlight the additional energy that Furay's presence added to a Poco show. More willing to take advantage of new technologies, Poco also performed a live set for XM satellite radio in September prior to a show at the RamsHead Tavern. In all, Poco performed at least one show in every month after beginning the tour in April. In between Poco shows, Jack Sundrud began work on a solo album with his former partner in Great Plains, Russ Pahl.

The year 2004 was expected to be a banner year for the band. There were several plans for an increased presence in the market, some by Rick Alter and some by Cotton's label Futuredge. The first move came early in the year when Futuredge secured the rights to finally release the 1977 live concert album THE LAST ROUNDUP. John Thaler went into the studio to digitally master the release from the ABC master tapes in the spring. The tapes located were of the final mix of the long-rumored vinyl release. Apparently, no multi-track tapes were found, which did not provide the opportunity for any additional tracks.

Futuredge released THE LAST ROUNDUP in September. The track listing showed that the acetate that had made the rounds among collectors was exactly what ABC had originally intended to release. The quality of the recording was excellent, although it was clear that a few repairs had been made by Poco in the studio after the 1977 tour was completed. Still, it was an accurate representation of Poco live in 1977 right before the departure of Tim Schmit. Perhaps the recording's most memorable moment was a remarkable live version of Rusty Young's innovative *The Dance*. The much-touted appearance by Richie Furay proved a disappointment as he's inaudible in the mix as he sings *Hoedown* with the group as the encore.

Meanwhile, Poco focused on the present as Rick Alter booked nearly 20 more live shows for the band during the course of the year. He also made a deal with Madacy Entertainment to release a live Poco DVD. The company wanted a greatest hits set to film to increase the commercial appeal and dictated the number of songs that would be included. Rusty Young felt that if the group couldn't put any of its new material on the DVD, they still should do something special. "We could have done the DVD ourselves, just myself, Paul, Jack and George, But I just thought it would be more special to involve Richie. Also from a fan's perspective it would be more interesting to have Richie involved."

The band filmed a live show at the Belcourt Theatre in Nashville on May 20 with Richie Furay in tow for the DVD. Young explains, "[Richie] came in and we rehearsed for three days before the show. We don't normally play Richie's songs every night so we had to do that little extra bit." The band also asked Phil Kenzie to sit in and recreate his sax solo for *Heart of the Night*. During the encore, Sky Kings alumni John Cowan and Bill Lloyd joined along on the Chuck Berry classic *Rock 'n' Roll Music*. The DVD was released in time for the holiday season. KEEPING THE LEGEND ALIVE was a spirited celebration of Poco's legacy with everyone clearly enjoying themselves. Despite Young's objections, Madacy did not include the Chuck Berry tune on the DVD.

Furay reflected on the experience. "This was a special and 'magic moment' for me and all of us, I hope," he said. "For me it was really a great opportunity to interact with the guys on a level I hadn't done for a long time. Also, to have George on stage was awesome – what a tremendous musician and person. It was also there that my friend Peter van Leeuwen and I discussed the making of my secular album, HEARTBEAT OF LOVE, although there was no title at that time."

During Poco's downtime, Paul Cotton finally got serious about compiling his long-awaited WHEN THE COAST IS CLEAR project. Peter Van Leeuwen had already nudged Furay into a recording project. Now he urged Cotton to finish the COAST project. "We saved what we could from the previous tracks up in Nashville," explains Cotton. "We put all the A-team on there, the best players in Nashville." He did recording throughout the year, stripping previously recorded tracks and adding tracks to the demos recorded back in 1994 and 1996. While many lead vocals were retained, backing vocals were added to the tapes. Thankfully, Cotton had worked on digital tape when he began the project. "We transferred it in Nashville. It was quite a learning curve for me. I'm pretty low-tech. Jack did such a great job on that." Jack Sundrud produced the album with help from Peter Van Leeuwen. Sessions took place in Hum Depot Studios in Nashville. In addition to the tracks recorded in 1994 and 1996, Cotton included a tune he recorded in October 1997 in San Juan Beach, Curacacao, entitled *Isle of Sirens*. He also re-recorded *Barbados* from LEGEND and *High Water* from CHANGING HORSES. "We mixed it at ZZ Top's studio in Houston with their producer, and he really did a number on it. And that was it!"

But to Poconuts, the year 2004 will forever be remembered for the events of July 29 in Springfield, Massachusetts. Poco was set to perform to a huge crowd in the town square as thousands of people packed the area. As the band began the second song of Poco's set, George Grantham began playing in an odd manner that drew the attention of Rusty Young. "We were playing the intro to the song, and there's this part where George comes in, and he missed the count, at least with his left hand," remembered Young. "I turned around to see what was going on. It was very scary, but it was also amazing, because he was still playing the high hat [cymbal] in time, with his right hand. Being the trooper he is, George said 'I'm OK, keeping going,' but I saw his left arm hanging down, and a confused look on his face, and I stopped the song and called out for a doctor." Sundrud helped Grantham to the floor and medical personnel from the audience began to assist. "I was personally devastated," Cotton recalls sadly. "We all were having to watch him slip behind the drums. Luckily we were three miles from the best hospital in the state." At first it was thought that Grantham had suffered heat stroke, but after EMT's arrived, it was clear it was something more serious. They transported Grantham to nearby Baystate Medical Center where doctors determined that he had suffered a stroke. Doctors performed emergency surgery to alleviate pressure on Grantham's brain shortly after his arrival.

Stunned by the turn of events, Poco remained behind and completed the show acoustically. With several thousand people in the audience, the band felt it owed it to them to perform. "We finished the show acoustically," Cotton recalled bleakly. "Luckily we had played trio stuff before so we knew it, but our heart wasn't in it. We figured we might as well give the people their money's worth. It was just the natural thing to do; there was nothing we could do to help him. We finished the set and ran to the hospital to see him. We couldn't see him so we talked to the doctor." Once it was clear that Grantham was in good hands, the group headed for their next tour stop. Young noted to Springfield *Republican* reporter Patrick Johnson that Grantham was lucky to have been stricken at the show within blocks of a hospital instead of in the middle of a long drive between shows. "If it happened in the back of the van, we would not have known it for hours." Cotton's thoughts ran to Poco and the long history they had shared together. "Boy, all I could think of was 'there goes that voice.' Because when I first saw those guys, it was George's voice that blew me away. I still miss him, really big-time, that voice was nothing for him. I'm so glad we did that DVD with him."

In Falmouth, the band recruited a local drummer Chuck Woodhams to make it though the next show. With a full slate of shows booked for the rest of the summer and early fall, Poco could not afford to cancel. Young contacted George Lawrence, who agreed to substitute on short notice. "I got a call in August 2004 from manager Rick Alter who asked, 'Are you the George Lawrence who played with Poco?' After telling me what had happened to George Grantham he asked me to fill in and if I could fly to Cape Cod the next day for a gig. It ended up that they could not get me there in time because of the traffic so they ended up using a local drummer. I met up with them several days later in California and finished out the year as a sub for George."

Lawrence flew to California and met the band there for their next series of dates. His first show was at the Coach House in San Juan Capistrano. "My first gig with the band was actually the next one in California," recalls Lawrence. "Rusty had faxed me a set list and I went and listened to a batch of CD's. We winged it that first night!" Poco had three shows booked in California with founder Richie Furay as the opening act.

The remainder of the summer touring season went well and Lawrence quickly fit into the scheme of things. As a veteran studio musician, Lawrence was also used to having to perform rescue missions. "I had made a reputation for myself in Nashville as a pinch hitter, filling in at the last minute for national acts like Tanya

Tucker, Diamond Rio, even Jack's group Great Plains." In September, George Grantham was allowed to return home to Nashville to continue his rehabilitation. In October, Rusty Young and Paul Cotton did their annual stint at the Wildwood Springs Lodge in Steelville, Missouri, bringing along Jack Sundrud. But this year, the engagement had a special twist. Rusty Young married his fiancée Mary Brennan, and Pastor Richie Furay performed the ceremony. Rusty debuted the new song *For the Love of Mary*, and Jack Sundrud did the new tune *Father's Day*. Unknown to those in attendance, Poco also recorded the shows for future use.

A few weeks later, Poco appeared on a very special bill in Solvang, California. The show was a benefit show for Arts Outreach that featured Richie Furay and Jim Messina along with Paul Cotton and Rusty Young of Poco. But Messina had another surprise up his sleeve. He brought along Kenny Loggins, and they performed together for the first time in decades. The night, which started on a bit of a down note by having to be moved indoors at the last minute due to the weather, ended up a night to remember. The show started with Kenny Loggins solo, and each artist joined him in turn on songs that they made famous. After a brief intermission, Loggins and Messina reunited for the first time since 1976. The show went so well and the personalities melded so well that it spurred a year-long reunion tour of the pair in 2005.

Meanwhile, Grantham's rehabilitation continued throughout the remainder of the year but it was clear that his ability to perform with a touring band had not returned. His left side was initially paralyzed; however initial treatments had gradually restored movement to his arm and hand. While Grantham continued to undergo treatment, Poco had to make other arrangements. Young offered George Lawrence a full-time position in Poco. Young also announced that Lawrence would share equally in artist royalties from any recorded project that he participated in.

As it turned out, that project was not far away. After a couple of shows early in the spring, Poco recorded a new live album at Dave Goodwin's Big Sky Ranch in Bozeman, Montana, on April 22-23, 2005. The band played unplugged and debuted some new arrangements to some old favorites, including a mandolin-driven version of *Under the Gun*. Paul Cotton also debuted *Bareback*, a tune he had written a few years earlier and had been considered for the title tune of the RUNNING HORSE album. *Bareback* provided the title of the live CD upon its release in September 2005. It was a memorable couple of days. "Dave is this big bear of a guy who has a 'den mother' approach to producing recordings," explains Lawrence. "Dave bought this big old house that is a bed and breakfast with a huge great room where the band rehearses and records. He built a studio on to the back of the house, and he basically records live concerts in an intimate 'unplugged' setting. I played a tiny little drum kit and lots of percussion toys: shakers and congas, etcetera. He sells about 100 tickets on Friday and Saturday nights, cooks for the band all week and the audience on the concert nights, and just really puts everybody in a great mood for some great music. In between rehearsing and playing the concerts, we went hiking up in the hills and hit the antique stores in the old downtown area. It was a great time."

The band reached another milestone when Rick Alter announced that he had successfully booked a European tour for Poco to take place in the spring. Poco had not engaged in a performing tour of Europe in decades, and the band was excited about the return. Right before the European tour, two members of Poco released solo projects. In April, the long-awaited release of Paul Cotton's WHEN THE COAST IS CLEAR project finally took place.

Jack Sundrud also released his first solo album entitled BY MY OWN HAND. The album was an excellent example of Sundrud's songwriting ability with modest instrumentation and minimal production. Several songs were of a personal nature, especially *Father's Day, Modern-Day Blacksmith*, and *I'm Living My Dream*. While the project had very little to do with Poco, it did highlight the tremendous talent that the band had to draw upon in future recording projects.

In May, Poco returned to Europe for their first full length tour since 1976. The tour opened in Copenhagen, Denmark, on May 5. Poco followed with three shows in France, including a date at the Olympia Theatre in Paris with Jefferson Starship. The tour played Germany, Italy, Belgium, and Holland before crossing the channel into England. Poco wound up the tour with a show in London on May 15. It was a long awaited return to Europe and European Poco fans were pleased that the band managed to perform in several different countries. It was a lightning strike tour as the band rarely had time for any sight-seeing as they hurried off for their next gig. Although the venues were generally small, the turnout was solid and led to other bookings later in the year. In general, the band considered it a successful tour and offered to consider future European dates. "It was fast and furious," Lawrence exclaims. "I am the only man alive to have toured the Louvre in 30 minutes! We didn't have nearly enough time to do sightseeing. We played an eclectic assortment of venues from the famous Olympia theatre in Paris to the promoter's garage in rural France to a dingy basement club in London. I think my favorite place was the 66 Club in Belgium. I really enjoyed that one. A real rock and roll roadhouse in a small town in Belgium. Who would have imagined it?" It was exhausting but it was a welcome visit to Poconuts in Europe.

After a quiet June dedicated to recovery, Poco hit the road again in July for a very busy summer touring schedule. It culminated with a prestigious and wildly successful engagement at B.B. King's Blues Club in New York City. It was Poco's first gig in New York City in several years and sold out.

BAREBACK AT BIG SKY was released in September. The CD included a number of surprises, including the band's take on the Tim Schmit song *Find Out In Time*. Paul Cotton came up strong with seven of the 15 tracks featuring his lead vocals. *Bareback* was finally released as part of the package. Jack Sundrud does a stellar job on *Shake It* and *Never Loved...Never Hurt Like This*. Big Sky Studio owner and co-producer Dave Goodwin added some harmonica to the obligatory J.J. Cale cover *Cajun Moon*. Rusty Young's contributions included *Nothing Less Than Love, What Do People Know*, and a sparkling acoustic version of *Save A Corner of Your Heart*. George Lawrence offers some workmanlike percussion throughout the set. Like its predecessor, the CD was distributed by Sony/RED. While most Poco fans appreciated the first unplugged Poco album, it didn't attract as much attention from critics as RUNNING HORSE had. Still, it managed to be named in the Top Ten of Indie CD releases for the year by Kweevak.com.

In October, Poco returned to Europe to play dates in Norway and Holland. Jack Sundrud's heritage was Norwegian, and this would be his first trip to the homeland. Sundrud flew out a few days in advance to do some sightseeing. "I went a few days early. I got to spend one beautiful autumn day touring Oslo, the Oslo waterfront, the Norwegian Folk Museum, Vigeland sculpture park, the museum of miniature liquor bottles, a little salmon, a little pastry – I had a wonderful time. The next day, my plan was to drive my rental car to the city of Gol to look up the farmstead of my ancestors. It was a good plan, but was thwarted by a freak snowstorm. I had to settle for bad Norwegian TV at a Quality Inn barely 45 minutes outside Oslo." After his brief sightseeing jaunt, Sundrud met up with the band in Lillehammer.

This return to Europe was supposed to be a real treat for Poco. After the whirlwind European tour in the spring, the band had planned to savor this additional visit. Instead, Poco found itself in an eerily similar situation as the previous year. On the eve of the first show in Lillehammer, Paul Cotton was stricken in his hotel room. He was rushed to the hospital and underwent immediate emergency treatment. "I had a heart attack," confirms Cotton, "which they fixed up with two stints within 10 days. The worst thing for me was a bleeding ulcer. I had that and almost bled out. I had only 30 percent left." His condition was pronounced critical, but he received excellent medical treatment that put him on the road to recovery. Poco was forced to play the shows in Norway and Holland as a trio. At the completion of the short tour, the band returned to the States to complete their tour without Cotton.

With four tour dates left on Poco's touring schedule, Rusty Young recruited former Sky King alumni Bill Lloyd to fill in for Cotton. Bill Lloyd explains, "I got a call from my old friend Rusty Young and he asked me to fill in some dates for recuperating Paul Cotton on a few Poco live dates, and I was happy to oblige. Having played a lot of the Poco material over the years with Rusty doing songwriters nights or Sky Kings gigs, I knew a lot of the songs already but there was still a lot to go over. Also, subbing for one of the principal members is a no-win situation because you can't BE someone else folks are expecting to see". Lloyd did some quick rehearsals after Poco's return to the States and filled in nicely.

After several weeks of treatment in Norway, Cotton returned to the U.S. and began convalescing at the home of his girlfriend in Florida. "The worst part was after I got back and got hit by pneumonia. Man, I don't ever want to deal with that again." Although Cotton's health problems had been serious, his recovery was strong and Rick Alter announced that Cotton would return to Poco in 2006.

The remainder of the winter was a quiet time for Poco. Cotton continued to recuperate, and all indications were that he would be back in action by spring. Just to be sure, Alter arranged for fewer bookings to avoid taxing Cotton, and also because Poco planned on recording a new studio album in the fall. As things turned out, Cotton was more than up to the task. Given the seriousness of his health problems, it was surprising to Cotton, as well as his bandmates, how quickly he was able to go back on the road. And with his return, Poco seemed to get a new boost of energy.

Poco's performing set list had grown to a point where any given show could contain surprises. The basic set list still revolved around fan favorites, but the band could now offer some additional tunes. Cotton would alternatively perform *Magnolia* or *Cajun Moon*. Jack Sundrud rotated between *Hard Country* or *Father's Day* during his solo set. Rusty Young offered *Old Hat* on occasion, as well as the Beatles cover *If I Needed Someone*. About mid-year, the band debuted a very creative arrangement to form a medley of Sundrud's *Shake It* with Cotton's *Barbados*. The highlight of 2006's touring year was Poco's first appearance at the Grand Ol' Opry in Nashville on April 7. Opry regulars Little Jimmy Dickens, Connie Smith, Bill

Anderson and Vince Gill shared the stage with Poco on this special night. Ironically, the only other time Rusty Young had played the Opry, it was when he was in Vince Gill's backing band. The next night, Poco and label mates Pinmonkey performed at the Mercy Lounge in Nashville. Bill Lloyd, Michael Kelsh, and Phil Kenzie all sat in with Poco during their set, making for a riotous night of music. On Sunday, the band spent a quiet afternoon with drummer George Grantham at his home sharing memories and friendship. Sundrud shared, "I mostly listened as Rusty, Paul and George reminisced. The talk and the memories were warm and fragrant as the day. Springtime in Tennessee."

Poco returned to Europe for a brief three-country tour in late May. As with their previous excursion, it was a quick visit with little time for vacationing. The band performed shows in Belgium, Holland, and France before returning to the States for a busy July and August. As late as the West Coast shows in August, Young was still talking about plans for the band to start recording a new Poco album in the fall.

However, the live offers continued, and Poco wound up adding additional live dates in the fall so a new studio offering was not in the mix. The release of solo albums by Cotton and Sundrud had tapped both songwriters for material for a Poco release. In addition, Rusty Young had been spending much of his down time starting work on a book project. Instead of a new studio effort, the band mixed a show recorded at the Wildwood Lodge in 2004 and released the intimate live CD THE WILDWOOD SESSIONS late in the year instead.

THE WILDWOOD SESSIONS was a short 10-song collection of acoustic versions of some standard Poco tunes with a couple of surprises. The intimate atmosphere of the Wildwood Lodge comes across in the recording, and the trio of Young, Cotton, and Sundrud sound loose and were enjoying themselves. The performances have a bit of a rough edge, which adds to their appeal. Sundrud's *Cain's Blood* and Cotton's *Do What You Do* are outstanding, and one can hardly listen to Young's *For the Love of Mary* without smiling with the realization that they were married during that engagement.

As if Poco wasn't busy enough, Jack Sundrud filled in on bass for Pure Prairie League during several shows throughout the year. Bassist Mike Reilly had fallen ill and Sundrud filled in when he could, doing double duty when the two bands shared the same bill. He also found time to record and release another album, this time with Craig Bickhardt, called IDLEWHEEL. Released in July 2006, it was a delightful mix of tunes.

The 2007 touring year was filled with additional highlights as Paul Cotton's revival seemed to energize the band. In February, Poco performed at a benefit for Pure Prairie League's Mike Reilly. Poco performed several shows in the spring as an acoustic trio, including a memorable three-day run at the Turning Point in Piermont, New York. The set lists featured some interesting selections, including a cover of the Beatles' *Baby's in Black*. Also in May, they shared the bill at the Wildwood Lodge with the Richie Furay Band for two nights before a return to New York City and the B.B. King Blues Club. Poco's set list included a rare reading of *I'll Leave It Up to You* and another Beatles cover *If I Needed Someone*. Rita Siwek, PR director of the club was quoted in *Hittin' the Notes* as praising Poco's performance, "They are a fantastic band. They did an incredible sold-out show. Considering how many choices a music fan has in NYC on any given night, Poco's success at the club is even more amazing." The band's performances continued to be top-notch. In October at Gulfstream Park in Hallendale, Florida Lee Zimmarman of the Miami *New Times* wrote, "With their venerable history, one that's brought them promise, disappointment, neglect and unexpected rebirth, seeing Poco in performance remains a rarified experience. Four members strong, their vocal harmonies still sound as sweet as ever, bringing their songs a warm embrace that remains intact after all these decades. The vocals, Cotton's in particular, still bear that rugged, assured richness, evidenced on his solo version of "Bad Weather," one of the band's most heart-wrenching ballads." The touring season extended into December with a New Years Eve show at the Swallow at the Hollow in Roswell, Georgia.

As the year drew to a close, one could sense that there was change in the air. Rusty Young moved into a new home in rural Missouri with his wife Mary. Jack Sundrud sold his cabin in Tennessee after extensive renovations. Paul Cotton and his fiancée Caroline were talking marriage. And Poco was on the verge of their 40th anniversary. The question was – would there be any change in store for Poco?

18
Where Did the Time Go?

The year 2008 marked Poco's 40th anniversary as America's premiere country-rock band. True to their nature, there was no hype, no gaudy stage costumes, no ego-filled reunion tours. There was no need for change within Poco. Instead, Rusty Young, Paul Cotton, Jack Sundrud and George Lawrence returned to the road in intimate settings to play Poco music for their fans and graciously conduct "meet and greets" after their shows to sign LP's, CD's, and newly minted merchandise. Poco remains a viable, creative band well into its fourth decade of existence. Their popularity still allows them to sell out shows in the media capital of New York City without a record on the charts. They truly love to play. Watching the band in live performances, one can see the sheer joy and fun that they have in performing. It's that joy that they easily convey to their audiences. Travel is now the limiting factor. With leader Rusty Young having moved into a new home in rural Missouri, he is now a two-hour drive from the nearest airport. Paul Cotton lives in Key West, Florida, and is a minimum of two flights away from any gig out of the state. The opportunity to spend time together and rehearse or record continues to dwindle. The days of Poco playing 40-50 shows a year are likely over. But what fans lose in frequency will never diminish the quality or the spirit that flows from a live Poco show.

While reflecting on the vast history of Poco, members of Poco continue to cite their friendship and admiration for each other's talents. Consequently from time to time, Poco dips into its past and invites former members to participate in projects or have the individual's talents grace their solo projects. Clearly there are bonds forged in the crucible of the rock and roll world that have endured. It is impossible to watch the 2004 Belcourt Theatre show on video and not see the story of Poco rooted deeply in the old friendships of Furay, Grantham, Young and Cotton. George Lawrence sums it up, "The last time we worked with Richie Furay we did a rehearsal with acoustic guitars in the dressing room. There was a look on Rusty's face that I had never seen before: a very enthusiastic and adoring smile as Richie sang through some of the old Poco staples. He looked at me and grinned about it as though to say; 'There it is, that is so cool, there's the shit that makes this special, do you hear it? Do you get it?' Hell yeah, I get it. It wasn't just Richie or Jimmie or Rusty or Tim or Grantham or any of the others that followed as members left to follow their own muse. It was the 'thing' that they all shared."

As for the future, Poco appears stronger than the sum of its parts. The talent and tenacity of Poco continue to endure. Jack Sundrud observes, "I see fun and frolic in the future. Our touring these days for me is about the joy of performing great songs - plus the fans are great and extremely supportive. I believe we will record some new music in the next year or two. No one knows how long we will stay at it, but I think Poco is enjoying the fruits of many years of hard work - with no plans to stop. Speaking for myself, I couldn't ask for a better gig." George Lawrence muses, "We will probably continue to perform as much as we can and do another album or two." Paul Cotton sees much the same, "I see us slowing down a bit. I love playing the shows but the traveling is really tough." One thing everyone agrees on. Rusty Young is the constant. He has been there every step of the way and personifies the Poco spirit and ensures that it survives. Cotton stresses, "If there's no Rusty, there's no Poco." Young himself has made the point with some pride that Poco has been on hiatus a few times in its history, but it never "broke up, and it never will."

The four-decade story of Poco has been filled with musical excellence tempered by frustrating near-misses and wildly improbable collapses. A fan can hardly have reached this point in the Poco story without asking "what if?" Any number of questionable decisions or ill-fated consequences could have gone the other way. Had Poco managed to reach the superstardom they so desperately craved in the 70's, what would have happened to them? Could they have maintained their profile for 40 years, or would they have exploded into pieces, victims of ego, greed, and drugs as so many of their contemporaries have? One can speculate, however it's not hard to state with some certainty that it's doubtful that Poconuts could have the kind of casual access to their heroes they now enjoy had Poco reached the upper echelons of rock stardom. The story of Poco is not so much about the frustrations of the past as the enjoyment of the future. Poco will continue on – content in their ability to make music on their terms and spread the Poco spirit wherever they go.

CREDITS

Photo Credits

Unless otherwise noted, photos are from the author's personal collection.

Page 1 bottom, courtesy of Richie Furay Archives; Page 3 top © Cindy Daiken; Page 3 bottom © www.rockflashbacks.com; Page 4 bottom and Page 5 top, courtesy of Bruce Poulos collection; Pages 6 top and bottom, Page 7 top © Kim Gottlieb-Walker; Page 7 bottom, Page 10 top © Steve Caraway; Page 7 bottom courtesy of Denny Jones; Page 9 bottom © Mark Rogers; Page 10 bottom, Page 11, Page 12 top courtesy of Denny Jones; Page 14 top and bottom courtesy of Jeff Steele; Page 15 top www.podipto.com; Page 16 top © Frank Canlin; Page 16 bottom, Page 17 top courtesy of Steve Casto collection; Page 17 bottom © Naomi Elkins; Page 18, Page 19 top © Julie Casto;
Page 20 top © Naomi Elkins; Page 21 top © Carl Linder; Page 21 bottom © Kate Lindop; Page 22 bottom © Mary Young; Page 23 bottom courtesy of George Lawrence; Page 24 © Doug Poore

Visit Kim Gottlieb-Walker's website: www.lenswoman.com and Steve Caraway's website: www.stevecarawayimages.com

Song Lyrics

"Saints and Sinners" Words and music by James Messina. © 1990. Reproduced by permission of James Messina. All Rights Reserved.

Cover Credits

Photo: Jerry Fuentes
Cover Design: Ronnie Fuentes

NOTES

Chapter 1 EARLY TIMES

1. *"It was the summer"* Richie Furay, "The Case of the Vanishing Buffalo Springfield," *Teen Screen*, August 1968.
1. *"By the time"* Richie Furay and John Einarson, *There's Something Happening Here: The Story of Buffalo Springfield*, Quarry Music Books, 1997.
1. *"I hit New York"* Stephen Stills to Allan R. McDougall, "Within Him, Without Him," *Rolling Stone*, March 4, 1971.
2. *"It was so different."* Richie Furay and John Einarson, *There's Something Happening Here: The Story of Buffalo Springfield*, Quarry Music Books, *1997*.
3. *"We did it grammatically incorrect"* Bill DeLugt, author interview, August 19, 1998.
3. *"Boenzee Cryque"* Rusty Young to Mick Skidmore, "Poco: Rusty Young Looks Back," *Goldmine*, August 2, 1985.
3. *"Rusty brought the country influence"* George Grantham, author interview, July 20, 1997.
4. *"One night in 1964"* Randy Meisner, as quoted in Marc Eliot, *To the Limit: The Untold Story of the Eagles*, Little, Brown & Company, 1998.
4. *"When we first"* Randy Meisner, Ibid.
4. *"Greene and Stone kept moving us"* Randy Naylor quoted in liner notes, THE POOR, Rev-Ola, 2003.

Chapter 2 LAST TIME AROUND

7. *"The moment the music,"* Jim Messina to Robert Stephen Spitz, *The Making of Superstars*, Anchor Press, 1978.
8. *"Richie and I"* Jim Messina, Ibid.
9. *"With Ahmet's cooperation"* Jim Messina to Willie G. Moseley, "Jim Messina: Been There, Done That, Part I," *Vintage Guitar* online, www.vguitar.com, 2000.
9. *"Miles called me up"* Rusty Young to John Einarson, *Desperados: The Roots of Country Rock*, 2001.
9. *"Jimmy was pretty much running"* Rusty Young, Ibid.
10. *"We flew Rusty out"* Jim Messina to Willie G. Moseley, "Jim Messina: Been There, Done That, Part II," Vintage Guitar online, www.vguitar.com, 2000.
10. *"Richie and I"* Jim Messina, author interview, August 12, 2002.
11. *"Those were demo sessions"* Jim Messina, Ibid.
11. *"Gram and I had conversations"* Richie Furay as quoted by John Einarson, *Desperados: The Roots of Country Rock*, 2001.
11. *"The difference is that"* Gram Parsons to Chuck Casell, Promotional Interview, 1972.
12. *"The Burritos play what I'd call barroom"* George Grantham to Bud Scoppa, "Poco, Yes Indeed," *Rock*, November 17, 1970.

12. *"Yeah, they always doing that ol' shuffle beat"* Richie Furay to Bud Scoppa, "Poco, Yes Indeed," *Rock*, November 17, 1970.

12. *"I know for myself"* Jim Messina, author interview, August 12, 2002.

12. *"George had been out looking"* Rusty Young to Jim Crockett, "Poco's Steel Guitar Stretching Out," *Guitar Player*, November/December 1972.

12. *"When Rusty decided to go"* George Grantham, author interview, July 20, 1997.

13. *"Rusty got in touch with me"* George Grantham, Ibid.

13. *"We got together, ran through some tunes"* George Grantham, Ibid.

13. *"Yeah, singing was a big part of it"* George Grantham, Ibid.

13. *"Eventually I just threw them away"* Jim Messina in Steve Caraway, "Jim Messina: Spanning Poco, Buffalo Springfield, Loggins & Messina," *Guitar Player*, February 1977.

14. *"You have to remember"* Rusty Young to Walter Tunis, "Faces Change, but Poco Keeps Playing," Lexington *Herald-Leader*, November 14, 2003.

14. *"It was amazing"* Rusty Young to Kurt Loder, *Rolling Stone*, May 17, 1979.

14. *"I thought that Jimmy and Richie"* Rusty Young to John Einarson, *Desperados: The Roots of Country Rock*, 2001.

15. *"I remember Neil coming over"* Rusty Young to John Einarson, *For What It's Worth: The Story of Buffalo Springfield*, Quarry Music Books, 1997.

15. *"I think it took only two or three days"* George Grantham, author interview, July 20, 1997.

15. *"I recall one session in particular"* Jim Messina, author interview, August 12, 2002.

15. *"The first set-up I used in Poco"* Jim Messina in *Guitar Player*, 1977.

16. *"We had a couple of people"* George Grantham, author interview, July 20, 1997.

16. *"I went up to Richie's house"* Randy Meisner, as quoted by John Einarson, *Desperados: The Roots of Country Rock*, Cooper Square Books, 2001.

16. *"I think there"* Jim Messina, author interview, August 12, 2002.

17. *"It was too intimidating"* Tom Phillips, author interview, March 27, 1998.

17. *"So the two of us drove over"* Tom Phillips, author interview, March 27, 1998.

17. *"I felt like"* Tim Schmit to Chris Macias, "A Wing and a Prayer," Sacramento Bee, May 1, 2001.

18. *"We used to ask him"* Tom Phillips, author interview, March 27, 1998.

18. *"I was really"* Tim Schmit to Barry Ballard in "Tim: We All Really Believe in Poco," *Omaha Rainbow's Poco Special*, 1975

18. *"Randy wound up taking the high harmonies"* George Grantham, author interview, July 20, 1997.

Chapter 3 WHEN IT ALL BEGAN

19. *"Before our first"* George Grantham, Ibid.

19. *"They played the Troubadour"* Richard Perry, author interview October 3, 2008.

20. *"During that year of transition"* Jim Messina in Caraway, *Guitar Player*, February 1977.

20. *"I think it took him awhile"* George Grantham, author interview, July 20, 1997.

20. *"Part of the hassles throughout"* Rusty Young, as quoted by Peter Frame, Poco Family Tree, *Zigzag*, 1972.

21. *"I used to think"* Richie Furay to Cameron Crowe, "Poor Poco: They Were 'The Next Big Thing' Four Years Ago," *Rolling Stone*, April 26, 1973.

21. *"We didn't want"* Rusty Young to William Ruhlmann, liner notes for FORGOTTEN TRAILS, 1990.

21. *"Our first name was R.F.D."* George Grantham to Michael Barackman, "Desperados: Poco Keeps on Tryin'," *Crawdaddy*, June 1977.

22. *"They were first"* Richard Perry, author interview, October 3, 2008.

22. *"I walked into the Troubadour"* Arnie Moore in Pete O'Brien, "The Arnie Moore Interview," *Omaha Rainbow*, April 29, 1974.

22. *"That was our coming out party there"* George Grantham, author interview, July 20, 1997.

22. *"Well, it was an incredibly exciting evening"* Jim Messina, author interview, August 12, 2002.

23. *"We had put"* Richie Furay, author interview, August 18, 2008.

23. *"It was quite an up evening"* Paul Cotton as quoted by John Einarson in *Desperados: The Roots of Country Rock*, 2001.

24. *"I didn't know it"* George Grantham, author interview, July 20, 1997.

24. *"I don't have a lot of fond memories"* Richie Furay and John Einarson, *For What It's Worth: The Story of Buffalo Springfield*, Quarry Music Books, 1997.

25. *"Walt Kelly took immediate offense"* Richie Furay to Pete Fornatale, *Jazz & Pop*, August 1971.

25. *"Thank you, Walt"* Richie Furay, author interview, August 18, 2008.

25. *"Anyway Bye Bye was"* Randy Meisner to John Einarson in *Desperados: The Roots of Country Rock*, 2001.

25. *When we talked"* Rusty Young to John Einarson in *Desperados: The Roots of Country Rock*, 2001.

26. *"Rusty didn't play"* Randy Meisner to John Einarson *Ibid*.

26. *"I have no idea"* Rusty Young quoted in Adam Dolgins, *Rock Names*, Carol Publishing Group, 1993.

26. *"Richie and I met with Atlantic"* Jim Messina, author interview, August 12, 2002.

26. *"It was touch-and-go"* Jim Messina, Ibid.

26. *"There were some"* Jim Messina, Ibid.

28. *"Every time we played the Troubadour"* Randy Meisner, to John Einarson in *Desperados: The Roots of Country Rock*, 2001.

28. *"I loved going out"* Rusty Young to John Einarson, unpublished portion of interview, 1997.

28. *"Poco was one of the most underrated groups."* John McEuen to John Einarson in *Desperados: The Roots of Country Rock*, 2001.

28. *"This was something that affected me personally"* Jim Messina, author interview, August 12, 2002.

29. *"By this time"* Jim Messina, Ibid.

29. *"It was my way"* Richie Furay, author interview, August 18, 2008.

29. *"I think a great part of our originality"* Rusty Young to John Einarson in *Desperados: The Roots of Country Rock*, 2001

29. *"Richie's songs were a lot different"* Randy Meisner to John Einarson in *Desperados: The Roots of Country Rock*, 2001.

30. *"The first album took a long time"* George Grantham, author interview, July 20, 1997.

30. *"It was such a new world for me"* Rusty Young as quoted by John Einarson in *Desperados: The Roots of Country Rock*, 2001.

30. *"Of course, Jimmy was producing"* George Grantham, author interview, July 20, 1997.

30. *"So now we get into the studio"* Jim Messina, author interview, August 12, 2002.

31. *"I really didn't like the sound"* Randy Meisner, as quoted by Richard Randall, KTTV - Colorado, January 10, 1995.

31. *"Randy is a very sensitive person"* Jim Messina, author interview, August 12, 2002.

32. *"They fired Randy"* Rusty Young as quoted in John Einarson, *Desperados: The Roots of Country Rock*, 2001.

32. *"We might have left one or two"* George Grantham, author interview, July 20, 1997.

32. *"They put a dog on the cover"* Randy Meisner, as quoted by Richard Randall, KTTV - Colorado, January 10, 1995.

32. *"That's Jimmy's dog, named Jasper"* George Grantham, author interview, July 20, 1997.

32. *"My dog was black"* Jim Messina, author interview, August 12, 2002.

32. *"There wasn't really much money at the time"* Randy Meisner, as quoted by John Einarson in *Desperados: The Roots of Country Rock*, 2001.

35. *"We had to fly in a Lear jet"* George Grantham, author interview, July 20, 1997.

36. *"What a Day was"* Richie Furay, 1975 tape interview.

37. *"I met Skip when I was living in Wilbraham"* Richie Furay to John Einarson, unpublished portion of interview, November 1997.

37. *"Certainly it was an innovative album"* Richie Furay to John Einarson in *Desperados: The Roots of Country Rock*, 2001.

39. *"In the early days we had very little money"* Rusty Young in Pete Senoff, "The World is Finally Catching Up With Poco (And About Bloody Time Too)," *ZigZag*, 1972.

39. *"We had a lot of problems"* George Grantham, author interview, July 20, 1997.

39. *"We got little"* Richie Furay, author interview, August 18, 2008.

39. *"I was at our"* Rusty Young to Mark Squirek, "Poco: Back on the Road," *Hittin' the Note*, Issue No. 47, 2005.

40. *"I don't know how"* George Grantham, author interview, July 20, 1997.

Chapter 4 PICKING UP THE PIECES

41. *"I thought we were crazy"* Rusty Young as quoted by John Einarson in *Desperados: The Roots of Country Rock*, 2001.

41. *"We couldn't think of anyone else"* George Grantham, author interview, July 20, 1997.

41. *"I saw Poco"* Tim Schmit in Bud Scoppa, "Poco's Deliverin' From the Inside," *Circus*, August 1971.

41. *"We were playing"* Tom Phillips, author interview, March 27, 1998.

42. *"I thought, fat chance"* Tim Schmit in TELL ME THE TRUTH press kit, 1990.

46. *"We rehearsed some"* George Grantham, author interview, July 20, 1997.

46. *"I used to make fifty bucks a week"* Tim Schmit in TELL ME THE TRUTH press kit, 1990.

47. *"Until Tim came"* Rusty Young as quoted by John Einarson in *Desperado: The Roots of Country Rock*, 2001.

43. *"I remember him calling and saying"* Tom Phillips, author interview, March 27, 1998.

47. *"After we arrived, I went backstage"* Tim Schmit, Diary, www.timothybschmit.com, 2006.

44. *"When Tim first joined the group"* George Grantham, in Bud Scoppa, "Poco's Deliverin' From the Inside," *Circus*, August 1971.

44. *"A couple of things"* Jim Messina, Author interview, August 12, 2002.

46. *"Dickie was a very"* Richie Furay, author interview, August 18, 2008.

46. *"He managed to offend"* Jim Messina, author interview, August 12, 2002.

46. *"Well, you know he was a personal friend of Richie's"* George Grantham, author interview, July 20, 1997.

46. *"David Geffen was extremely fond"* Richie Furay, *Picking Up the Pieces*, 2007.

46. *"I told him that"* Jim Messina, author interview, August 12, 2002.

47. *"One day he brought"* Richie Furay, author interview, August 18, 2008.

47. *"Todd Shiffman was"* Jim Messina, author interview, August 12, 2002.

47. *"The thing Todd and Larry were good at was booking"* Richie Furay in Jerry Gilbert, "The World Still Hasn't Caught Up With Poco and Now They're Pickin' Up the Pieces Again," *Zigzag*, September 1974.

48. *"Alex really liked"* Jim Messina, author interview, August 12, 2002.

48. *"Well, this particular album is an experiment with me"* Jim Messina, as quoted by Pete Senoff, unidentified British magazine clipping, 1970.

48. *"There was an unspoken feeling"* Jim Messina, as quoted by John Einarson in *Desperado: The Roots of Country Rock*, 2001.

49. *"I think I may have intimidated him"* Jim Messina, author interview, August 12, 2002.

49. *"I think he sang a little"* George Grantham, author interview, July 20, 1997.

49. *"This guy came"* Richie Furay, 1975 interview.

50. *"If you listened to that song"* Richie Furay to John Einarson, *For What It's Worth: The Story of Buffalo Springfield*, Quarry Music Books, 1997.

50. *"On that track"* Rusty Young to John Einarson, *Desperado: The Roots of Country Rock*, 2001.

50. *"It was our way"* Richie Furay, *Picking Up the Pieces*, 2007.

50. *"I think Dewey"* Richie Furay, 1975 interview.

50. *"We were trying to find an identity"* George Grantham to Robyn Flans, "George Grantham," *Modern Drummer*, August 1985.

51. *"El Tonto de Nadie, which was Nobody's Fool"* Jim Messina, author interview, August 12, 2002.

51. *"The second album is really hard to pull out of the context"* Rusty Young to John Einarson in *Desperado: The Roots of Country Rock*, 2001.
52. *"It was amazing"* George Grantham, author interview, July 20,1997.
52. *"That night, we played"* Rusty Young to Mark Squirek, "Poco: Back on the Road," *Hittin' the Note*, Issue No. 47, 2005.
54. *"That must have been what got it all started"* George Grantham, author interview, July 20, 1997.
54. *"Playing Shea Stadium Peace Show"* Richie Furay to Bud Scoppa, "Poco, Yes indeed," *Rock*, November 17, 1970.

Chapter 5 CONSEQUENTLY, SO LONG

55. *"I couldn't help"* Jim Messina, author interview, August 12, 2002.
55. *"I though that"* Jim Messina to Jerry Gilbert, "Kenny Loggins (with Jim Messina Sittin' In) Talkin' About...," *Zigzag*, January 1974.
55. *"Richie really wanted"* Jim Messina, Ibid.
56. *"When people are afraid"* Messina in Tom Nolan, "There's Gold in the Middle of the Road," *Rolling Stone*, February 27, 1975.
56. *"The group was very"* Jim Messina, to Jerry Gilbert, "Kenny Loggins (with Jim Messina Sittin' In) Talkin' About...," *Zigzag*, January 1974.
56. *"Jim was touring"* Clive Davis with James Willwerth, *Clive: Inside the Record Business*, 1975.
57. *"We kept hearing"* George Grantham, author interview, July 20, 1997.
57. *"They were just things"* George Grantham in David Procktor, "Poco Live in London," *Dark Star*, 1977.
57. *"We had been rehearsing"* Grantham, author interview, July 20, 1997.
57. *"I don't remember"* Richie Furay, author interview, August 18, 2008.
58. *"I was probably the one"* Jim Messina, author interview, August 12, 2002.
58. *"We had worked with Paul"* Grantham, author interview, July 20,1997.
59. *"The Speed Press was"* Paul Cotton, author interview, September 3, 2008.
59. *"I actually said"* Paul Cotton, Ibid.
59. *"When Paul came"* Richie Furay, author interview, August 18, 2008.
60. *"Jimmy had showed"* Paul Cotton, author interview, September 3, 2008.
60. *"Jimmy left"* Richie Furay in Pete Fornatale, "Poco Power," *Jazz & Pop*, August 1971.
61. *"I got away"* Paul Cotton, author interview, September 3, 2008.
61. *"As far as I'm concerned"* Richie Furay to John Einarson, *Desperados: The Roots of Country-Rock*, 2001.
62. *"I think it was one"* George Grantham, author interview, July 20, 1997.
63. *"I had a vision"* Richie Furay in Cameron Crowe, "Poco," *San Diego Door*, August 17-September 17, 1972.
64. *"As it ended up"* Rusty Young to John Tobler, "Rusty Young & Poco," *Omaha Rainbow*, Spring 1979.
64. *"We wrote eight of the songs"* Richie Furay in Jerry Gilbert, "Richie Furay," *Sounds*, February 1972.
64. *"We toured for six months"* Rusty Young to William Ruhlmann, liner notes for FORGOTTEN TRAIL, 1990.

64. *"I'm not sure the album"* Rusty Young in Jerry Gilbert, "No Boundaries for Poco's Music," *Sounds*, 1971.

65. *"It's not a Memphis blues record"* Richie Furay in Lynn Randall, "Trying to Relieve the Tensions," *Hit Parader*, 1971.

65. *"The reason we weren't happy"* Rusty Young in untitled magazine clipping, "Laid Back Longevity," 1976.

65. *"When I came in"* Tim Schmit in Mary Campbell, "Poco: 'We're Happy When People Smile,'" Associated Press as printed in Tacoma *News Tribune*, June 20, 1971.

65. *"We were at Transmaximus"* Paul Cotton, author interview, September 3, 2008.

65. *"Paul's made it better"* Tim Schmit to Elen Mandell, "Interview: Poco," *Action World*, May 1971.

66. *"Richie was going through"* Paul Cotton to John Einarson in *Desperado: The Roots of Country Rock*, 2001.

66. *"My first show"* Denny Jones, author interview, August 5, 2008.

66. *"I first noticed it in New York"* Paul Cotton to David Procktor, "Poco Live in London," *Dark Star*, 1976.

68. *"In those days"* Rusty Young to William Ruhlmann, liner notes to FORGOTTEN TRAILS, 1990.

68. *"It does get old"* Richie Furay in Craig Moddereno, "Poco Still Picking Up the Pieces," *Rolling Stone*, December 24, 1970.

69. *"I did most of the writing"* Richie Furay in Jerry Gilbert, "Richie Furay," *Sounds*, February 1972.

69. *"You'd think he would have been satisfied"* Paul Cotton to David Procktor, "Poco Live in London," *Dark Star*, 1976.

69. *"Actually, that came"* Paul Cotton, author interview, September 3, 2008.

69. *"We first talked about moving"* George Grantham, author interview, July 20, 1997.

69. *"From my perspective"* Richie Furay, author interview, August 18, 2008.

70. *"That move created"* Denny Jones, author interview, August 5, 2008.

71. *"When it came time"* George Grantham, author interview, July 20, 1997.

71. *"We recorded two"* Richie Furay, author interview, August 18, 2008.

71. *"I'd never been"* Paul Cotton, author interview, September 3, 2008.

Chapter 6 A GOOD FEELING TO KNOW

73. *"They just didn't agree"* George Grantham, author interview, July 20, 1997.

73. *"We went to CBS"* Richie Furay and Michael Roberts, *Pickin' Up the Pieces*, 2007.

73. *"Well, we never"* Richie Furay, author interview, August 18, 2008.

74. *"I was the only guy"* Denny Jones, author interview, August 5, 2008.

74. *"It was brutal"* Jones, Ibid.

75. *"The highlight was playing"* Jones, Ibid.

75. *"We'd finished playing"* Grantham, author interview, July 20, 1997.

76. *"It was like Stranger in a Strange Land"* Grantham, Ibid.

76. *"We had a big case"* Denny Jones, author interview, August 5, 2008.

76. *"Well, we never"* Richie Furay, author interview, August 18, 2008.

77. *"Our record company"* Rusty Young in Peter Knobler, "Poco: All We Need is a Hit Single", *Crawdaddy,* January 1973.

77. *"Singles are so much fun"* Richie Furay in Mary Campbell, "Poco: We're Happy When People Smile,' Tacoma *News Tribune*, June 20, 1971.

77. *"The band was living in Boulder"* Jack Richardson, author interview, August 28, 2002.

77. *"Good Feelin' to Know was designed"* Richardson, Ibid.

78. *"It was a blow to me"* Richie Furay in Cameron Crowe, "Poco Was the Next Big Thing Four Years Ago," *Rolling Stone*, April 26, 1973.

78. *"I've been writing songs"* Richie Furay in *Crawdaddy*, June 1972.

78. *"The rumors were "* Furay in Cameron Crowe, "Poor Poco: They Were 'The Next Big Thing' Four Years Ago," *Rolling Stone*, April 26, 1973.

79. *"There was no golf"* Denny Jones, author interview, August 5, 2008.

80. *"That was a lot of fun"* George Grantham in David Proctor, "Poco Live in London," *Dark Star*, 1977.

81. *"This one is so much better"* Paul Cotton to Jim Esposito, "Poco – A Good Fat Feeling To Know," unknown magazine clipping, 1972.

81. *"I'm opposed"* Paul Cotton to David Procktor, "Poco Live in London," *Dark Star*, 1976.

81. *"It was the same"* Jack Richardson, author interview, August 28, 2002.

82. *"I did a live album"* Jack Richardson, author interview, August 28, 2002.

83. *'Everybody had had it"* Denny Jones, author interview, August 5, 2008.

Chapter 7   HERE WE GO AGAIN

85. *"I suppose I"* Richie Furay with Michael Roberts, *Pickin' Up the Pieces*, 2007

85. *"David listened" Richie Furay*, Ibid

86. *"Geffen wanted acts"* Rusty Young, "Rusty Young & Poco," *Omaha Rainbow*, Spring 1979.

86. *"David had"* Ned Doheny to Fred Goodman, *Mansion on the Hill*, 1997.

86. *"Geffen told us"* Tim Schmit to Cameron Crowe, "Poor Poco: They Were 'The Next Big Thing' Four Years Ago," *Rolling Stone*, April 26, 1973.

87. *"He wanted these"* Paul Cotton in David Procktor, "Poco Live in London," *Dark Star*, 1976.

87. *"When I suggested"* Jack Richardson, author interview, August 28, 2002.

88. *"We were cutting"* Richie Furay with Michael Roberts, *Pickin' Up the Pieces*, 2007.

88. *"That's a really good"* George Rayne as quoted in Richie Furay with Michael Roberts, *Pickin' Up the Pieces*, 2007.

90. *"That one was supposed"* Jack Richardson, author interview, August 28, 2002.

90. *"It would have to be"* Richie Furay to Jerry Gilbert, "One of the Great Mysteries of Rock," *Sounds*, September 1973.

91. *"I talked with Don Ellis"* Jack Richardson, author interview, August 28, 2002.

92. *"I think it will be fun"* Richie Furay to Jerry Gilbert, "One of the Great Mysteries of Rock," *Sounds*, September 1973.

92. *"It all happened pretty fast"* George Grantham in David Procktor, "Poco Live in London," *Dark Star*, 1976.

92. *"Right up to the day"* Paul Cotton in Jerry Gilbert, "Poco's Rebirth," *Sounds*, December 1973.

93. *"Gram hadn't recorded"* Richie Furay to John Einarson in *Desperados: The Roots of Country Rock*, 2007.

94. *"Stephen was always crazy"* Paul Cotton in David Procktor, "Poco Live in London, *Dark Star*, 1977.

94. *"We got Stephen"* Jack Richardson, author interview, August 28, 2002.

Chapter 8 YOU'VE GOT YOUR REASONS

97. *"Tim, Paul, George and I"* Rusty Young to Steve O'Donnell, "The Rusty Young Interview," *A Good Feelin' to Know*, Issue 4, December 1998.

98. *"They came to us"* Rusty Young to John Tobler, "Rusty Young & Poco," *Omaha Rainbow*, Spring 1979.

98. *"It was Richie's band"* Chris Hillman to Todd Everett "Exclusive First Interview: The Souther-Hillman-Furay Band," Los Angeles *Free Press*, June 14, 1974.

99. *"I know the feeling"* Tim Schmit in Jerry Gilbert, "Poco – Return to Simplicity," *Sounds*, 1972.

99. *"Oh man, I didn't think"* George Grantham, Author interview, February 11, 1998.

99. *"Whew! Those were"* Paul Cotton, author interview, September 3, 2008.

99. *"I did"* Paul Cotton in David Procktor, "Poco Live in London," *Dark Star*, 1977.

99. *"I think since we have"* Tim Schmit in *Guitar Player*

99. *"It's really been fun"* Paul Cotton in Jerry Gilbert, "Poco's Rebirth," *Sounds*, December 1973.

100. *"We became quite"* Paul Cotton, author interview, September 5, 2008.

100. *"When we started"* Tim Schmit in "Poco Happy Working as Quartet," *Scene Magazine*, November-December 1974.

101. *"Who was going"* Denny Jones, author interview, August 5, 2008.

102. *"It was not a pleasant"* Jack Richardson, author interview, August 28, 2002.

103. *"They were not"* Richardson, Ibid.

103. *"The record was heavier"* Richardson, Ibid.

103. *"It was a really dark album"* Richardson, Ibid.

105. *"POCO SEVEN was certainly"* Paul Cotton to John Einarson, *For What It's Worth: The Story of Buffalo Springfield*, Quarry Music Books, 1997.

106. *"I don't think,"* Rusty Young to Jan Press, "Looked Like Bad Weather," The Scarlet, Clark University newspaper, April 5, 1974.

107. *"We had the whole album"* Tim Schmit in "Poco Happy Working as Quartet," *Scene Magazine*, November-December 1974.

117. *"We were trying"* Tim Schmit in Ellen Mandell, "Poco – On the Brink of Superstardom," *Good Times*, February 4-February 18, 1975.

107. *"He just kind of sat"* Tim Schmit to Elen Mandell, *Good Times*, February 4-February 18, 1975.
108. *"I hated that"* Tim Schmit, Ibid.
108. *"Rusty, of course, stepped in"* George Grantham, author interview, February 11, 1998.
109. *"The song has nothing to do"* Paul Cotton, author interview, September 3, 2008.
110. *"The songwriting responsibilities"* George Grantham to Dean Sciarra, "For 8 Years, It's Been Worth the Wait," *Distant Drummer*, July 20, 1976.
110. *"What we did was"* Tim Schmit to Barry Ballard, "Tim: We All Believe in Poco," *Omaha Rainbow Poco Special*, 1975.

Chapter 9   SITTIN' ON A FENCE

111. *"I was recruited"* Vince Marchiolo, author interview, November 7, 1997.
111. *"Talk is cheap"* Rusty Young in Paul Kendall, "Poco Keep on Tryin' (And Wind Up Making Good)," Zigzag, 1975.
112. *"The president of ABC"* Young, Ibid.
112. *"The newly appointed"* Tim Schmit to Barry Ballard, "Tim: We All Believe in Poco," *Omaha Rainbow Poco Special*, 1975.
112. *"It's one of my favorite"* George Grantham, author interview, February 11, 1998.
112. *"It was something"* Tim Schmit, to Barry Ballard, "Tim: We All Believe in Poco," *Omaha Rainbow Poco Special*, 1975.
113. *"Getting a hold of Garth"* Tim Schmit, Ibid.
113. *"It was a real personal tune"* Rusty Young, in Paul Kendall, "Poco Keep on Tryin' (And Wind Up Making Good)," Zigzag, 1975.
113. *"He like things real sparse"* Grantham, author interview, February 11, 1998.
113. *"Tim had been doing sessions"* Paul Cotton in to Kingsley Grimble, *Omaha Rainbow's Poco Special*, 1975.
113. *"I called Donald Fagen"* Tim Schmit to Barry Ballard, "Tim: We All Believe in Poco," *Omaha Rainbow Poco Special*, 1975.
113. *"It was supposed to be"* Grantham, author interview, February 11, 1998.
115. *"It was a little risky"* Grantham, Ibid.
115. *"I think we've grown"* Tim Schmit to Barry Ballard, "Tim: We All Believe in Poco," *Omaha Rainbow Poco Special*, 1975.
115. *"God, I was blown away"* Grantham, author interview, February 11, 1998.
115. *"On this last tour"* Rusty Young in Paul Kendall, "Poco Keep on Tryin' (And Wind Up Making Good)," Zigzag, 47, 1975
116. *"To this day"* Grantham, author interview, February 11, 1998.
116. *"He played with us"* Rusty Young to Peter O'Brien, *Omaha Rainbow's Poco Special*, 1975.
117. *"We have a huge following"* Paul Cotton to Kingsley Grimble, *Omaha Rainbow's Poco Special*, 1975.
118. *"They said, Hey!"* Al Garth to Pete O'Brien, *Omaha Rainbow 11*, December 1976.

118. *"We were going to have"* George Grantham, author interview, February 11, 1998.

118. *"I got a little bit creative"* Al Garth to Pete O'Brien, *Omaha Rainbow* 11, December 1976.

118. *"I think it was more exciting"* Grantham, author interview, February 11, 1998.

120. *"I wanted to create a song"* Rusty Young as quoted by John Einarson in *Desperado: The Roots of Country Rock*, 2001.

120. *"After we did"* Rusty Young to John Einarson, unpublished portion of interview, 1997.

120. *"Paul's going through"* George Grantham to Dean Sciarra, "For 8 Years, It's Been Worth The Wait," *The Drummer*, July 20, 1976.

121. *"I wanted to do some"* Paul Cotton to David Procktor, "Poco Live in London," *Dark Star*, 1976

121. *"One of the amazing things"* Mark Harman in Tom Lott, "Poco is Like a Blowfish at 40,000 Feet," *Sounds*, October 23, 1976.

121. *"We played all over"* Denny Jones, author interview, August 5, 2008.

122. *"That's when we"* Denny Jones, Ibid.

123. *"After Atlanta,"* Randy Locke as quoted in Willie Nelson with Bud Shrake, *Willie: An Autobiography*, Cooper Square Press, 2000.

123. *"I jumped in the band"* Al Garth to Pete O'Brien, *Omaha Rainbow* 11, December 1976.

124. *"We were thinking"* Paul Cotton to Jerry Gilbert, "Poco's Rebirth,' *Sounds*, December 22, 1973.

124. *"When you come over here"* George Grantham to David Procktor, "Poco Live in London," *Dark Star*, 1976

124. *"I remember doing a T.V. show"* Rusty Young to Steve O'Donnell, "The Rusty Young Interview," *A Good Feelin' to Know*, Issue 4, December 1998.

125. *"That was a great tour"* Denny Jones, author interview, August 5, 2008.

125. *"We are all very different"* Tim Schmit to Tom Lott, "Poco is Like a Blowfish at 40,000 Feet," *Sounds*, October 23, 1976.

Chapter 10   LIVIN' IN THE BAND

127. *"I think the thing with Al"* George Grantham, author interview, February 11, 1998.

127. *"There were some"* Paul Cotton, author interview, September 3, 2008.

128. *"I guess that's what it is"* Paul Cotton to David Procktor, "Poco Live in London," *Dark Star*, 1976.

128. *"We haven't really talked"* Tim Schmit to Michael Barackman, "Desperados: Poco Keeps on Tryin'," *Crawdaddy*, June 1977.

128. *"Oh, I think it would have been"* Grantham, author interview, February 11, 1998.

128. *"It happens"* Richie Furay to Michael Barackman, "Desperados: Poco Keeps on Tryin'," *Crawdaddy*, June 1977.

128. *"ABC is submitting"* Paul Cotton to David Procktor, "Poco Live in London," *Dark Star*, 1976.

128. *"It will be about 10 to 12 minutes"* Rusty Young to David Procktor, "Poco Live in London," *Dark Star*, 1976.

129. *"We're not the richest band"* Tim Schmit in Michael Barackman, "Desperados: Poco Keeps on Tryin'," *Crawdaddy*, June 1977.

129. *"Because of a certain chain of events"* Schmit, Ibid.

129. *"Tim and I never got along"* Rusty Young to John Einarson, *Desperado: The Roots of Country Rock*, 2001.

129. *"I know we're talented enough"* Tim Schmit to Kenny Weissberg, "Poco Mysterious Frustrating," *RMME*, September 1977.

129. *"We have two albums left"* George Grantham to Kenny Weissberg, "Poco Mysterious Frustrating," *RMME*, September 1977.

130. *"That was really out there"* George Grantham, author interview, February 11, 1998.

130. *"We had the hard rock"* Paul Cotton to John Einarson in *Desperado: The Roots of Country Rock*, 2001.

131. *"The obvious single"* George Grantham to Kenny Weissberg, "Poco Mysterious Frustrating," *RMME*, September 1977.

132. *"The week the album came out"* Rusty Young to Art Smith, "It Took 10 Years for Times to Catch Up With Poco," Denver *Post*, September 16, 1979

132. *"ABC quickly thought of them"* Vince Marchiolo, author interview, November 7, 1997.

132. *"INDIAN SUMMER"* Paul Cotton, author interview, September 3, 2008.

132. *"I think the tour"* Paul Cotton, Ibid.

Chapter 11 THE LAST GOODBYE

133. *"I got a phone"* Tim Schmit to Charles M. Young, "A Good Year in Hell," *Rolling Stone*, November 29, 1979.

133. *"He told me first"* Paul Cotton, author interview, September 3, 2008.

133. *"I remember one night"* George Grantham, author interview, February 11, 1998.

134. *"I though that"* George Grantham, Ibid.

134. *"We thought that"* Paul Cotton, author interview, September 3, 2008.

135. *"The roadie from Poco"* Charlie Harrison, author interview, November 1, 1998.

135. *"That bass line"* Charlie Harrison, Ibid.

135. *"Steve and I"* Charlie Harrison, Ibid.

135. *"Ah yes,"* Paul Cotton, author interview, September 3, 2008.

136. *"She had auditioned"* Kim Bullard, author interview, October 28, 1998.

136. *"These guys are players"* Paul Cotton to David Seays, "Poco: In Praise of Perseverance," *BAM Magazine*, April 20, 1979.

136. *"They're musicians"* Rusty Young to Richard Wootten, *Omaha Rainbow* 21, Summer 1979.

136. *"They weren't great"* Paul Cotton, author interview, September 3, 2008.

137. *"Some changes"* George Grantham, author interview, February 11, 1998.

137. *"Well, Steven and Charlie"* Rusty Young to Richard Wootten, *Omaha Rainbow* 21, Summer 1979.

138 *"I hope they never"* Rusty Young to Mick Skidmore, "Poco: Rusty Young Looks Back," *Goldmine*, August 2, 1985.

138. *"They were rehearsing"* Richard Orshoff, author interview, May 3, 2008.

138. *"I felt that"* Richard Orshoff, Ibid.

138. *"They were used"* Richard Orshoff, Ibid.

139. *"We sat around"* Richard Orshoff, Ibid.

139. *"We cut some country tunes"* Rusty Young to Richart Wootten, *Omaha Rainbow* 21, Summer 1979.

139. *"Rusty played"* Steve Chapman, author interview, October 17, 1997.

139. *"There was no pressure"* Steve Chapman, Ibid.

139. *"Based on how"* Richard Orshoff, author interview, May 3, 2008.

139. *"We went to"* Paul Cotton, author interview, September 3, 2008.

140. *"It almost has a Picasso feel"* Phil Hartmann, Las Vegas *Sun*, May 28, 1998.

140. *"We were looking"* Rusty Young on BBC Radio, unknown date, 1979.

140. *"Heart of the Night"* Rusty Young to Richard Wootten, *Omaha Rainbow* 21, Summer 1979.

141. *"Crazy Love originally"* Richard Orshoff, author interview, May 3, 2008.

141. *"We tried a lot"* Steve Chapman, author interview, October 17, 1997.

141. *"There were two or three"* Paul Cotton to David Seays, "Poco: In Praise of Perseverance," *BAM Magazine*, April 20, 1979.

141. *"This album barely"* Richard Orshoff, author interview, May 3, 2008.

142. *"They were just the kind"* Rusty Young to Richard Wootten, *Omaha Rainbow* 21, Summer 1979.

142. *"I remember we were"* Kim Bullard, author interview, October 28, 1998.

142. *"We chose to play clubs"* Rusty Young to Richard Wootten, *Omaha Rainbow* 21, Summer 1979.

142. *"Rusty and Paul wanted"* Steve Chapman, author interview, October 17, 1997.

143. *"We toured all"* Denny Jones, author interview, August 5, 2008.

143. *"It was a great song"* Steve Chapman, author interview, October 17, 1997.

143. *"I really don't enjoy"* Rusty Young to Richard Wootten, *Omaha Rainbow* 21, Summer 1979.

144. *"It hurt the single"* Rusty Young to Richard Wootten, *Omaha Rainbow* 21, Summer 1979.

144. *"FM stations"* Richard Orshoff, author interview, May 3, 2008.

144. *"I remember one"* Denny Jones, author interview, August 5, 2008.

145. *"We had the month"* Rusty Young to Richard Wootten, *Omaha Rainbow* 21, Summer 1979.

145. *"That was a really disgusting"* Kim Bullard, author interview, October 28, 1998.

145. *"We did this Raleigh thing"* Steve Chapman, author interview, October 17, 1997.

146. *"It was a union"* Denny Jones, author interview, August 5, 2008.

146.   Information on the Cotton Carnival comes from http://www.oidar.com, 2000.

146.   *"That was a huge"* Denny Jones, author interview, August 5, 2008.

147.   *"I recall Richie"* Kim Bullard, author interview, October 28, 1998.

147.   *"There was never,"* Richie Furay to Art Smith, "It Took 10 Years for Times to Catch Up with Poco," Denver *Post*, September 16, 1979.

147.   *"I think I was making"* Charlie Harrison, author interview, November 1, 1998.

148.   *"Rusty rang me"* Charlie Harrison, Ibid.

148.   *"That thing went'"* Paul Cotton, author interview, September 3, 2008.

148.   *"I'm real proud"* Rusty Young in M.U.S.E. program, 1979.

148.   *"Yeah that was a lot of fun"* Kim Bullard, author interview, October 28, 1998.

148.   *"Well, this is what happened"* Charlie Harrison, author interview, November 1, 1998.

149.   *"I do remember"* Kim Bullard, author interview, October 28, 1998.

149.   *"We were against the wall"* Paul Cotton to Richard Randall, KTTV, June 1, 1992.

149.   *"Rolling Stone"* Paul Cotton, author interview, September 3, 2008.

Chapter 12   UNDER THE GUN

151.   *"We put together"* Steve Chapman, author interview, October 17, 1997.

152.   *"It was basically"* Steve Chapman, Ibid.

152.   *"We approached"* Richard Orshoff, author interview, May 3, 2008.

152.   *"Mike had done records"* Charlie Harrison, author interview, November 1, 1998.

152.   *"Mike's big pitch"* Steve Chapman, author interview, October 17, 1997.

153.   *"Mike was the"* Paul Cotton, author interview, September 3, 2008.

153.   *"A major difference"* Rusty Young in *The Independent*, undated clipping, 1980.

153.   *"It wasn't a great marriage"* Kim Bullard, author interview, October 28, 1997.

153.   *"We trusted his perception"* Rusty Young in *The Independent*, undated clipping, 1980.

153.   *"He had a very"* Denny Jones, author interview, August 5, 2008.

153.   *"Rusty had a feeling"* Kim Bullard, author interview, October 28, 1997.

154.   *"We recorded at Village"* Steve Chapman, author interview, October 17, 1998.

154.   *"We kept the strengths"* Rusty Young in *The Independent*, undated clipping, 1980.

154.   *"The song came about"* Paul Cotton in *The Independent*, undated clipping, 1980.

154.   *"Made of Stone"* Rusty Young in *The Independent*, undated clipping, 1980.

155.   *"We went up"* Kim Bullard, author interview, October 28, 1998.

155. *"It was a conceptual piece"* Steve Chapman, author interview, October 17, 1997.

155. *"I broke a bone"* Kim Bullard, author interview, October 28, 1998.

156. *"The reason was"* Steve Chapman, author interview, October 17, 1997.

157. *"That was a fun tour"* Kim Bullard, author interview, October 28, 1998.

157. *"Poco like to party"* Denny Jones, author interview, August 5, 2008.

157. *"He and Paul"* Kim Bullard, author interview, October 28, 1998.

157. *"Rusty was"* Denny Jones, author interview, August 5, 2008.

157. *"We were into"* Kim Bullard, author interview, October 28, 1998.

158. *"I think when it didn't sell"* Kim Bullard, Ibid.

158. *"Here's what happened"* Kim Bullard, Ibid.

159. *"I don't know"* Richard Orshoff, author interview, May 3, 2008.

159. *"Those were throw away albums"* Kim Bullard, author interview, October 28, 1998.

160. *"Well, it's about the Civil War"* Rusty Young to Jim Ladd, *InnerView*, syndicated radio show, 1981.

160. *"Blue and Gray"* Rusty Young to Robert Klein, syndicated radio show, 1981.

161. *"The whole thing"* Rusty Young to Chris Willman, "Poco Explores the Civil War," *BAM Magazine*, September 25, 1981.

161. *"Yeah, that's just one-on-one"* Paul Cotton to Jim Ladd, *InnerView*, syndicated radio show, 1981.

161. *"Widowmaker" became"* Paul Cotton, author interview, September 3, 2008.

161. *"Shows what we do"* Rusty Young to Chris Willman, "Poco Explores the Civil War," *BAM Magazine*, September 25, 1981.

161. *"We covered a lot"* Kim Bullard, author interview, October 28, 1998.

162. *"It was one of the better"* Charlie Harrison, author interview, November 1, 1998.

162. *"I think it was probably"* Charlie Harrison, Ibid.

162. *"It doesn't matter"* Rusty Young to Chris Willman, "Poco Explores the Civil War," *BAM Magazine*, September 25, 1981.

163. *"No, They didn't"* Kim Bullard, author interview, October 28, 1998.

163. *"Never. No way"* Charlie Harrison, author interview, November 1, 1998.

163. *"He was the wild card"* Denny Jones, author interview, August 5, 2008.

163. *"I never even thought"* Steve Chapman, author interview, October 17, 1997.

Chapter 13 SHOOT FOR THE MOON

165. *"I think the reason"* Steve Chapman, author interview, October 17, 1997.

165. *"They would always say"* Kim Bullard, author interview, October 28, 1998.

166. *"I think we were still"* Steve Chapman, author interview, October 17, 1997.

166. *"Yeah, we made it"* Kim Bullard, author interview, October 28, 1998.

166. *"We had noticed"* Rusty Young to Barry Alfonso, liner notes for GHOST TOWN/INAMORATA, Rhino Records.
167. *"I usually had one song"* Rusty Young, Ibid.
167. *"Back in 1980"* Paul Cotton to Barry Alfonso, liner notes for GHOST TOWN/INAMORATA, Rhino Records.
167. *"We were doing these very long tours"* Cotton, Ibid.
168. *"It made the Top 40"* Steve Chapman, author interview, October 17, 1997.
168. *"At that time"* Denny Jones, author interview, August 5, 2008.
169. *"God, it was like Spinal Tap"* Kim Bullard, author interview, October 28, 1998.
169. *"Yeah, you'd have tour routing"* Charlie Harrison, author interview, November 1, 1998.
169. *"It was dangerous"* Denny Jones, author interview, August 5, 2008.
170. *"I think it had a lot to do"* Rusty Young to Mick Skidmore, "Poco," *Relix*, October 1984.
170. *"I think at that"* Steve Chapman, author interview, October 17, 1997.
171. *"I was ecstatic"* Kim Bullard, author interview October 28, 1998.
171. *"I didn't wish"* Kim Bullard, Ibid.
171. *"We wanted to see"* Rusty Young to Mick Skidmore, "Poco," *Relix*, October 1984.
171. *"I call that"* Paul Cotton, author interview, September 3, 2008.
171. *"Richard Landis started off"* Rusty Young to Barry Alfonso, liner notes for GHOST TOWN/INAMORATA, Rhino Records.
171. *"Richard Landis"* Paul Cotton, author interview, September 3, 2008.
172. *"Richard just felt he wanted"* Chapman, author interview, October 17, 1997.
172. *"Yeah, I did a lot of work"* Bullard, author interview October 28, 1998.
173. *"To me, the Poco sound"* Paul Cotton to Barry Alfonso, liner notes for GHOST TOWN/INAMORATA, Rhino Records.
173. *"Well, you know"* George Grantham, author interview, February,11, 1998.
173. *"It was a fun"* Richie Furay, author interview, August 18, 2008.
173. *"Reed's a friend of mine"* *Young* to Barry Alfonso, liner notes for GHOST TOWN/INAMORATA, Rhino Records.
173. *"We cut that track"* Young to Alphonso, Ibid.
174. *"I was really into Robert Plant's"* Cotton to Barry Alfonso, liner notes for GHOST TOWN/INAMORATA, Rhino Records.
174. *"Tim Schmit blended nicely"* Cotton to Alphonso, Ibid.
174. *"I'm not sure we got"* Young to Alphonso, Ibid.
174. *"That song is kind of my blue-collar"* Cotton to Alphonso, Ibid.
174. *"I think it's one of the four or five"* Young to Alphonso, Ibid.
175. *"I really don't understand"* Rusty Young to Holly Gleason, "Poco Still on Country Trail," Miami *Herald*, September 14, 1984.
175. *"The band got back together"* Chapman, author interview, October 17, 1997.
176. *"I had known him a short while"* Harrison, author interview, November 1, 1998.
176. *"I should have quit two years before"* Harrison, Ibid.

177. *"The next morning"* Harrison, Ibid.
177. *"The first person"* Jeff Steele, author interview, October 22, 2007.
177. *"They came down"* Steele, Ibid.
177. *"The band left"* Steele, Ibid.
178. *"A lot of people are real curious"* Rusty Young to Justin Mitchell, "Poco at the Beach," New York *Daily News*, August 23, 1984.

Chapter 14 ONE OF THESE DAYS

181. *"We thought that"* Rusty Young to Josepf Woodard, "Change the 'g' to 'c': Poco is born," Santa Barbara *News-Press*, July 5, 1987.
181. *"I kind of had"* Paul Cotton, author interview, September 3, 2008.
182. *"It feels good to be back"* George Grantham in Robyn Flans, "George Grantham," *Modern Drummer*, August 1985.
182. *"A few days later"* Jack Sundrud, author interview, March 22, 2000.
182. *"These guys moved"* Jack Sundrud to Pete Fornatale, *Mixed Bag* radio show, July 1986.
182. *"We rehearsed a lot"* Sundrud, author interview, March 22, 2000.
182. *"I was surprised"* Sundrud, Ibid.
183. *"Jack was a great guy"* George Grantham, author interview, February 11, 1998.
183. *"Great voice"* Paul Cotton to Richard Randall, KTTV, June 1, 1992.
183. *"We had a handshake"* Paul Cotton, author interview, September 5, 2008.
183. *"We supposedly had a record deal"* Grantham, author interview, February 11, 1998.
183. *"It was one of those music business things"* Sundrud, author interview, March 22, 2000.
183. *"When I came"* Rusty Young to Jim Beal Jr., "Spirit-filled Folk: Poco's Energy to Hit Kerrville Fest Stage," San Antonio *Express-News*, May 25, 2001.
184. *"We recorded quite a few times"* Sundrud, author interview, April 17, 2000.
184. *"We started recording"* Paul Cotton, author interview, September 3, 2008.
184. *"Chasin' Love"* Jack Sundrud, author interview, April 17, 2000.
185. *"He used to say"* Paul Cotton, author interview, September 3, 2008.
186. *"I had to get"* Grantham, author interview, February 11, 1998.
186. *"We only toured in summer time"* Steve Chapman, author interview, October 17, 1997.
187. *"I thought it"* Jack Sundrud, author interview, April 17, 2000.
187. *"In fact, it was from seeing me"* Sundrud, Ibid.
188. *"I just remember"* Chapman, author interview, October 17, 1997.
188. *"After the initial burst"* Sundrud, author interview, April 17, 2000.
189. *"Crime of the Century was a blues-rock"* Sundrud, Ibid.
189. *"I wouldn't say the mood"* Sundrud, Ibid.
189. *"I don't think they told me"* Sundrud, Ibid.
190. *"Nashville is insecure"* Paul Cotton to John Einarson, unpublished portion of interview, December 1997.

Chapter 15   LEGACY

191.   *"That deal came"* Paul Cotton, author interview, September 3, 2008.
191.   *"In fact he lived"* Jeff Steele, author interview, October 22, 2007.
192.   *"I went into"* Paul Cotton, author interview, September 3, 2008.
192.   *"I was doing"* Paul Cotton as quoted by Mark Gould, *Sound Waves*, September 2000.
192.   *"The guy with the money"* Paul Cotton, author interview, September 3, 2008.
192.   *"They wanted my album"* Paul Cotton, Ibid.
192.   *"There was no help"* Paul Cotton, Ibid.
193.   *"I talked with Jimmy"* Rusty Young in Lydia Carole DeFretos, "An Interview with Rusty Young and Jim Messina of Poco," *Harmonies*, October 1989.
193.   *"We decided it was going to be"* Rusty Young, Ibid.
193.   *"I spoke with Timmy"* Jim Messina, author interview, October 14, 2002.
194.   *"One of my first calls"* Rusty Young in Lydia Carole DeFretos, "An Interview with Rusty Young and Jim Messina of Poco," *Harmonies*, October 1989.
194.   *"I think that"* Richie Furay, author interview, August 18, 2008.
194.   *"RCA President"* Jim Messina in Dave DiMartino, "Poco Reclaims Its Musical 'Legacy'", *Billboard*, September 30, 1989.
195.   *"Things started"* Jim Messina, author interview, October 14, 2002.
195.   *"They told me"* Messina, Ibid.
195.   *"Alan Kovac said"* Rusty Young in Lydia Carole DeFretos, *Harmonies*, October 18, 1989.
195.   *"They chose the material"* Jim Messina in Mick Skidmore, "Poco 1989," *Relix*, December 1989.
195.   *"Call it Love was not"* Jim Messina, author interview, October 14, 2002.
196.   *"I had just gone through"* George Grantham, author interview, February 11, 1998.
197.   *"We had to find someone"* Jim Messina, author interview, October 14, 2002.
198.   *"That one"* George Grantham, author interview, February 11, 1998.
198.   *"The chorus is extremely high"* Richie Furay and Michael Roberts, *Pickin' Up the Pieces*, 2007.
199.   *"We did travel all over"* Randy Meisner to John Beaudin, SmoothJazz.com interview, 2004.
199.   *"I'm dumbfounded"* Jim Messina, October 14, 2002.
201.   *"Richie Furay is a minister"* Randy Meisner to John Beaudin, SmoothJazzNow.com interview, 2004.
201.   *"I agreed to change"* Jim Messina, author interview, October 14, 2002.
201.   *"When it came"* Rusty Young in William Ruhlmann, "Poco: Siftin' Through the Pieces," *Relix*, Vol.18, No. 3, 1990
201.   *"We probably never"* Rusty Young, Ibid.
202.   *"I'm glad that Richie's not along"* Rusty Young to anonymous fan, July 1990.

202. *"I don't blame anybody"* Jim Messina to Willie G. Moseley, "Jim Messina: Been There, Done That, Part II," *Vintage Guitar* online, www.vguitar.com, 2000.
202. *"After the Richard Marx tour"* Jack Sundrud, author interview, March 22, 2000.
203. *"It was great"* Jack Sundrud, author interview, March 22, 2000.
204. *"That was written"* Jim Messina, author interview, October 14, 2002.
205. *"The audiences were very polite"* Jack Sundrud, Ibid.
206. *"The time when"* Jim Messina to Willie G. Moseley, "Jim Messina: Been There, Done That, Part II," *Vintage Guitar* online, www.vguitar.com, 2000.
206. *"Alan Kovac made some commitments"* Jim Messina, October 14, 2002.
207. *"By the time"* Jim Messina, Ibid.
207. *"Let me tell you what really happened"* Randy Meisner to John Beaudin, SmoothJazzNow.com interview, 2004.
208. *"Randy and I and Rusty"* Jim Messina, October 14, 2002 .
208. *"The reason I chose"* Jim Messina, Ibid.

Chapter 16 WHEN THE COAST IS CLEAR

210. *"At RCA, the guy"* Rusty Young to Steve O'Donnell, "The Rusty Young Interview: 16 October 1998," *A Good Feelin' To Know*, Issue 4.
210. *"Larry Larson"* Paul Cotton, author interview, September 3, 2008.
211. *"It was just a way"* Paul Cotton, Ibid.
212. *"I thought that"* Paul Cotton, Ibid.
212. *"Richard tends to overplay"* Paul Cotton, Ibid.
212. *"Yeah, that thing"* Paul Cotton, Ibid.
213. *"It was too hard"* Paul Cotton, Ibid.
213. *"We are not an act"* Rusty Young to Calvin Wilson, Kansas City *Star*, July 11, 1993.
214. *"Poco is one part of my life"* Rusty Young to Brenda Woody, "Poco Will Help Alaskans Shake Their Cabin Fever," Anchorage *Daily News*, March 4, 1994.
214. *"The whole project"* Paul Cotton, author interview, September 3, 2008.
214. *We had to learn"* Paul Cotton, Ibid.
215. *"I personally never"* Rusty Young to Neil Haislop, "The Sky Kings Get off the Ground," *Country Weekly*, August 13, 1996.
216. *"This will be the"* Rusty Young to Ben Eicher, "Deadwood Jam Marks Poco's Last Performance," Rapid City *Journal*, September 15, 1995.
218. *"Rusty really shut"* Paul Cotton, author interview, September 3, 2008.
218. *"I was Rusty's neighbor"* George Lawrence, author interview, May 29, 2008.
218. *"I stayed at Jim's"* George Lawrence, Ibid.
218. *"I contacted Paul"* John Thaler to John Brindle, "Firebird, The Return of Paul Cotton," *A Good Feeling to Know*, No. 6, Summer 2000.
219. *"The correspondence"* Paul Cotton, author interview, September 3, 2008.

219. *"We tried"* Paul Cotton, Ibid.
220. *"We felt that"* John Thaler, to John Brindle, "Firebird, The Return of Paul Cotton," *A Good Feeling to Know*, No. 6, Summer 2000.
220. *"I think the new album"* Paul Cotton to Jim Ciborski, "Paul Cotton Interview," *A Good Feeling to Know*, No. 6, Summer 2000.

Chapter 17   A HORSE THAT'S RUNNING

221. *"Sony has said"* Rusty Young to Steve O'Donnell, "Rusty Young Interview, 16 October 1998," *A Good Feelin' To Know*, Issue 4, December 1998.
221. *"Tim Smith and I"* Richard Neville, Internet mailing list, June 2000.
222. *"We had become"* Paul Cotton, author interview, September 3, 2008.
222. *"Where we're at"* Rusty Young to Mark Faulkner, "Poco's Singer Recall's Group's Past," *Shorelines*, February 21, 2001.
223. *"Paul and I"* Rusty Young, Ibid.
225. *"We did this CD"* Rusty Young to Jim Lundstrom, "Poco: A Pioneer of Blending Country with Rock 'n' Roll," Appleton Post-Crescent, June 12, 2003.
225. *"We don't set out"* Rusty Young to Misha ben-David, "Poco's Horse Till Running Strong," www.vintagerock.com.
226. *"We're not youngsters,"* Rusty Young to Jim Lundstrom, "Poco: A Pioneer of Blending Country with Rock 'n' Roll," Appleton Post-Crescent, June 12, 2003.
227. *"We could have done"* Rusty Young to Steve O'Donnell, *A Good Feelin' to Know*, Poco Fanzine, Issue 11, Autumn 2004.
227. *"[Richie] came in"* Rusty Young to Steve O'Donnell, Ibid.
227. *"This was a special"* Richie Furay, author interview, August 18, 2008.
228. *"We saved what"* Paul Cotton, author interview, September 3, 2008.
228. *"We transferred it"* Paul Cotton, Ibid.
228. *"We mixed it"* Paul Cotton, Ibid.
228. *"We were playing the intro"* Rusty Young to Mark T. Gould, "George Grantham Interview," poconut.com, June 2006.
228. *"I was devastated"* Paul Cotton, author interview, September 3, 2008.
229. *"We finished the show"* Paul Cotton, Ibid.
229. *"If it happened in the back"* Rusty Young to Patrick Johnson, Springfield *Republican*, July 31, 2004.
229. *"Boy, all I could"* Paul Cotton, author interview, September 3, 2008.
229. *"I got a call"* George Lawrence, author interview, May 28, 2008.
229. *"My first gig"* George Lawrence to Steve O'Donnell, A Good Feelin' to Know, Poco Fanzine, Fall 2005.
229. *"I had made a reputation"* George Lawrence, author interview, May 28, 2008.
230. *"Dave is this big"* George Lawrence, Ibid.
231. *"It was fast"* George Lawrence, Ibid.
232. *"I went a few"* Jack Sundrud, Blahg, www.jacksundrud.com, 2005.
232. *"I had a heart attack"* Paul Cotton, author interview, September 3, 2008.
233. *"I got a call"* Bill Lloyd, www.billlloyd.com, 2005.
233. *"The worst part"* Paul Cotton, author interview, September 3, 2008.

233. Plans on recording a new studio album came from a conversation with Rusty Young by the author, August 19, 2006.
234. *"I mostly listened"* Jack Sundrud, Blahg, www.jacksundrud.com, 2006.
235. *"They are a fantastic"* Rita Siwek to Mark Squirek, "Poco: Back on the Road," *Hittin' the Note*, Issue No. 47, 2005.

Chapter 18   WHERE DID THE TIME GO?

266. *"The last time"* George Lawrence, author interview, September 10, 2008.
266. *"I see fun"* Jack Sundrud, author interview, September 16, 2008.
266. *"We will probably"* George Lawrence, author interview, September 10, 2008.
266. *"I see us"* Paul Cotton, author interview, September 3, 2008.
266. *"If there's no Rusty"* Paul Cotton, Ibid.

ACKNOWLEDGEMENTS

I would like to extend my sincere thanks and appreciation to all the people quoted in this book for their willingness to share their time and memories in interviews with me. I am especially grateful to Denny Jones, Poco's longtime road manager, for not only sharing his memories, but also providing access to his Poco files. Steve Chapman was especially helpful in providing contact for his fellow Poco members. Mary Young has been especially helpful with photos and some very insightful comments on the manuscript.

And special thanks to George Grantham. George was my first Poco interview back in 1997. His friendly nature and earnest efforts to recall the misty details for an overzealous Poco fan/author helped to ease me into a tremendously challenging part of researching this book. My prayers are with you.

John Einarson has provided me with substantial assistance including sharing interview material, helpful advice, and tremendous friendship throughout the long gestation process for this book. My humble thanks to you for your generosity and friendship. I am forever in your debt.

My editor, Lynne Stevenson, did an exceptional job of turning this into a readable and informative story. Her enthusiasm and energy helped me through some challenging times. We make a pretty good team, Lynne. Let's do it again, sometime.

Being a Poco fan has provided me with some tremendous friendships. Steven Casto and I became friends back in 1985 and our friendship remains strong today. Steve and wife Julie supplied feedback on the draft manuscript and several photographs. My thanks to you both.

My dear friends Joe and Libby Field have been supporters of mine for many years, including supporting my choice of a wife. They looked over the manuscript in draft form and provided some key insights. God bless the both of you.

Additional acknowledgement is due to other Poconuts who have provided information, support, and friendship: Corey Bearak, Jon Rosenbaum, Dennis Richards, Mark Gould, Stu Rosenberg, Poco Jim McCaffrey, Pat Marshall, Joe Crawford, Jim Ciborski, Sue Klulan, Karen Mott, Naomi Elkins, Johnny Norris, Pete Long (for countless European Poco clippings), Torbjörn Orrgård, Christopher Hjort, Doug Hinman, Greg Shaw, Grace Grantham, Mike Stelk, Ben Eicher, Terry Barkley, and a host of others. Make no mistake that after 20 years there are many more people who qualify to be listed here. My thanks to you all, named or unnamed.

I spent countless hours doing research for this book in libraries and archives around the country. My special thanks to the

266

California State Library, California Room, California State University, Sacramento Library, the Dick Clark Productions Archives, the Musician's Union, Local #47 Archives, Pennsylvania State Library, Texas State Library, Dallas Public Library, Seattle Public Library, and countless others.

And special thanks to my family. My wife Kim has steadfastly supported this effort to see my dream in print. I could not have done it without you, babe. Thanks also to my sons Nick and Ronnie and daughter Melissa for their love, support and interest. Special kudos to Ronnie for providing the cover design and Groundhog Press logo.

ABOUT THE AUTHOR

Jerry Fuentes is a professional historian and author of feature articles on Buffalo Springfield, Neil Young, and Poco for periodicals such as *Goldmine, Broken Arrow,* and *A Good Feelin' to Know.* His research into rock concerts and band chronologies have been used by authors John Einarson, Doug Hinman, Christopher Hjort and Pete Long. He is the acknowledged expert on Poco. *LEGEND: The Story of Poco* is his first book.

Jerry lives in Stockton, California with his wife, Kim, sons Nick and Ronnie, and daughter Melissa and works for the U.S. Army Corps of Engineers in Sacramento as a historian and planner.

Visit Jerry Fuentes' website documenting Poco's concert history at:

www.angelfire.com/rock3/deliverin/pocoindex.htm

For other publications visit Groundhog Press at

www.booksatgroundhog.com

And visit Poco's official website at:

www.poconut.com